Death
Without Fear

DEATH WITHOUT FEAR

*Collective Wisdom for Making
Peace with Mortality*

L. Saxon Elliott, Psy.D.

Jefferson, North Carolina

ISBN (print) **978-1-4766-9660-7**
ISBN (ebook) **978-1-4766-5554-3**

LIBRARY OF CONGRESS CATALOGING DATA ARE AVAILABLE

Library of Congress Control Number 2025017075

© 2025 L. Saxon Elliott, Psy.D. All rights reserved

No part of this book may be reproduced or transmitted in any form or by any means, electronic or mechanical, including photocopying or recording, or by any information storage and retrieval system, without permission in writing from the publisher.

Front cover image: © Yalcin Sonat/Shutterstock

Printed in the United States of America

Toplight is an imprint of McFarland & Company, Inc., Publishers

Box 611, Jefferson, North Carolina 28640
www.toplightbooks.com

*To Conrad,
light of my life,
beneficiary of my
posthumous royalties*

A man traveling across a field encountered a tiger. He fled, the tiger after him. Coming to a precipice, he caught hold of the root of a wild vine and swung himself over the edge.

The tiger sniffed at him from above. Trembling, the man looked down to where, far below, another tiger was waiting to eat him. Only the vine sustained him.

Two mice, one white and one black, little by little started to gnaw away the vine. The man then saw a luscious strawberry near him. Grasping the vine with one hand, he plucked the strawberry with the other.

How sweet it tasted.

—Zen Proverb

Table of Contents

Preface	1
Introduction	5
Part I. The Problem of Death Anxiety	9
Chapter 1. The Elephant in the Room	12
Chapter 2. Death Anxiety 101	28
Part II. Philosophical Approaches	49
Chapter 3. The Epicureans	52
Chapter 4. The Stoics	61
Chapter 5. The (Pre)Existentialists	96
Part III. Spiritual Approaches	105
Chapter 6. The Afterlife: World Religions	107
Chapter 7. Death Rituals	117
Chapter 8. Death Meditation	129
Part IV. Psychological Approaches	137
Chapter 9. Cognitive Behavioral Therapy	138
Chapter 10. Acceptance and Commitment Therapy	155
Chapter 11. Existential Approaches	165
Chapter 12. Altered States of Consciousness	185
Part V. Functional Approaches	197
Chapter 13. Death Education and Literacy	198

Chapter 14. Ready to Go: Practical Considerations   216
Chapter 15. More(tality): Alternative Perspectives   231

Epilogue: The Last Bite   248
Appendix: The Revised Collett-Lester Scale   251
References   253
Index   261

Preface

It was a typical New England summer day in all respects, except for my brush with death. That Monday morning in June, I was going about my business, oblivious to my precarity, when I was stopped in my tracks by a massive heart attack. At age 59, absent any family history or known risk factors, I could not have seen this coming—nor did I, even as it was. Cardiac catheterization and stent of a wholly blocked artery saved my life, which I was granted the daunting privilege of resuming and rebuilding, though on altogether different terms. Prior to this interruption, I hadn't given mortality much thought. Not mine, anyway. Now, having dodged the proverbial bullet, it was staring me in the face.

You might wonder what I did with this sobering wake-up call. It transformed me, no doubt. But not in the way you'd think. I'd like to say that I took the opportunity to come to terms with my mortality, to face and accept the inevitability of my death. But alas, dear reader, I doubled down on my denial of death and instead committed myself to avoid it. Resolving not to die isn't all bad, of course. I made a number of lifestyle and pharmacological changes that, at least statistically, improved my odds of survival. But I had failed to balance efforts to preserve life with acceptance of its finitude. I met my near-death with defiance rather than reckoning.

And then, a couple of years into my new lease on life and next-level death denial, I had an epiphany. It came from my day job.

I'm a clinical psychologist by trade. In my 40+ years of practice, I've treated the entire spectrum of mental illness, specializing in anxiety disorders. Consider these clinical vignettes from my practice, paraphrased for brevity and clarity.

56-year-old female with debilitating panic attacks
ME: What's the most distressing symptom of a panic attack for you?
PATIENT: Heart palpitations. I'm scared I'm going to die of a heart attack.

32-year-old male with obsessive-compulsive disorder (OCD), manifesting in compulsive handwashing with skin breakdown
ME: What if you stopped washing your hands so frequently?
PATIENT: Germs will cause a fatal infection.

25-year-old female with a phobia of flying
ME: What exactly makes you anxious about flying?
PATIENT: I could die in a plane crash.

72-year-old depressed male with existential despair
PATIENT: My life has no meaning. I don't see the point of it.
ME: Are you having thoughts of suicide?
PATIENT: Yes, but I'd never do it. I'm afraid I'd go to hell.

8-year-old child with separation anxiety
ME: When mom drops you off at school, what happens when she leaves?
PATIENT: I get scared she'll be killed in a car accident on the way home.

49-year-old female with hypochondriasis who requests repeated medical testing
ME: What would happen if you stopped seeking diagnostic tests?
PATIENT: My doctor will miss a life-threatening illness.

19-year-old female with post-traumatic stress disorder (PTSD) following an assault
ME: What triggered your flashback on Friday evening?
PATIENT: I heard footsteps behind me and thought I was being followed. I was afraid I'd be attacked again and wouldn't survive this time.

Are you noticing a recurring theme? When I've scratched the surface of seemingly unrelated disorders with diverse symptoms, fear of death frequently lurked underneath. As a seasoned (old) practitioner, I've treated hundreds of patients, and yet not a single one showed up at my office complaining of death anxiety. How can this be? The simple answer is that they weren't aware of it. It was masked or eclipsed by other symptoms and concerns. It's also possible that those consciously struggling with fear of death don't deem it to be a problem amenable to psychotherapeutic intervention, just something to live with.

I've come to understand that numerous and varied mental illnesses serve as proxies for an underlying, unconscious fear of death. Had I been treating the manifest symptoms—often quite successfully—but missing the existential issue at the core? Though death anxiety came up in sessions, as illustrated above, how was I to treat it? Surely not in the same ways I treated garden-variety anxiety disorders. Not to minimize their seriousness and felt impact, but now we're talking about THE BIG ONE—the mother of all fears. Unlike so many worries that are unlikely to happen, death is a certainty. Unlike other threats that are survivable—or at least manageable—I was up against the one insoluble human condition: mortality. How was I to address this pervasive, if not universal, source of suffering, this oft' unarticulated fear of the inevitable?

At a loss, I did what anyone would do who had both a deep personal and professional stake in this whole mortality matter—I became a death expert.

In the years since my brush with death, I've shifted from my initial, default position of avoidance and aversion to one of curiosity. Rather than keeping death at arm's length, I decided to lean in, to get as close to it as I could. So I undertook training to become a death doula and began to companion those in their final weeks, days, and moments of life. Though ministering to the dying might seem noble, I must admit that, at least initially, it was yet another way of denying my own mortality. Perhaps I thought that if I stood really close to the monster, it wouldn't see me. If Death was busy visiting someone else, I'd be safe. Yes, even shrinks are guilty of magical thinking sometimes.

Concurrently, I studied death as if my life depended on it. I discovered Thanatology—the scientific study of death (who knew?)—

and became an avid apprentice. I took the courses, read the books, listened to the lectures, attended death cafes, interviewed death workers and mortuary professionals, and talked to the real experts—the dying. Though seemingly a brave new (under)world, this quest was a natural extension of my clinical practice. I was an expert in anxiety but lacked death literacy. Recognizing the ubiquity of fear of death, I wanted remedies—for myself, my patients, and you. Finding scant literature on the subject of death anxiety for the lay reader, I mined the three disciplines with the most to say about death—philosophy, spirituality, and psychology—for answers.

Convinced that our death-phobic Western culture is implicated in instilling and perpetuating fear of death, I took on a mission to "out" the death taboo, to normalize and de-mystify the source of such pervasive fear and disdain. I wanted to address Death's branding problem. Though I'd long been in the trenches of clinical work, a solitary enterprise, my passion for changing our relationship with death had me pivoting to outreach for broader impact. I became an end-of-life educator, public speaker, and facilitator of frank, squirmy conversations about death and dying with unsuspecting victims (i.e., friends, family, strangers), and I founded The Examined Death™—a suite of death literacy and death anxiety resources. The book in your hand is the cornerstone of this mission-driven ecosystem.

And so, as it turns out, that fateful New England summer day was not my time to die. Instead, it was my time to birth this book—the coalescence of a lifetime of clinical practice, a heart attack, and a journey to acquaint myself with Death. Please allow me to introduce you.

Introduction

What if I told you that you're going to experience something that you've never experienced before and that you won't know when, where, or how it will happen? You'll have no idea what to expect because no one who's experienced it has provided an account. You won't know what it will feel like, or what will happen after. Oh, and it will be permanent. After your vehement, utterly predictable "No thanks!," what if I told you it was going to happen anyway? These are, essentially, the very contours and conditions of death. We can't predict it, we can't control it, we can't even imagine it. Nor can we opt out. All of this is problematic because we humans are wired for certainty. We tend to fear the unknown, and that which we don't understand. And death is the ultimate unknown and unknowable; it's simply beyond comprehension. There's no greater mystery in life than death. And, as a society, we've kept it that way. Until recently.

Now, death is coming out of the closet. Against the backdrop of our death-denying, death-averse Western culture, we're finally peeking out from behind our collective fingers to face the last great taboo. Our attitudes toward death are undergoing dramatic change. We're increasingly viewing death not as a tragedy to be feared, but as a life-affirming inevitability to be accepted and embraced—and prepared for. The many manifestations of the burgeoning death positive movement, spawned by mortician Caitlin Doughty's founding of The Order of the Good Death, include the emergence of death cafes, coffin clubs, alternative funeral and burial options, living funerals, popularization of the role of death doulas, Swedish death cleaning, and TED talks and books about death and dying (e.g., *New York Times* bestsellers *When Breath Becomes Air* and *Being Mortal*). The widespread exposure to death wrought by COVID-19 reminded us of the fragility of life and instilled a sense of urgency to come to terms with our mortality. Now more than ever, those who fear death are ready to acknowledge it, talk about it, and address it. It's your time, and the zeitgeist is with you.

And yet, despite these encouraging sociocultural developments, death anxiety is quite a private pain, a dark-night-of-the-soul existential issue. When you contemplate death, what thoughts and images come to mind? What about associations? Memories? Visceral sensations? Many of our ideas about death are negative and disturbing, evocative of fear and dread. Most of us can't even bear to think about our death for very long. It's a bit like staring directly at the sun, isn't it? We have to look away. But, for better or worse, only a small fraction of us—10 to 20 percent—will die without warning. The rest of us will know what's going to end our lives. We'll have opportunity to think about it—or avoid thinking about it.

Given that you've picked up this book, it's safe to assume that the prospect of death—your own or others'—unsettles you, or maybe even terrifies you. Perhaps this fear is buried in the dark recesses of your mind. Or, perhaps, you're unable to stop thinking and fretting about your eventual demise. Regardless, you're in good company, as fear of death is a normal part of the human experience. But if your death anxiety feels painfully excessive, or is interfering with your enjoyment of life, rest assured that there are answers. And they're accessible to you—right here, right now.

Informed and inspired by 40+ years of clinical psychology practice and my work as a death doula and end-of-life educator, this book is a curated compilation of powerful remedies to death anxiety, drawn from the collective, crowdsourced wisdom of multiple disciplines, perspectives, and voices, from ancient to contemporary. I've gathered and distilled the most resonant and potent philosophical, spiritual, psychological, and practical approaches to fear of death, offering you a menu of solutions from which to select those best suited to your concerns. Whether you fear your own death or the death of loved ones, whether you fear the process of dying or being dead, whether your orientation is spiritual or secular, there's something here for anyone who's confounded (or freaked out) by their finitude.

This book is primarily intended for those whose death anxiety is robbing them of life's vitality. If you find yourself avoiding thinking about, talking about, or planning for the end of life, or, alternatively, if you're obsessively preoccupied with death and dying, this book is for you. If your death anxiety is causing you some degree of mental and emotional pain and/or behavioral constriction, this book is for you. If you're concerned that you're not living life in the fullest, most meaningful way or worried about experiencing regrets at the end of life, you're in the right place. This book is also for the "death-curious" reader who, though not necessarily fearful, is mindful of their ephemerality and wishes to explore death's meaning and mysteries. Though it's written by a clinical psychologist, you needn't be suffering from a diagnosable mental illness or be psychotherapy-savvy to benefit, as no prior condition, experience, or knowledge is assumed. However, this book is not a substitute for one-on-one professional help if you should need it, and can also be used as an adjunct to psychotherapy.

Designed to inform and transform, this book's overarching goal is to alleviate your fear of death and to break through the denial and avoidance that prevent you from living freely and fully. To that end, its content is driven by the following objectives:

- To normalize and de-stigmatize your fear of death
- To help you assess, identify, and understand the particular bases of your death anxiety
- To educate you about death and dying and debunk myths that perpetuate fear
- To empower you to boldly face your mortality
- To equip you with tools to reduce anxiety and distress related to end-of-life issues
- To engender a more accepting and peaceful attitude toward death
- To inspire mindful awareness of mortality to live a richer, more meaningful life

So, my agenda for you is a bit more ambitious and expansive than mere relief from death anxiety.

To orient you to the scope and organization of the book, it begins by exploring the nature of death anxiety—its historical and sociocultural context, and its defining characteristics, causes, and consequences. Because any prescribed intervention is best preceded and informed by a comprehensive understanding of the problem, this foundational first step is crucial to optimizing the direction, precision, and effectiveness of subsequent problem-solving efforts. The balance and bulk of the book is focused on answers to death anxiety, organized into four broad categories: philosophical, spiritual, psychological, and functional. Each chapter within these four parts consists of a stand-alone approach for your consideration and application. I'm generally a proponent of avant-garde composer John Cage's dictum to "begin anywhere." However, I advise starting at the beginning and proceeding in sequence to maximize benefit and facilitate synthesis. Though the book's content is primarily didactic and prescriptive, you'll encounter experiential opportunities throughout. Whether through self-assessment tools, self-reflective prompts, thought experiments, or actionable applications, I encourage you to fully engage with the material, even when it's difficult. Especially when it's difficult.

Facing mortality isn't for the faint of heart, and I commend you for embarking on this journey. It takes courage and fortitude to face your fears, whatever they are. But replacing fear with wisdom, freedom, and peace is the greatest gift you can give yourself. My intent is to inspire hope and confidence that your fear of death, whether background noise or deafening disruption, can be overcome, or at least attenuated. Coming to terms with your mortality and that of those you love may be one of the most challenging—and rewarding—things you ever do. But you don't have to do it alone. You have access to a roadmap and a tour guide. I hope to be a supportive and convivial companion on your death-facing journey of self-exploration and growth. Though I haven't yet died myself, I know the terrain.

Part I

The Problem of Death Anxiety

What is it, if anything, that makes us uniquely human? At first glance, our intelligence may seem to be the defining factor. Perhaps it's our capacity for language. Or our opposable thumbs. But there's something more profound. Unlike other species, the central perplexity of human beings is their awareness of their mortality. As 19th-century Scottish poet Alexander Smith (1863) asserts in his essay *Dreamthorp*, "It is our knowledge that we have to die that makes us human." No one knows exactly when in our evolutionary history this awareness emerged, but at some point, the human brain developed the capacity for consciousness of mortality. Humans began to realize that they weren't going to live forever. And the trouble started.

Awareness of mortality has haunted us ever since, as evidenced by humanity's oldest surviving work of literature—*The Epic of Gilgamesh* (ca. 2750–2500 BCE/1998)—inscribed into clay tablets four thousand years ago in ancient Mesopotamia. In the epic poem, Gilgamesh wrestles with this timeless issue: "I am going to die! Am I not like Enkidu? Deep sadness penetrates my core, I fear death, and now roam the wilderness." Our Babylonian hero, distressed over the death of his best friend Enkidu, undertakes a long and perilous journey in quest of the secret of eternal life, lest he suffer the fate of his friend. An immutable part of the human condition, death has featured prominently in art, drama, poetry, literature, philosophy, psychology, sociology, theology, anthropology, archeology, and every other human discipline throughout recorded history. A popular, ubiquitous theme, death.

Awareness of our finitude is both an evolutionary marvel and a curse. Self-awareness enables us to think deeply about our existence, to imagine things that don't yet exist, to innovate, to create, and to explore the bounds of the known universe, physical and metaphysical. However, the ability to think abstractly and symbolically also enables us to project into the future and to contemplate our inevitable nonexistence. We can't escape the fact that, ultimately, we're simply ashes to ashes and dust to dust, just like all the other animals. As expressed by existential psychiatrist Irvin Yalom (2008) in his book *Staring at the Sun: Overcoming the Terror of Death*, "Our existence is forever shadowed by the knowledge that we will grow, blossom, and inevitably, diminish and die." Thus, self-awareness, a supreme gift, comes at a heavy price. This is the shared burden with which we all live—the knowledge that each of us will die, and so will the people we love. This is what makes us uniquely human. And this, according to American philosopher William James, is "the worm at the core" of human existence.

Stephen Cave (2012), in his book *Immortality: The Quest to Live Forever and How It Drives Civilization*, describes the "mortality paradox":

> Our awareness of ourselves, of the future, and of alternative possibilities enables us to adapt and make sophisticated plans. But it also gives us a perspective on ourselves that is at the same time terrifying and baffling. On the one hand, our powerful intellects come inexorably to the conclusion that we, like all other living things around us, must one day die. Yet on the other, the one thing that these minds cannot imagine is that very state of nonexistence; it is literally inconceivable. Death therefore presents itself as both inevitable and impossible.

The correlate to *awareness* of death is *fear* of death. To know we will die is to know death anxiety. We're programmed to live and to do everything we can to survive against all odds. And just as this survival instinct resides in our DNA, so does the fear of death. Death terror is primal and archetypal, the manifestation of an innate, instinctual tendency toward the perpetuation of life. It's normal—to a certain extent—to be wary of death. In fact, it has great evolutionary value. Being fearful of death has kept our species alive for hundreds of thousands of years. This universal fear has also inspired and informed human endeavors from great art to brutal warfare. Indeed, as you'll soon discover, the looming specter of death drives and motivates everything we do. How we as a species, as a society, as a culture, and as individuals deal with this "worm at the core" is the essence of this book.

Chapter 1

The Elephant in the Room

Death is a common occurrence. According to the *World Population Review* (2024), approximately 167,000 people per day are doing it, worldwide. And people have been doing it for a very long time. Perhaps death is so common because there are so many ways to die. The *International Classification of Diseases* (*ICD-11*), used by healthcare professionals and researchers worldwide to classify and code causes of death for statistical and epidemiological purposes, catalogs countless (literally, I tried) codes and combinations of codes for causes of death (World Health Organization, 2019). Poetically quantified by Jacobean playwright John Webster in *Duchess of Malfi*, "Death hath ten thousand several doors for men to take their exits."

Historically, death was much more commonplace than it is today. Life was precarious for our predecessors, cut short by disease and war. As recently as five hundred years ago, the risk of infection was a reality of daily life. Eating a meal or drinking a glass of water could be fatal. As we shifted to indoor city life, outbreaks and pandemics tore through society with alarming regularity. At one point, major epidemics of plague occurred approximately every thirty years in England, killing about one-fifth or more of London's population each time. Throughout the 1800s, pandemics of cholera occurred around every decade or two. In the last one hundred years of its existence, smallpox outbreaks are estimated to have killed five hundred million people (Pannu & Swett, 2023). Life expectancy was also adversely impacted by high infant and maternal mortality rates.

Because virtually no family was left untouched by the untimely death of a loved one, death was far more visible. As recently as the 1800s, people died in their homes, not in hospitals. With the

Chapter 1. The Elephant in the Room

prevalence of multi-generational households, the dying were surrounded by family members, including children and grandchildren. The dead were cared for by the family, who cleaned, dressed, and prepared them for burial. Their bodies were laid out in the home parlor where wakes were held, open to the community. Black curtains were hung over doors and windows to signify a family in mourning, and the entire community participated in death rituals alongside the bereft family. The family cared for the dying, and the community cared for the family. Cemeteries were located close to home, usually associated with churches, and graveyard visitations were a common part of everyday life.

Around 1900, with the advent of funeral parlors, the *Ladies Home Journal* advocated changing the home parlor to the living room we know today. The modern living room became the "living" room because it was no longer the room for laying out the dead. Now, death is something that happens offstage, sequestered from our view. But this is a fairly recent development.

Several factors account for this shift. First, advances in medicine, nutrition, and sanitation have allowed people to live much longer. With increased life expectancy comes an implicit sense of immortality, or at least the belief that modern medicine, with all its miracles, has answers for everything. Death is now seen as a problem to be solved, and the solution is prolonging life at all costs. No longer surrounded by death as a part of everyday life, its reality has receded from our consciousness. In the West, we often hear about death, we see it in movies and video games, but rarely do we face it directly. When we witness death through mass media, it's heavily filtered. Whether someone dies at home or in a hospital, we don't typically spend time with the body before it's whisked away to the morgue or funeral home. If there's an open casket for mourners to view the body one last time, it's likely to be pumped full of embalming chemicals and covered in makeup to make the corpse appear more presentable (i.e., alive). Because we're so insulated from death, it's something we can easily avoid or postpone thinking about. Hence, the recent COVID-19 pandemic posed a shock to our systems as we watched in horror as the TV news displayed stacks of body bags. Death was, once again, in our living rooms.

Second, with the disbursement of families and the virtual disappearance of multi-generational households, care of the dying has been outsourced to medical professionals and care of the dead has been outsourced to mortuary professionals. With the advent of modern hospitals, dying is no longer staged in homes, among the living. Today, many people die in hospitals, alone and sometimes far from their families. Tragically, this phenomenon was exacerbated by the COVID-19 pandemic, as loved ones were robbed of the opportunity to be with the dying or to participate in funerals and burials.

Finally, for Western societies in particular, traditional rites and rituals have been usurped by the forces of modernity. The medicalization of dying and the commercialization of funerals have supplanted the sacred and communal aspects of death and dying. As death has become increasingly sanitized, we've lost touch with the naturalness of dying as part of life. Other forces, such as the spread of dominant cultural values and global capitalism, have also had an impact on Western society's relationship with death and dying. In developing countries, direct exposure to death is far more common and more widely accepted as an everyday reality. As Dasho Karma Era, President of the Centre for Bhutan Studies and Gross National Happiness Research, points out in a recent BBC interview, "Rich people in the West, they have not touched dead bodies, fresh wounds, rotten things. This is a problem. This is the human condition. We have to be ready for the moment we cease to exist" (Weiner, 2022).

All of these Western sociocultural developments have served to distance us from the reality of death. Hidden from our view, we don't know what death looks like anymore. It's mysterious, even secretive. Contemporary society has tried to push death and dying out of sight, out of mind, and out of our conversation. This stigmatization of death has had a profound impact on our society at large, and on each of us as individuals. Banishing an inevitable part of our human experience has created unnecessary aversion and avoidance. Though death is as natural as birth, our societal fear of it is palpable.

We live in a death-denying, death-defying, death-illiterate, death-phobic culture. The many manifestations of this dysfunctional relationship with death include our language around death and dying, the quest for eternal youth and immortality, and prevailing myths and misconceptions surrounding the end of life. Let's examine each of these in depth so that you can better understand your own fear of death and what you're up against in overcoming it.

The D–Word

> One great use of words is to hide our thoughts.—Voltaire

When I was a young girl, my maternal grandmother came to live with us near the end of her life. One morning, my mother entered my room and tearfully announced, "We lost Granny last night." Though I had no idea how she got lost or where she might be, I felt compelled to go looking for her, to find her. After adult reflection (and plenty of therapy), I concluded that my mother's intention was not to deceive or confuse me. Rather, she wished to protect me from the pain of my beloved grandmother's death. She chose her words accordingly.

Euphemisms provide a way to convey something unpleasant or embarrassing without using specific language that may be considered too harsh, blunt, or direct. We substitute a softer, more innocuous word or phrase for one generally considered offensive or insensitively explicit. The social benefit of euphemism is that it allows discussion of taboo topics without upsetting or offending others. Hence, the words "dead," "death," and "dying" are cloaked in language that's more palatable and protective. In the case of my grandmother, "lost" was substituted for "dead."

As a general rule, the more taboo a topic, the more euphemisms there are for it. And though there are plenty of delicate subjects that we tend to discuss in roundabout ways (e.g., sex, money, bodily functions), there's no topic more "euphemized" than that of death. A quick Google search yields over one hundred alternative English words and phrases to the word "dead." To experience the magnitude of this linguistic obfuscation for yourself, see how many you and your friends can generate at your next gathering—a fun party game to liven things up. The lexicon of death is remarkably imaginative and wide-ranging, encompassing clinical, descriptive, polite, irreverent, old-fashioned, whimsical, religious, humorous, and even mobster variants. But the function is always the same: to avoid naming death as death. We go to great linguistic lengths to avoid direct reference to "the fate from which there's no escape." (See what I did there?)

The euphemization of death is so pervasive that even "death pros" avoid speaking of death and dying directly. For example, funeral directors refer to our dead loved ones as "the dearly departed." Medical professionals describe their dying patients as declining, not doing well, failing to respond to treatment, seriously ill, and candidates for comfort care. I recently attended a lecture by a hospice nurse who substituted "passed" for "died" for an entire hour. In all of these examples, language is used to disguise or sugarcoat the reality and finality of death.

Why is it so common in our culture to refer to death and dying by any number of other names? If we understand that the word "euphemism" derives from the Greek word *euphemismos* or "words of good omen"—in context, the superstitious avoidance of bad luck words during religious ceremonies of the 17th century—it makes sense that we're so careful to avoid direct references to death. Because words are so powerful, we may hold the superstitious belief, conscious or unconscious, that to name death is to invoke or manifest it. The notion that uttering a word makes it so, a type of magical thinking, is deeply embedded in our cultural mythology.

Euphemisms for death serve social and psychological functions as well. Wishing to avoid being perceived as rude or insensitive, we tread lightly to protect the feelings of others. Speaking covertly about death also enables us to avoid dealing with our own feelings of fear, aversion and grief. Finally, euphemisms that refer to an afterlife (e.g., "passed to their eternal reward") serve as a comforting reminder to those of certain faiths.

One can tell a lot about a culture by studying its language, as language is undergirded by the cultural values from which it evolved. In turn, words color and inform cultural perceptions and attitudes. Eloquently expressed by Princely H. Glorious, African video essayist, "Language is the audible soul of culture." Examples of this mutually influential relationship between language and culture abound. In Eskimo culture, there are 40 to 50 Inuit/Yupik words for snow.

At the other extreme is the absence of words for certain phenomena in some cultures. Of words that don't even exist in the English language, the Japanese word *wabi-sabi* is my favorite. Wabi-sabi refers to the beauty in imperfection and impermanence. In Japanese culture, wabi-sabi is not merely a word, but a way of looking at things. It's the underpinning philosophy of *Kintsugi*, the Japanese art of repairing broken objects with gold lacquer, not to restore their former beauty but to enhance it. What does it signify that there's no word for this concept in English?

Euphemistic expressions for death are certainly not limited to the English language or to modern times. The discomfort evoked by the subject of death has been with us since time immemorial. To this day, in many parts of the world, language is used to distance people from the harsh reality of mortality. Consider these charming cross-cultural euphemisms for death, assembled by League of the Lexicon (2022):

- Gone to sell salty duck eggs (China)
- Thrown out your best skates (Russia)
- Thrown a spoon in a corner (Finland)
- Gone to the land of no hats (Haiti)
- Have no more toothache (France)
- Wearing wooden pajamas (Portugal)
- Woken up under a cypress (Italy)
- Closed the umbrella (Swiss German)
- Put aside your clogs (Denmark)
- Fallen with the flowers (Japan)
- Handed in the key (Hungary)

As language shapes culture and vice versa, it follows that how we talk—or don't talk—about death in our contemporary Western society reflects prevailing attitudes about the subject. The use of euphemisms for death is both cause and consequence of death denial. In other words, our denial of death drives avoidance of using the d-word and, in turn, using euphemisms for death perpetuates our denial. This cycle persists because death is a fear-based taboo.

Death Is for Losers

> Do not go gentle into that good night. Rage, rage against the dying of the light.—Dylan Thomas

"She lost her battle to cancer."
"He died after a courageous battle with kidney disease."
"She beat cancer."
"They put up a good fight."

How often have you heard these kinds of statements? Whether read in an obituary, stated in a eulogy, or overheard at a cocktail party, we're all familiar with these references to a combative, adversarial relationship with illness and death. It's expected that we'll "go down swinging."

Humanity has forever been at war with death. The use of militaristic language in death-speak has a long and illustrious history, dating back thousands of years. For example, the Bible refers to death as "the last enemy to be destroyed." During the Renaissance, cancer was thought of as a worm or wolf, eating the body of the afflicted who was compelled to slay the beast. But since President Nixon "declared war" on cancer and signed the National Cancer Act into law in 1971, the military metaphor for illness and death took firm hold. Over the 20th century, scientists and politicians alike have declared war on diabetes, AIDS, and obesity. COVID-19 is now the target of our warfare, the latest enemy to be defeated. As a society, we've "taken on" most of the diseases that threaten to kill us.

Today, war metaphors for illness and death are embedded in language surrounding healthcare. Their use is pervasive, extending well beyond the medical community to the culture at large. We "battle" and "struggle against" disease and decline. When diagnosed with a terminal illness, we vow to "fight" it. We use weaponry (e.g., an "armamentarium" of drugs and "magic bullet" cures) to combat disease. In the case of cancer, chemo and radiotherapy are known for "killing" cells, both malignant and healthy. The body is a battlefield. How ironic that the language of healing is so interwoven with the language of warfare. How strange that at a time when people are at their most vulnerable, we resort to violent rhetoric.

This hostile attitude toward death has infused our entire modern healthcare system. Death is considered a failure and a defeat—even a source of embarrassment. In its perennial battle against death, the medical establishment's core mission and primary raison d'être is to avoid or postpone it for as long as possible. Death must be suppressed, controlled, denied, and defeated at all costs (Diamond, 2016). And the cost is tremendous. Let's examine the implications of this antagonistic narrative surrounding illness and death, as well as the tragic consequences for our struggle with mortality and our fear of death.

First and foremost, framing our relationship with disease as adversarial implies that those who beat their illness are winners and those who die are losers. Battle metaphors put responsibility for the trajectory and outcome of an incurable illness squarely on the patient. The idea that people can "beat" disease implies that they're in control of their prognoses. Regrettably, the implication that illness can be defeated if one just tries hard enough or thinks positively enough can be tremendously burdensome. An afflicted person is compelled to summon strength, endurance, and courage—characteristics of a warrior—when beaten down by illness. If they don't respond well to treatment, this constitutes a personal defeat, leading to feelings of failure and guilt. Necessary changes in treatment protocols are viewed as "setbacks" or "lost ground" in the context of warfare. As an end-stage cancer patient expressed it, "I feel weighed down by people expecting me to win a battle I didn't choose." In reality, strength and skill have no bearing on disease prognosis.

Militaristic language can even inadvertently blame or shame those who end up dying from their illness. Whether intended or not, there's too often a judgmental element implicit in such language. Didn't they fight hard enough? Weren't they brave enough? Did they give up too soon? These questions are an inherent criticism of the deceased. "Losing the battle" to illness blames the person who died. Conversely, "winning the battle" suggests that it's possible to do so and casts judgment on those who don't. Following the recent death of Jimmy Buffet, I heard his longtime friend Carl Hiaasen say, "I truly thought he could beat this because he had such a phenomenal attitude." No, Carl.

Zooming out a bit, it's important to note that this misplacement of blame becomes even more unfair when we consider the disproportionate impact of racial and socioeconomic factors on health outcomes. For example, it has been well documented that the millions of people in the United States without health insurance are more likely to be diagnosed at a later stage of illness and to fare more poorly. Yet we hold the disadvantaged among us equally responsible for fighting and winning their battles against disease.

In the 17th century, rhetoric framing cancer as an "enemy" led doctors to treat it aggressively with poisons such as arsenic and mercury, in hopes that they'd kill the cancer before they killed the patient. Those were, effectively, the first chemotherapies. The adversarial narrative we've inherited from history has led to an emphasis on aggressive, heroic cures for cancer and other illnesses. Emphasis is placed on sexy new drugs or surgical procedures, and qualifying for a clinical trial of an untested treatment protocol is often seen as a status symbol.

Battle metaphors for illness also imply that it's unacceptable, even shameful, to "surrender." When it comes to fighting disease, giving up is considered anathema to the life-sustaining goal of healthcare. When death constitutes failure, and failure is not an option, a brave warrior fights on, no matter what. But what if a patient with terminal illness is weary of subjecting themselves to invasive treatments with side effects that are adversely impacting their quality of life in exchange for, perhaps, a brief extension? What if the treatment is worse than the disease itself? In these cases, the use of militaristic language by healthcare providers can be experienced as authoritarian and disempowering. At the "command" of their doctors, patients often feel compelled to bravely "soldier on," even in the face of incurable disease. Tragically, this focus on "the fight" can color or delay important conversations about the end of life, as well as decisions to seek palliative or hospice care.

Finally, and most relevant to our concern, metaphors that frame death as an enemy to be vanquished serve to perpetuate our culture's fraught relationship with death and our aversion to it. Linguistic imperatives to conquer death compel us to deny its inevitability and undermine our acceptance of it as a normal part of life. They perpetuate the medicalization of death, removing what is natural and sacred about the end of life. They reinforce the death taboo and, hence, our collective fear of death.

Research suggests that the use of battle metaphors has a direct impact on how patients experience the end of life, and that language of struggle is antithetical to death acceptance. As part of the project "Metaphor in End of Life Care," researchers at Lancaster University conducted extensive interviews with 15 hospice managers across the U.K. They discovered that the difference between "good" and "bad" deaths is expressed via contrasting metaphors. A good death was described as involving "freedom" from pain, and the end of a "journey." In contrast, a bad death was described as a "struggle" or "fight" (Demjén et al., 2016).

Metaphors matter. Like euphemisms, their linguistic cousin, metaphors inform the narrative around unpleasant or intolerable realities. They shape our thinking and, in so doing, color our lived experiences. As with euphemisms for death and dying, battle metaphors reflect and perpetuate the denial and avoidance of death so prevalent in our Western culture. With regard to death anxiety, hiding death behind language makes matters so much worse.

The Quest for Immortality

> Our culture's zeal for longevity reveals our incredible collective fear of death.—Ram Dass

Since the dawn of time, humans have sought to overcome or outwit death. From the epic quest of Gilgamesh, to the sly Sisyphus of Greek mythology, to modern Silicon Valley tech giants, humans have long been on the case. This quest for immortality—or at least extreme longevity—is directly related to death denial, a cause and consequence of death anxiety. Defiance of death, in all its manifestations, reflects our pervasive fear and disdain of death.

Let's first consider the FOGO (fear of getting old) phenomenon. If we're living, we're aging. And yet, as a culture, we're obsessed with arresting or reversing this process. We're conditioned to remain youthful—in appearance, ability, and attitude. We're bombarded with words and images glorifying youth, typically offering solutions to combat bagging, sagging, wrinkling, graying, and other vestiges of (normal) aging. The revenue of the U.S. cosmetic industry was estimated to amount to $49 billion in 2022 (Petruzzi, 2023). That's a lot of lotions, potions, and hair dye to maintain the illusion of youth. For those seeking more durable remedies to aging, there's cosmetic surgery, generating over $8.5 billion in the U.S. in 2022 (Yang, 2024). "Anti-aging" is an entire industrial complex and a movement. Those who aren't on board are left behind, shrinking into invisibility and obsolescence. Our cultural ageism and failure to "see" our aging population is yet another manifestation of our fear of death.

For some, however, it's not enough to *appear* youthful. A more extreme form of death denial and defiance is the Life Extension Movement, proponents of which have declared an all-out war on aging. These biohacking "super-agers" are combatting mortality on several fronts. The calorie minimizers limit food intake to lower body temperature and slow metabolism. The compulsive exercisers are sweating their way to immortality. The supplementarians hope to arrest or reverse aging with vitamins, minerals, herbs, and antioxidants. The cryonicists pay as much as $200,000 to have their heads or their entire bodies frozen in a tank of liquid nitrogen until science finds a way to resurrect them (Wong, 2016). Responding to the growing interest in "aging medicine," scientists offer various anti-aging protocols for people willing to spend upwards of $100,000 per year at longevity clinics. For the budget-conscious, there's Equinox—a high-end gym chain with a newly launched longevity program—for a mere $40,000 annual membership fee. Immortality doesn't come cheap.

According to a recent study published in the scientific journal *Aging*, researchers at Harvard Medical School, led by geneticist and longevity expert David Sinclair, made an anti-aging breakthrough in the form of "chemical cocktails" with the potential to reverse the aging process in human and mouse skin cells (Sexton, 2023). Other advances in the quest for immortality include 3D organ printing, nanobots that can replicate the immune system, blood injections that supposedly extend life, and even cold saline resuscitation. Stem cells, genetic engineering, and nanotechnology also hold promise for reversing aging. The eternal quest for the fountain of youth, as old as civilization itself, persists in an increasingly inventive fashion.

Meanwhile, a number of Silicon Valley tech billionaires are betting heavily on the death-defiance cause (Friend, 2017; Isaacson, 2015). Larry Ellison, co-founder of the software company Oracle, finds accepting mortality "incomprehensible." Peter Thiel, co-founder of PayPal, has admitted that he's "against" the idea of death and is investing millions in the quest for eternal life. Sergey Brin, co-founder of Google, hopes to someday "cure death." Jeff Bezos, former Amazon CEO, has reportedly invested millions in immortality via Altos Labs, a startup with the stated purpose of reversing the aging process.

One has only to follow the money to conclude that anti-aging initiatives will soon succeed in making us immortal. Billionaires in quest of immortality have funded a variety of research programs and secret labs, offering millions of dollars in grant funding for anti-aging research (Varanasi, 2023). Perhaps the most ambitious immortality project of them all is Russian billionaire Dmitry Itskov's "2045 Initiative," the goal of which is to "create technologies enabling the transfer of an individual's personality to a more advanced non-biological carrier, and extending life, including to the point of immortality" by (you guessed it) 2045 (2045 Initiative, n.d.).

Not surprisingly, artificial intelligence (AI) has been enlisted to challenge death's finality. Innovations include "digital heirs" that reason and respond like their human "originals," as well as chatbots, virtual replicas, and three-dimensional holograms that mimic dead loved ones. Most notably, inventor and futurist Ray Kurzweil (2005) is banking on immortality through *the singularity*, that point in time when all advances in technology, particularly AI, will produce machines smarter than human beings and transcend our biological limitations. Kurzweil, profoundly impacted by the early death of his father, has preserved fifty boxes of his effects—from letters and photographs to electric bills—in hopes of someday creating a virtual avatar of his father (Friend, 2017).

Though rarely mentioned in the literature on death-defying measures, a fascinating example can be found in a religious context. As a college student of sociology, I had the opportunity to conduct field research in North Carolina's Appalachian mountains. There, in a Pentecostal worship service, I observed participants handling poisonous snakes and drinking strychnine poison, purportedly as a demonstration of faith. Pitting religious belief against death was, to me, the ultimate act of death defiance.

A less dramatic (and safer) manifestation of death defiance is *symbolic immortality* (Wong, 2016). To cope with the fear of extinction, we attempt to live forever through our progeny (biological immortality), through our belief in an afterlife (spiritual immortality), through our accomplishments (creative immortality), through our return to nature after death (natural immortality), through identification with institutions or traditions which outlive us (cultural immortality), and through our digital presence which persists beyond our biological existence (digital immortality). Social media profiles are forever.

I hope you're as impressed as I am with the lengths to which we mortals go to deny and defy the immutable reality of death. From surgery to supplements, cryogenics to chemicals, we are "raging against the dying of the light." Unfortunately, none of these measures do anything to engender our acceptance of death or to allay our fear of it. They only seek to postpone or avoid it altogether, which is just another form of denial. Death-defying measures represent a refusal to accept the inevitability of death and, thereby, exacerbate our fear of it.

Death Illiteracy and Mythology

> The oldest and strongest emotion of mankind is fear, and the oldest and strongest kind of fear is fear of the unknown.—H.P. Lovecraft, *Supernatural Horror in Literature*

Yet another manifestation of our death-denying, death-phobic culture is its pervasive death illiteracy. Because we avoid thinking and talking about death and dying, we really don't know very much about it. Unlike the many facts of life to which we're exposed and in which we're schooled, we're simply not well-versed in death. And,

Chapter 1. The Elephant in the Room 25

until recently, there weren't many available resources to remedy this state of affairs. It's notable, even strange, that we have driver's education and sex education, but no death education. Likewise, there are courses in financial literacy, digital literacy, media literacy, and cultural literacy, but no such offerings in death literacy. Though over 80 percent of pregnant Americans create a birth plan, only an estimated 22 percent have documented their desires for end-of-life care (Sarazin, 2023). Even though 100 percent of us will have to navigate death and dying at some point, nobody teaches us what to expect or how to prepare for it, much less manage our fear of it.

In a death-illiterate culture, the prospect of death is hypothetical and conditional, as reflected in our language. It's not "*When* I die...," it's "*If* I die..." We've all heard people say, "In case of my death..." or "X can increase the likelihood of death." If? In case? Likelihood? More linguistic evidence of death denial. Consider this television commercial (for which, appalled, I looked up the script):

> If you're watching this Gerber Life Guaranteed Life Insurance commercial, there's a good chance you're still alive. Now I know what you're thinking. Life insurance? I'm going to live forever. Death is what happens to other people. When you stop, I mean, *if* you stop watching TV, your family can use the insurance money...

An interesting consequence of death illiteracy and mythology is "morbid" curiosity. For example, are we not all a bit fascinated with the death of celebrities? Think of the last time you read or heard that a prominent figure died—perhaps someone you idolized or saw as being somehow immortal. After your initial shock and disbelief, what happened next? You needed to know why and how. You required details. Was the cause of death natural or unnatural? Was it accidental, self-inflicted, or caused by a fatal disease? If it was cancer, what type? Did they suffer? Could it have been prevented?

Even when we learn of the death of someone we know personally, we scan the obituary or social media feed for the cause of death. This compulsive, reflexive "need to know" relates directly to our cultural death denial and associated death illiteracy. We want to peek behind the curtain and solve the mystery. We want to know—sort of—what's in store for us. If they died, whether celebrity or mere mortal, so could we. These reminders of our mortality trigger our latent death anxiety. The cause of death matters because we need to reassure ourselves that it probably won't happen to us—at least not that way. For example, it's easier to distance ourselves from death by (preventable) overdose than death by (unpreventable) disease. We like to know that the deceased's situation just doesn't apply to us. A smoker died of lung cancer? Okay, I'm safe. I don't smoke. Bearing witness to the deaths of others allows us to perceive death from a relatively safe distance as an abstraction, as something that always happens to someone else (Diamond, 2016).

Due to our cultural illiteracy, myths and misconceptions about death and dying abound. Assumptions arise to fill voids in knowledge. Rumors, typically horrific, are spread and embellished. Our imaginations run wild. Unfortunately, these misunderstandings, perpetuated by popular culture, can serve to fuel fear about the end of life. Some of the most common are as follows:

- Dying is always painful.
- Dying is traumatic.
- Dying looks like television and movie depictions.
- Dying is a medical event requiring medical personnel and resources.
- Talking about death and dying will hasten it or bring it about.
- All dying people lose their mental faculties.
- Going on hospice means giving up or hastening death.
- Hospice hastens death by administering morphine.
- Hospice hastens death by withholding nutrition and hydration.
- Dying is a somber occasion.
- Everyone wants to die in peace and quiet.
- Nobody wants to die alone.
- Science and modern medicine can prevent or control death.

These are all examples of mortality mythology. Which do you believe? Are any of these misconceptions contributing to your fear of death? Our lack of exposure to and acquaintanceship with death perpetuates our fear of it. Like the bogeyman under the bed, the shadow in the dark, we fear the unknown and the unseen. As long as we're unfamiliar with death and dying, as long as it remains the great mystery, the great unmentionable, the more fearful we'll be. But in the wise words of Mister Rogers, "Anything that's human is mentionable, and anything that is mentionable can be more manageable."

Though all of these societal manifestations of death denial and aversion—from linguistic, to attitudinal, to behavioral—are interesting in their own right, how are they relevant to *your* fear of death? In providing a larger historical and sociocultural context for your personal struggle with mortality, I hope to normalize and demystify it. I want you to begin this journey with a big, fat "NO WONDER I'm afraid of death!" When our entire death-dysfunctional dominant culture is designed to instill and perpetuate distance from death, ignorance of death, and defiance of death, do your own fear and avoidance not make perfect sense? Why wouldn't you be fearful of the greatest taboo of Western culture?

The good news is that there are many alternative ways to think about and engage with your mortality and, thereby, free yourself from death anxiety. Having (hopefully) destigmatized your suffering a bit, let's proceed to the starting point of solving any problem: defining it, understanding its precise nature, and taking a measure of it.

Chapter 2

Death Anxiety 101

And the Winner Is...

Americans love competition. "Top 10" lists are a source of fascination, as books, billionaires, and beauty contestants jockey for position. Film buffs anxiously await the Oscars, hoping their favorite actor wins. Likewise, colleges and universities hold their collective breath in anticipation of the annual *U.S. News & World Report* rankings. Ditto sports fans biting nails over their team's standing. But as a social science nerd, *my* anxious anticipation occurs every October when *The Chapman University Survey of American Fears* (*CSAF*) drops, revealing the top 10 fears in America. Conducted annually, the *CSAF* is an unprecedented, ongoing study of American fears, now in its ninth year. The survey asks a representative national sample about more than 90 fears, and ranks them by the percent of respondents who report being "afraid" or "very afraid." It follows trends over time and identifies new fears as they emerge. The *CSAF* has been cited in over 1,000 print, broadcast, and online media, making it the #1 top-ranked fear survey. Irony!

Now that you're on the edge of your proverbial seat, the 2023 results reveal that 7 of the top 10 fears in America are—directly or tangentially—related to death. Fears ranked #5 and #6 are "People I love becoming seriously ill" and "People I love dying," respectively. Fears regarding war and terror ranked #3 (Russia using nuclear weapons), #4 (the U.S. becoming involved in another world war), #8 (biological warfare), and #9 (cyber-terrorism). The #7 ranked fear (pollution of drinking water) reflects environmental concerns (Chapman University, 2023). Whether by illness, war, or destruction of our planet, Americans are terrified of annihilation.

Americans are more fearful of the death of loved ones (50.4%) than they are of their own death (26.2%). The same relationship holds when looking at fear regarding illness. Of those surveyed, only 35 percent were afraid of becoming seriously ill themselves, while 50.6 percent were afraid of a loved one becoming seriously ill. Incidentally, fear of public speaking has always ranked higher than fear of death, inspiring comedian Jerry Seinfeld to quip, "This means to the average person, if you go to a funeral, you're better off in the casket than doing the eulogy."

Having put your death anxiety in proper statistical (and comical) perspective, let's begin to examine the phenomenon—definitionally, diagnostically, demographically—so we can approach it from a solid base of understanding.

Death Anxiety: What, Who, When, Why?

Death anxiety, also called *thanatophobia*, is emotional distress aroused by reminders of mortality. The medical term thanatophobia derives from two ancient Greek words: *Thanatos* (the god of death) and *phobos* (fear or terror). The American Psychological Association (2015) defines thanatophobia as a "persistent and irrational fear of death or dying," which can be focused either on one's own death or the death of loved ones. It has been described as a feeling of dread, apprehension, or extreme concern when thinking about the process of dying or detaching from life, as well as what happens after death (Firestone & Catlett, 2009).

If you're fearful of death or dying, you're not alone. Death-related anxiety is quite common and experienced by many, if not most, people at some point in their lives. Feeling uneasy or apprehensive about extinction is as natural a part of being human as any other concern over our well-being. We're biologically hardwired to fear death, and that wiring will, inevitably, short-circuit and produce a jolt of terror from time to time.

Notably, the American Psychiatric Association doesn't officially recognize thanatophobia as a distinct disorder. That is, it doesn't appear in the *Diagnostic and Statistical Manual of Mental Disorders*,

Fifth Edition (*DSM-5*), the catalog of diagnosable psychiatric conditions published by the American Psychiatric Association (2013). If preferring to live isn't irrational or pathological, does this mean that your death anxiety isn't a real problem? Should you put down this book? Not so fast!

Though thanatophobia isn't a separate clinical diagnosis, as with most phobias, fear of death can exist anywhere on a spectrum ranging from mild and manageable to extreme and debilitating. Death anxiety only becomes a real problem when it causes significant, persistent emotional distress and/or interferes with day-to-day functioning. When fear of death is so intense as to pose a notable negative impact on mental well-being and quality of life, it may constitute a diagnosable phobia, classified as an anxiety disorder in the *DSM-5*. The *DSM-5* categorizes phobias into three groups: specific phobias, social phobias, and agoraphobia. Thanatophobia is classified as a specific phobia. Other examples of specific phobias you've probably heard of are *claustrophobia* (fear of small, confined spaces) and *arachnophobia* (fear of spiders). Specific phobias are quite common. In fact, according to the National Institute of Mental Health (n.d.), an estimated 12.5 percent of adults in the U.S. will experience a specific phobia at some point in their lives. Interestingly, the focus of nearly every specific phobia (e.g., snakes, heights, needles, flying) has the potential to result in death.

According to the *DSM-5*, a *specific phobia* is characterized by intense and irrational fear of a specific activity, object, or situation. For an individual's fear of *death* to be classified as a phobia, it must meet the following diagnostic criteria:

- Thoughts of death (or exposure to death-related stimuli) almost always provoke *immediate fear or anxiety*.
- Thoughts of death (or exposure to death-related stimuli) are *actively avoided* or endured with intense fear or anxiety.
- The fear or anxiety is *out of proportion* to the actual danger posed by thoughts of death (or exposure to death-related stimuli).
- The fear, anxiety, or avoidance is *persistent*, typically lasting for six months or more.

- The fear, anxiety, or avoidance causes clinically significant *distress or impairment* in social, occupational, or other important areas of functioning.

So, whether normal, garden-variety death anxiety devolves into diagnosable thanatophobia is a matter of intensity, duration, and degree of disruption.

Thanatophobia should not be confused with other death-related but distinct specific phobias. While thanatophobia is a fear of death in general, *necrophobia* is a fear of dead things (corpses), as well as things associated with corpses (e.g., graveyards, coffins, tombstones). *Taphephobia* is a fear of being buried alive, and *athazagoraphobia* is an intense fear of forgetting someone or of being forgotten, most commonly associated with a fear that you or a loved one will develop a disease that affects memory, such as dementia. These unpronounceable phobic conditions aren't mutually exclusive.

Symptoms of acute thanatophobia are similar to those of other phobias, including a number of physical symptoms of a panic attack, such as rapid or irregular heartbeat, shortness of breath, dizziness, trembling, upset stomach, dry mouth, sweating, agitation, fear of losing control, and a sense of dread or impending doom. However, death anxiety is not always experienced as sudden and intense. Chronic, lower-level anxiety about death can be experienced as persistent physical tension, difficulty relaxing, insomnia, fatigue, difficulty concentrating, social withdrawal, and generalized worry or obsessive rumination.

In addition to the above mental, emotional, and physical symptoms, death anxiety is invariably accompanied by several notable behaviors. Chief among them is avoidance of internal and external reminders of death. These can include death-related thoughts and images, places associated with death (e.g., hospitals, funeral homes, cemeteries), media that feature death (e.g., books, articles, movies, news), activities or situations associated with perceived risk of death (e.g., heights, exposure to contaminating substances), conversations about death (e.g., estate planning, discussing end-of-life preferences), and images or symbols of death (e.g., skulls, coffins, blood, dead animals).

Death anxiety is also commonly associated with intrusive thoughts and disturbing images about one's own or others' deaths, reassurance-seeking behaviors, safety-seeking behaviors, compensatory behaviors designed to ward off death (e.g., excessive exercise, compulsive hand-washing), preoccupation with physical health, compulsive information-seeking about death and dying, maintaining conduct to avoid feared punishment in an afterlife, and self-medicating with substances, retail therapy, or comfort eating. As you can imagine—or, perhaps, know—these behaviors can be extremely time-consuming and disruptive.

Given this broad array of symptoms, it's not surprising that thanatophobia can manifest in a variety of ways. In some people, death anxiety is overt and easy to recognize, while in others, it's more subtle or disguised, hidden behind seemingly unrelated symptoms or concerns. Often, other psychological conditions serve as surrogates for fear of death. Symptoms of thanatophobia may come and go over an individual's lifetime, and various triggers can activate or exacerbate an underlying or mild case of death anxiety.

Death anxiety isn't a unidimensional construct or homogeneous affliction. While thanatophobia is defined as a general fear of death, there are many different types and bases of this anxiety, and individuals fear death for varying reasons. While some experience overwhelming concerns about their own mortality, others have an excessive fear of losing their loved ones. For some, death anxiety centers on things that may result in their death, such as contamination, dangerous situations, or contracting a terminal illness. Others are preoccupied with the process of dying or what happens after death. Still others worry about leaving loved ones behind after they die.

Growing empirical evidence points to the central role of death anxiety in numerous diagnosable mental health conditions (Iverach et al., 2014; Menzies et al., 2019). As a transdiagnostic construct, thanatophobia is commonly associated with other anxiety disorders, depressive disorders, somatic disorders, eating disorders, obsessive-compulsive disorder (OCD), and post-traumatic stress disorder (PTSD). Not surprisingly, death anxiety is most frequently linked with *hypochondriasis* (now called *illness anxiety disorder*), characterized by excessive worry about becoming seriously ill. The notion that death anxiety underpins numerous mental illnesses may explain the "whack-a-mole" phenomenon in clinical practice, wherein the successful resolution of one disorder is followed by the popping up of another, seemingly-unrelated set of symptoms. It's as if the underlying fear of death is determined to find expression, in one way or another.

The inter-relationship between thanatophobia and other, co-occurring, conditions is complex and multifactorial. Though a compelling body of research suggests that fear of death may indeed underlie much, if not all, psychopathology, the causal relationship remains unclear. It has been argued that the relationship is indirect, with symptoms of mental illness reflecting maladaptive coping strategies to manage death anxiety (Iverach et al., 2014). Specific phobias, in particular, may represent an unconscious attempt to cope with underlying, amorphous death anxiety by focusing on smaller, more discrete, and more manageable threats, such as spiders or germs. Displacement, in other words. Regardless, it's important to note that death anxiety rarely occurs in a vacuum, and must be understood against the backdrop of each person's unique psychological makeup and lifetime of experiences.

The purpose of this clinical exposition is not to pathologize normal human concerns regarding mortality. Whether your anxiety is merely the ambient hum of everyday life or the crashing terror that wakes you up in the wee hours, these definitions, descriptions, and classifications are designed to help you determine where you fall on this continuum. Whether or not you meet the formal diagnostic criteria for a specific phobia (thanatophobia), your death anxiety is a problem if *you* experience it to be. The solutions contained in this book are designed to benefit all who are concerned about their own or others' mortality, no matter where they fall on the spectrum, no matter the bases of their fears. Now that you better understand the *what* of death anxiety, let's move on to the *who*, the *when*, and the *why*.

Who Fears Death?

Death anxiety varies widely among individuals and can be influenced by factors such as age, gender, educational and socioeconomic status, culture, religion, health, personality, and life experiences. Some people are more prone to fear death than others, and life events tend to interact with these predispositions. Early childhood experiences that can contribute to death anxiety include having anxious, overprotective, or inattentive caregivers; hearing adults talk about death in negative or catastrophic ways; or not hearing adults talk about death at all. Exposure to specific adverse events can give rise to thanatophobia, including significant illness, abuse, trauma, or witnessing a sudden or traumatic death. And yet, not everyone who experiences these life events develops a fear of death. Thus, death anxiety appears to be a classic case of "nature + nurture."

What are the risk factors for developing thanatophobia? A landmark study on the effects of age and gender on death anxiety revealed that death anxiety peaks for both men and women during their 20s and declines as they age. Interestingly, the same study found that women in their 50s often experience an unexpected second spike of death anxiety that men do not. In general, women show a greater tendency to fear death than men, perhaps because they're more likely to acknowledge and discuss such fears. Regardless of gender, once the age of 60 is reached, death anxiety seems to decrease and level off (Russac et al., 2007).

Though anyone can develop death anxiety at any age, it appears to be more common in people who:

- have other phobias or mental health disorders
- are routinely exposed to illness, trauma, violence, or death in their jobs, such as first responders or healthcare providers
- are in poor health or have been diagnosed with a serious or terminal illness
- have friends or family members who are elderly, ill, or dying
- have low self-esteem
- feel a sense of dissatisfaction with their life or lack of fulfillment
- lack close connections to family or friends

Who is *least* afraid of death? A review of the literature (Kastenbaum, 2000; Wu, 2020) reveals some interesting, even counterintuitive, findings regarding the following variables:

Age. Older people tend to fear death less. Though you might assume that those closer to death would fear it more, older age is more associated with acceptance of death than fear of death. Having experienced more of life, seniors might have less concern about missing out. Navigating the deaths of others might decrease fear through exposure and familiarity. It's also possible that death is seen as an escape from the health issues, pains, and losses associated with old age (Russac et al., 2007).

Religion. Religion isn't necessarily the hedge against death anxiety that we'd expect. Though it might seem that religious people who believe in an afterlife are less afraid of death than nonreligious people, the relationship between religiosity and fear of death is more complicated. A study published in the journal *Religion, Brain, & Behavior* suggests that the relationship is curvilinear (an inverse-U). That is, those least afraid of death are the very religious and the not-at-all religious (e.g., atheists), while the moderately religious (those in the middle of the curve) are most fearful of death (Jong et al., 2018).

Experience with Danger. Interactions with danger also impact fear of death in a curvilinear fashion. Though having some dangerous experiences results in less death anxiety, too much exposure to danger increases fear. In a study comparing skydivers with varying levels of experience, researchers found that beginner (student) skydivers were much more fearful of death than intermediate (average of 90 jumps) skydivers. But, surprisingly, expert skydivers (over 700 jumps) were more scared of death than intermediate skydivers. This suggests that simply risking death more doesn't decrease fear of it (Griffith et al., 2018).

Physical Health. People with better physical health tend to fear death less. Researchers have found a correlation between physical health and mental health, as well as an increased sense of meaning in life, all of which serve as protective factors against death anxiety (Ding et al., 2020).

Attachment Style. Attachment styles, usually shaped early in life, describe the ways people behave in close relationships. Securely attached people tend to be trusting, communicative, and comfortable with both emotional closeness and independence. Insecurely attached people tend to be anxious and clingy, distant and avoidant, or a mix of both. The quality of our relationships determines the degree of threat we perceive regarding mortality. People with secure attachment styles fear death less than people with insecure attachment styles (Mikulincer et al., 1990).

Culture. People who live in cultures in which death is openly discussed and even celebrated are much less fearful of death than those who live in cultures in which death is a taboo subject, shielded from public view and discourse.

Reviewing these risk factors for death anxiety, which predispositions and/or life experiences apply to you?

When Do We Fear Death?

Though awareness of mortality can remain covert for much of life, certain developmental milestones, life events, and circumstances inevitably bring this awareness to the surface and force us to reckon with the impermanence of our existence. Some of these "triggers" are obvious and tend to be processed consciously. Others are more subtle and metabolized out of our awareness. Regardless, many life experiences evoke *mortality salience,* the term social scientists use for awareness of the inevitability of one's death. Mortality salience, in turn, sparks and manifests our latent death anxiety. Hence, we can be going about our business, oblivious to our vulnerability, and one of the following might precipitate an existential crisis:

Close Encounters. Perhaps there's nothing more catalyzing of death anxiety than receiving a life-limiting diagnosis or facing imminent death. The terminal illness, death, or near-death of someone we love, or even someone we know, is a close second. Accidents, injuries, health scares, and other such close calls can be activating events as well.

Time Running Out. With advanced age comes awareness that we have less time to live than we've already lived. Though birthdays are the most common provocateurs of this awareness, the passage of sand through the hourglass can also become more clear in the face of loss, failure, or unfulfilled aspirations that we may not have time to actualize. Reviewing a bucket list longer than our remaining timeline can provoke heightened awareness of mortality.

Trauma or Loss. A major, irreversible threat to one's safety (e.g., physical or sexual assault, robbery, car accident, fall) or to one's basic security (e.g., divorce, unemployment, bankruptcy) can precipitate acute awareness of fragility and impermanence.

Empty or Meaningless Life. The realization that one has failed to live a life that has mattered, to contribute to something greater than oneself, or to create a legacy that will live on, brings mortality into sharper focus. A sense of meaninglessness, often correlated with a "mid-life crisis," is strongly associated with higher levels of death anxiety.

Assaults to Ego. Vulnerability—feeling small, insignificant, or insecure—stirs up death anxiety by adversely impacting feelings of worth and self-esteem. Experiences of humiliation, demotion, failure, or rejection puncture the illusion of immortality through strength and power. We're reminded that we're not invincible, after all.

Signifiers of Aging. Many people experience the "mortality alarm" in their 50s and 60s, as these decades are replete with symbolic reminders of aging and mortality. Consciously or unconsciously, we process birthdays, anniversaries, school reunions, children leaving home, retirement, estate planning, annual physical exams, aches and pains, sexual dysfunction, our reflection in the mirror, death of a parent, and death of a contemporary as wake-up calls to our finitude. Personally, as a boomer, watching Joni Mitchell sing "Both Sides Now" at the 2024 Grammys did it for me.

Natural Disasters and Acts of Terrorism. Disasters, whether acts of nature (e.g., fires, floods, earthquakes) or of humans (e.g., plane crashes, terrorist attacks, mass shootings), all serve as reminders of the fragility of life.

Public Health Emergencies. Widespread threats to health and safety, such as those inherent in a global pandemic (e.g., COVID-19), inevitably provoke a wave of mortality salience.

Reflecting on your own death anxiety, can you attribute its inception or exacerbation to any of these "triggers" or activating life events?

Why Do We Fear Death?

Social scientists have long pondered the underlying causes of death anxiety and, as social scientists do, have come up with a variety of theories to account for humans' fraught relationship with mortality. Without getting too bogged down in etiological considerations, a brief survey of theoretical perspectives will further our understanding of the problem we're preparing to address.

Psychoanalytic Theory

Sigmund Freud, the father of psychoanalysis, was the first theorist to tackle thanatophobia. According to his classical psychoanalytic theory, it's not actually death that people fear, because the unconscious mind cannot fathom the passage of time or conceive of its annihilation. He reasoned that because one can't fear that which one has never experienced, fear of death must be a disguise for some deeper fear stemming from unresolved childhood conflicts.

Developmental Theory

Developmental psychologist Erik Erikson's psychosocial theory of development posits that death anxiety represents a failure to successfully navigate the last in a series of eight distinctive developmental stages or *crises* (turning points) that humans pass through during their lifespan: *ego integrity vs. despair*. According to Erikson, when a person reaches late adulthood, they begin to conduct a review of the life they've lived. At this juncture, they either conclude that they've lived a life of meaning and purpose (ego integrity), or they conclude that their life was a series of misfortunes and failures and experience bitterness and regret (despair). Successful resolution of this stage enables a person to reflect on their life with a sense of closure, completeness, and coherence, and to accept death without fear. Conversely, those who have lived an unfulfilled life fear dying more.

Existential Psychology

Existential theorists, such as Otto Rank, Rollo May, and Viktor Frankl, posit that death anxiety is a fundamental aspect of the human condition. They understand death anxiety within the context of humans' struggle with the big existential issues of life, including freedom, responsibility, isolation, meaning, and mortality. Blessed/cursed with free will, humans must struggle with perpetual choices regarding the realities of life and death, including the dichotomy between awareness of mortality and finding meaning and purpose in a finite life. How they manage this existential dilemma will determine the degree to which they experience death anxiety, as well as the general nature of their psychological adjustment and well-being. According to existential theorists, facing and embracing mortality is the key to an authentic and fulfilling existence.

Meaning Management Theory (MMT)

According to Meaning Management Theory, first proposed by Canadian psychologist Paul T.P. Wong, human beings are meaning-seeking and meaning-making creatures with two primary motivations: to survive and to find reasons for survival (Wong, 2007). Wong's "Death Attitude Profile" identifies three possible orientations to death: Escape (i.e., death as an escape from suffering), Approach (i.e., death as a gateway to a better life), and Neutral (i.e., death as a natural, inevitable part of life) (Wong et al., 1993). Of these three orientations, Neutral is most strongly correlated with reduced death anxiety. MMT catalogs numerous bases of death anxiety, including the finality of death and uncertainty of what follows. However, when individuals create meaning and purpose in life, they're better equipped to confront the existential reality of death. As awareness of mortality is viewed as life-affirming, MMT falls under the umbrella of "positive psychology."

Terror Management Theory (TMT)

Terror Management Theory is the leading psychological framework for understanding the fear of death and its impact on human behavior. Proposed by social psychologists Jeff Greenberg, Tom Pyszczynski, and Sheldon Solomon in 1986 and expanded in their bestselling book, *The Worm at the Core: On the Role of Death in Life*, TMT is based on the earlier work of cultural anthropologist Ernest Becker. His Pulitzer Prize–winning book, *The Denial of Death*, posits that all of human civilization is ultimately based on defense mechanisms against the awareness of our finite existence. According to Becker (1973), fear of death—and attempts to ignore or evade it—drive nearly everything we do, including behaviors that don't appear to be even remotely associated with mortality. In other words, our attitudes, beliefs, and cultural practices are all designed to deny death and to keep our fear of it at bay—hence, "terror management" theory.

According to TMT, awareness of mortality produces intense existential anxiety, and humans have developed two defense mechanisms to cope with this crippling terror: cultural worldviews (i.e., shared values and belief systems of an in-group) and self-esteem (i.e., feeling like a valued member of the culture through fulfilling the expectations of the cultural worldview). This anxiety-buffering system creates a sense of permanence (in the form of symbolic immortality), meaning, belonging, security, and personal significance in the face of powerlessness over death (Greenberg et al., 2014).

To test whether people who were reminded of their mortality would respond by clinging more tenaciously to their cultural worldviews, the researchers behind TMT first experimented with municipal court judges and prostitutes (Rosenblatt et al., 1989). Judges were randomly divided into two groups, and half of them were reminded of their mortality via mortality-priming questions embedded within various filler questionnaires. Both groups were then shown a hypothetical prostitution case—the most common crime in their municipality at the time—and asked how much bail they'd set. The judges in the control group set bail at $50, the average bail for that crime at the time. The judges confronted with their mortality set bail at nine times higher, an average of $455. Essentially, they upheld the law more vigorously and sought to punish women who had violated the norms of their culture. When debriefed at the end of the study, the judges were incredulous that the death questionnaire had impacted the way they adjudicated the case, reinforcing the notion that the terror management mechanism operates largely unconsciously.

In another representative study investigating the effects of mortality awareness, students were asked to write about their political beliefs and then given a bogus paragraph, either supporting or attacking their beliefs, allegedly written by a fellow participant. The students were then instructed to allocate an amount of hot sauce to the fellow participant, who was described as disliking spicy food. Mortality-primed students allocated twice as much hot sauce to the students they believed to have written worldview-inconsistent paragraphs than they did to perceived writers of worldview-consistent paragraphs. Non-mortality-primed participants allocated roughly equal amounts (McGregor et al., 1998). In another study, participants who were subliminally presented with the word "death" on a computer screen more strongly endorsed the worldview of their own ethnic group or nation and denigrated members of groups with differing worldviews (Solomon et al., 2015).

Hundreds of other studies testing the mortality salience hypothesis have demonstrated that people go to great lengths to avoid thinking about their mortality and that reminders of death cause them to double down on their cultural worldviews, driving a vast array of human behaviors, including political affiliations, consumer choices, mate selection, risk-taking behaviors, creative expression, relational attachments, sexual behavior, leadership preferences, procreative tendencies, and prosocial versus antisocial behaviors (Burke et al., 2010; Jonas et al., 2002). In the real world beyond the laboratory, TMT has been used to explain sociocultural phenomena as diverse as denial of climate change (Wolfe & Tubi, 2019) and xenophobia targeting Asians during COVID-19 (Menzies & Menzies, 2020).

So how does this work? In short, reminders of death compel us to seek immortality. By identifying with a cultural group and complying with the sociocultural norms associated with that group, we feel part of something eternal and larger than ourselves, thereby transcending death. Because embracing culturally constructed belief systems and values serves a death-denying function, threatening these constructs—via experimental or real-world reminders of mortality—invokes defense mechanisms to restore a state of psychological equilibrium (i.e., feelings of invulnerability). To protect our illusion of immortality, we respond more positively toward those who uphold our cultural values, and more negatively toward those who violate them. Reminders of mortality cause us to cling more intensely to the institutions we're a part of, and the worldviews we hold.

Undoubtedly, terror management has inspired the best of humanity, as manifest in art, innovation, philanthropy, perpetuation of the species, and prosocial behavior. But there's a dark side. Managing death-terror by bolstering the scaffolding we've built around our identities can lead to troubling consequences, such as prejudice, intolerance, and even aggression against anyone designated as "other," and therefore seen as posing a threat to our cultural worldview. This polarizing defensive maneuver can occur along lines of nationality, race, religion, politics, age, or any number of other self-identifying variables.

Though these five theories of death anxiety vary significantly, they share the premise that fear of death is an inexorable part of the human condition and, by whatever means, for better or worse, profoundly influences a wide range of human behaviors.

So What?

Now that you better understand the larger historical and sociocultural context for your fear of death—as well as the whats, whos, whens, and whys of death anxiety—you may be wondering how all of this applies to you, and why it matters. And you're right to wonder. Before undertaking the laborious, sometimes painful, process of tackling any problem, it's important to consider the costs and the benefits of doing so and, perhaps more importantly, the costs of *not* doing so. So let's examine some of the adverse consequences of unaddressed death anxiety for quality of life and health. As you'll see, death anxiety—and the denial/avoidance that both assuage it (temporarily) and perpetuate it (indefinitely)—come at great cost.

During my residency training on an inpatient psychiatric unit, I encountered a patient with a condition so rare that I haven't seen it again in all my years of clinical practice. That patient was afflicted with *Cotard's syndrome* (aka *walking corpse syndrome*), characterized by the delusional belief that they're dead, rotting flesh, or don't exist. Though this is, obviously, an extreme psychiatric disorder, an analogous state is all too common in our death-denying culture. When we deny our temporality and fail to draw a clear distinction between being alive today and dead tomorrow, it's easy to sleepwalk through life, on autopilot. We're neither dead nor fully alive.

Because most of us find it difficult, if not impossible, to tolerate facing our mortality directly, we've developed an astonishing array of strategies—some conscious, some unconscious—to temper our fear of death. Some of these defense mechanisms are effective and adaptive, but many are unreliable and maladaptive. And though there are likely as many coping strategies as there are individuals, management of death anxiety typically takes one of two forms.

At one extreme are those who live life as if death doesn't exist. They're not so much avoiding death, but awareness of death. Feeling invincible, as if they're going to live forever, they may take unnecessary risks, abuse their bodies, neglect their health, and avoid medical care. They maintain their denial with incessant busyness and frenetic activity as if running from death. They distract themselves with mindless pursuits or numb themselves with substances. Financially, they spend like there's no tomorrow. They fail to plan for the future, including the end of life, because doing so requires that they face their mortality. They accumulate wealth, status, power, and material possessions as a hedge against mortality, or they deny the finality of death by living through their children or embracing religious dogma. Operating under the illusion of unlimited time, they fail to prioritize what really matters. They fritter away time, preoccupied with trivialities or pseudo-problems. They postpone meaningful activities and connections and take their loved ones for granted. Most significantly, they take life itself for granted, failing to live each day fully and purposefully.

At the other extreme are those who are acutely aware of their mortality and consciously fearful of death, as if imminent. They're prone to "catastrophizing" and contemplating worst-case scenarios. Feeling vulnerable, they live a rigid, restricted, and constricted life, opting to play it safe rather than take risks that might engender a richer, more meaningful existence. These individuals may be over-attentive to their health and safety, over-seeking medical attention and reassurance. It's not uncommon for people with death anxiety to be preoccupied, even obsessed, with their health, constantly scanning for signs of illness and consulting "Dr. Google." They engage in magical thinking, believing their hypervigilance serves to ward off peril. Relationally, they tend to avoid forming and maintaining meaningful attachments for fear of loss and abandonment or, conversely, they cling to loved ones in anxious, symbiotic attachment. They may believe they'll be saved by a relationship partner, a political figure, a guru, or a divine being—in exchange for their autonomy and self-determination.

These two extreme "styles" of mortality management aren't necessarily discreet or mutually exclusive. An individual can, and usually will, adopt a mixture of both postures and everything in between. So, if these defensive strategies serve a protective function against the unbearable pain of finitude, what are the downsides? First, they're difficult to pull off consistently and don't always work. Especially when confronted with undeniable mortality triggers, the defenses may not hold, resulting in feelings of vulnerability and exposure. Additionally, both those who deny the inevitability of death and those who are overtly fearful of it are slaves to the tyranny of avoidance—the former compelled to avoid all reminders of death, and the latter compelled to avoid death itself. Besides being exceedingly time-consuming, energy-depleting, and life-limiting, avoidance invariably makes matters worse. Though avoidance may provide relief in the short term, it serves to perpetuate a vicious cycle of more fear and more avoidance. Finally, and most significantly, defensive strategies designed to manage mortality steal life's vitality.

It's impossible to fully embrace life without acknowledging its limit. Ultimately, failure to wholeheartedly engage with life results in one of the worst pains a human can experience: regret at the end of life. Alternatively, shifting from denial to acceptance of death not only reduces anxiety and frees up psychic energy—it enables us to get the most juice out of life.

If you weren't already sufficiently motivated to face your mortality and tackle your fear of death, I hope you're now fully on board and ready to engage with the solutions ahead. Though you've likely been applying abstract, generalized elements of this overview to your own case, it's time to personalize your experience. Let's identify which specific elements of death—your own or others'—are the primary sources of your fear.

What About Me?

To borrow a metaphor from Acceptance and Commitment Therapy (Chapter 10), facing death is like confronting a giant monster made of tin cans and string. The 50-foot behemoth is so loud and menacing, it's almost impossible to stare him down. But if we disassemble him into his component parts—all the cans and string and wire and bubble gum he's made of—we can deal with each of these pieces one at a time. So let's break down death anxiety into its constituent elements and determine exactly what it is about death that scares you the most. Once you know why you're afraid, the monster isn't quite so daunting, and you're in a better position to choose strategies that target your particular fears.

At the most macro level, death anxiety falls into two broad categories: fears regarding one's own death and fears regarding the death of others, presumably loved ones. Comprising fears regarding one's own death are two categories: fears regarding the dying process and fears regarding being dead. Beyond these broad categories, there's little agreement among theorists about the precise components of death anxiety and no definitive list. However, research studies and clinical experience reveal the following themes:

Fears Regarding One's Own Death:

- Dying process (pain and suffering, immobility, dependency, loss of dignity, loss of control, vulnerability, and/or helplessness)
- Dying in a particular way or of a particular disease
- Dying prematurely
- Dying alone
- Losing mental faculties at the end of life
- Annihilation or nonexistence (not being, thinking, feeling, experiencing)
- Missing out
- Unfulfilled ambitions, unfinished projects or plans, and/or unattained milestones
- What happens to the body after death, including decomposition and being buried alive
- What happens to the soul after death, including eternal punishment in the afterlife
- Unknown, uncertainty, and unpredictability of death in general
- Loneliness or isolation, during or after dying
- Impact on loved ones, such as causing others grief or sadness, or being a burden
- How we'll be remembered after death
- Our absence won't be felt
- What will happen to dependents (children, pets)
- Loss in general (capacity, relationships, possessions, status, future, identity)
- Wasted life, regrets
- Finality/permanence of death

Fears Regarding the Death of Others:

- Talking to a loved one about their death
- Witnessing the dying process of a loved one
- Handling caregiving responsibilities
- Seeing the dead body of a loved one
- Emotional pain of loss; unbearable grief

- Loneliness
- Logistical considerations such as settling the estate, making funeral arrangements, etc.
- Financial or emotional dependency on a loved one
- Guilt

Are you surprised by the number and variety of reasons people fear death? How many of these do you identify with? You may have one or two specific types of fears, or perhaps you're bothered by multiple aspects of death and dying. Though most people who report experiencing death anxiety identify one or more of these elements as the primary source(s) of their fear, sometimes fear of death feels like a nebulous, undifferentiated monolith of terror. Or, for some people, it's "death just creeps me out." Regardless, I invite you to go a step further and take an actual measure of your death anxiety—both to quantify exactly where your anxiety falls on the nagging-to-debilitating continuum and to obtain a baseline of your degree of distress and disruption before proceeding to solutions. If interested, I direct you to the self-assessment tool—*The Collett-Lester Fear of Death Scale* (Lester, 1990)—in the Appendix. This clinically validated death anxiety test is not intended to be used as a diagnostic instrument in this context, but rather as a way to assess the benefits of the interventions ahead and to track your progress. It's not your absolute score that matters, but rather a comparison between your "before" and "after" scores. Just as you might take a blood test to measure your baseline cholesterol before starting a statin, assessing a psychological problem is a good first step to solving it. Thankfully, no blood is required for this test.

And now, let's explore what the sages, the shamans, and the shrinks have to say about overcoming the fear of death. Onward!

PART II

Philosophical Approaches

When you think about the discipline of philosophy, what comes to mind? Perhaps visions of bearded old white dudes sitting on massive rocks and contemplating their navels? Dusty tomes containing dry, unfathomable "blah-blah-blah" with no relevance to modern times, let alone your life? Perhaps you think of that pothead philosophy major from college who's now working as a barista at Starbucks and living in a van?

Regardless of your associations, all well founded, I contend that philosophy, and the ideas within its purview, is an utter goldmine when it comes to addressing fear of death. I'll go a step further to suggest that death is philosophy's muse and raison d'être. This is not a new idea. Over two thousand years ago, Socrates opined, "Ordinary people seem not to realize that those who really apply themselves in the right way to philosophy are directly and of their own accord preparing themselves for dying and death" (Plato, ca. 360 BCE/1977). Through the application of critical reasoning and logical analysis, the discipline of philosophy provides us with invaluable tools for doing just that.

Philosophy, as we know it, hearkens back to ancient Greece where rock stars like Socrates, Plato, and Aristotle lived and breathed. This was a time and place of great intellectual accomplishment, (in)forming the bedrock of philosophy to this day (Scott, 2021). Socrates, arguably Athens's most famous practitioner, had a lot to say about death and, in the end, mastered it. Believing the soul to be immortal, he welcomed the death of his body as freedom from the limitations imposed by the physical world. Sentenced to die by execution for charges of impiety and corrupting the youth of Athens, he famously met his death with calm indifference. Prior to his forced suicide via poison hemlock, he delivered his final lesson on the nature of the afterlife, took a bath (so that his body wouldn't have to be cleaned postmortem), and bid farewell to his wife and three sons. He drank the poison calmly and chastised his friends for their weeping. His last words were uttered to his friend about paying a debt of chickens: "Crito, we owe a cock to Asklepios. Pay it and do not neglect it." Wow. I want whatever he had. (Not the hemlock, of course.)

Socrates believed that philosophy—essentially, the study of wisdom—was the most important pursuit in life. It was he who uttered the famous dictum: "The unexamined life is not worth living." An unexamined life, as he intended it, is a life without wisdom. And wisdom addresses the fundamental existential questions of how to live a good life and prepare to die a good death. As he (and other ancient philosophers) saw it, the art of living and the art of dying are inextricably connected—two sides of the same coin.

Many of Socrates' fellow philosophers exemplified the art of dying well as they faced their own ends, sometimes in spectacularly chill fashion. First-century Stoic philosopher Julius Canus is a prime example. When sentenced to death by Emperor Caligula for an alleged plot against him, he responded, "Most excellent prince, I tender you my thanks." Ten days later when a centurion came to take him to his execution, he was found playing checkers. To his companion, he said, "Don't cheat after I die and say you won." To the centurion, he said, "You are witness that I am one piece ahead." Chrysippus, another Stoic philosopher, famously died from laughing at one of his own jokes. Apparently, during the 143rd Olympiad, he caught a donkey eating a basket full of his figs. Finding the image amusing, he cried out, "Now give the donkey a drink of pure wine to wash down the figs," whereupon he fell to the ground and died in a fit of laughter. Clearly, he himself had tipped a few goblets.

There are many other examples of stellar deaths among ancient philosophers, the subject of an entire book—*The Book of Dead Philosophers*—by modern philosopher Simon Critchley (2008). Herein he explores the contention of ancient philosopher Marcus Tullius Cicero that "to study philosophy is nothing but to prepare one's self to die." In an interview with *The Guardian*, Critchley says, "It is the ambition of *The Book of Dead Philosophers* to show that often the philosopher's greatest work of art is the manner of their death" (Reed, 2008). Indeed, one of the things I most admire about the ancient philosophers is that they embodied the wisdom they imparted. Perhaps these old dead guys have something to teach us about facing death with equanimity, even humor.

You may question the relevance of ancient philosophies for your life and your problems. How could words written two millennia ago apply in a world with indoor plumbing and next-day delivery? Seneca, a Roman Stoic philosopher you'll soon meet, maintains that by studying philosophy, we can draw on the rich and timeless wisdom of the ages for guidance on the challenges we face today. He elaborates on the benefits of mining the writings of humanity's greatest thinkers:

> By the toil of others, we are led into the presence of things that have been brought from darkness into light. We are excluded from no age, but we have access to them all; and if we are prepared in loftiness of mind to pass beyond the narrow confines of human weakness, there is a long period of time through which we can roam... None of these will force you to die, but all will teach you how to die. None of them will exhaust your years, but each will contribute his years to yours. What happiness, what a fine old age awaits the man who has made himself a client of these! [Seneca, ca. 49 CE/2005]

Throughout the ages, there has been one constant, immutable reality and ubiquitous concern: our mortality. Philosophy, the study of wisdom and mindful living, may well be the most reliable anchor for our existential precariousness. In the chapters ahead, I'll survey various philosophical approaches to the problem of mortality, from the ancient Epicureans and Stoics to modern practitioners.

Despite any reservations you may have regarding relevance, at the very least, you can derive comfort from knowing that great minds have been grappling with fear of death since the beginning of recorded time. Recognizing the universality of your concerns—that people over two thousand years ago were plagued with the same fears you're struggling with today—can help you feel not so alone in your struggles. So hug a philosopher/barista, and prepare to contemplate death in good company.

Chapter 3

The Epicureans

Epicureanism was a school of philosophy, founded around 307 BCE by Epicurus, a Greek philosopher of the Hellenistic period. After Epicurus' death, Epicureanism became one of two major schools of thought in classic Greek philosophy, alongside Stoicism. On the analytic side, both schools addressed the nature of the universe, matter, and the soul. On the practical side, both left a remarkable legacy of instruction for living a good life and facing death without fear.

Epicurus and Lucretius are the most well-known Epicureans. Lucretius, a Roman poet and philosopher, was a devoted follower and proponent of Epicurus' philosophy. He's best known for his epic poem *De Rerun Natura* (*On the Nature of Things*), a didactic, six-volume work written over two hundred years after Epicurus' death. A comprehensive exposition of the Epicurean worldview, the poem reveals crucial insight into the ideas of his predecessor, much of whose work had been lost. Since its publication over two thousand years ago, *De Rerun Natura* has influenced the thinking of heavy hitters such as Michel de Montaigne, John Locke, Thomas Jefferson, Karl Marx, and Albert Einstein. Fun fact: Horace—the Roman poet who penned the Latin aphorism *carpe diem* in his *Odes* (23 BCE)—was a card-carrying Epicurean.

Though Epicureanism is often mischaracterized as an exclusively pleasure-seeking, hedonistic approach to life, Epicurean philosophy is actually focused on the eradication of pain and anxiety. As fear of death was believed to be the root cause of human suffering, the Epicureans made it their business to address it with their philosophy. They proposed two classic arguments to face death with calm indifference: the *experiential blank argument* and the *symmetry argument*.

Chapter 3. The Epicureans

Lights Out

> He alone rated himself beyond diamonds and rubies. Diamonds and rubies are gone, spread out on the deck to be washed away by a bucket of sea-water, and he does not even know that the diamonds and rubies are gone. He does not lose anything, for with the loss of himself he loses the knowledge of loss.—Jack London, *The Sea Wolf*

Can you imagine living in constant fear of the wrath of the gods? Such was the plight of the citizens of ancient Greece. They viewed their mortal lives as temporary and believed that their sins would be punished with eternal torment by temperamental and vengeful deities. This prevailing view was predicated on belief in the immortality of the soul—as espoused by both Plato and Socrates—and pre-dated the medieval Christian view of an afterlife, complete with gory hell iconography designed to scare believers into submission. Needless to say, the prospect of death was terrifying.

Enter Epicurus (341–270 BCE), born approximately seven years after Plato's death. He began his philosophical journey as a rebellious teenager in revolt against his teachers. He founded a philosophy school called "The Garden," near Plato's "Academy" in Athens, one of the first philosophical establishments to welcome both women and slaves. Very progressive. Epicurus vehemently condemned contemporary religious leaders who, to bolster their power, threatened believers with punishment in an afterlife for failure to adhere to their rules. He wasn't very popular in ancient Greece.

Epicurus posited that the world is constructed entirely of empty space and atoms—over two thousand years before science discovered them—and attempted to explain all natural phenomena in atomic terms. He believed the universe to be logical and predictable, and that true knowledge is to be found empirically, through the senses—a precursor to the modern scientific method. His reliance on observable, objectively verifiable phenomena contradicted the commonly held notion that mythology and religion are the true sources of knowledge. A strong proponent of free will, Epicurus maintained that the lives of humans are self-determined and that the gods have no influence on them. He rejected the prevailing views of an afterlife and an immaterial, immortal soul.

The absence of an afterlife meant no one needed to fear suffering after death or worry about pleasing vengeful gods. In eschewing the prospect of life after death, Epicurus encouraged his students to focus on enjoying their mortal lives. He believed that the purpose of human life is to achieve *eudaimonia*—the absence of physical pain (*aponia*) and freedom from mental disturbance (*ataraxia*). In the Epicurean view, the only thing preventing us from enjoying a life of peaceful contentment is our omnipresent fear of death. Because it pervades our thoughts and "leaves no pleasure undisturbed," it's the worst fear we face in life. Epicurus believed that reason alone has the power to banish fear of death. Asserting that the fear of death is natural but not rational, he formulated a series of well-constructed arguments to alleviate death anxiety, memorized and recited by his students like a creed.

According to Epicurus' *experiential blank argument*, the first step to overcoming fear of death is to try to imagine what it would be like to be dead. In so doing, you'll encounter an immutable contradiction: Because death is the absence of existence, there's nothing to imagine. From nothingness, there's no perspective, no point of reference. You can't perceive—or even imagine—nonexistence from a state of existence. There's no there there. Through this thought experiment, Epicurus was inviting his students (and us) to realize that being dead isn't an experience, that death itself isn't really a thing at all (Dresser, 2020).

Central to this Epicurean argument is the notion of death as total annihilation, the end of being. Lights out. Sounds harsh, but bear with me for the upside. Epicurus believed the human soul to be made of atoms, presumably dispersed throughout the body. Because consciousness (the soul) interacts closely and dynamically with the body, the soul's existence is linked inextricably to the body's fate. The soul cannot exist without the body. Thus, at the time of death, the soul evaporates entirely. Consciousness perishes with the body. This conclusion—the mortality of the soul—is in direct opposition to that of Socrates who, facing his execution 100 years previous, was comforted by his belief in the immortality of the soul and looked forward to eternal communion with like-minded people.

Chapter 3. The Epicureans

For Epicurus, accepting death as the end of existence is the key to peace and happiness. If indeed death marks the end of consciousness and sensation, both positive and negative, we'd experience no emotional or physical pain. Because feelings of fear, sadness, grief, regret, or deprivation are not possible after we die, then it makes no sense to dread death. "We" won't be around to experience it. Epicurus argues further that if death doesn't cause us any pain when we're dead, it's foolish to allow the fear of it to cause us pain while we're alive.

Epicurus' philosophy of death is encapsulated in a surviving letter to one of his students, Menoeceus:

> Accustom yourself to believe that death is nothing to us, for good and evil imply awareness, and death is the privation of all awareness; therefore a right understanding that death is nothing to us makes the mortality of life enjoyable, not by adding to life an illimitable time, but by taking away the yearning after immortality. For life has no terror for those who thoroughly apprehend that there are no terrors for them in ceasing to live. Foolish, therefore, is the person who says that he fears death, not because it will pain when it comes, but because it pains in the prospect. Whatever causes no annoyance when it is present, causes only a groundless pain in the expectation. Death, therefore, the most awful of evils, is nothing to us, seeing that, when we are, death is not come, and, when death is come, we are not. It is nothing, then, either to the living or to the dead, for with the living it is not and the dead exist no longer [Epicurus, n.d./2019].

In other words, death isn't bad for the living since they're not dead; neither is it bad for the dead since they don't exist.

Let's break down Epicurus' formal argument (Scott, 2021):

1. Things are only bad for us if they are experientially unpleasant.
2. The dead have no experience.
3. Therefore, by 1 and 2, nothing can be bad for the dead.
4. It is irrational to fear what will not be bad.
5. Therefore, by 3 and 4, it is irrational to fear death itself.

For Epicurus's argument to be persuasive, you must accept two premises: First, that death is the end of consciousness which doesn't transcend the body, and second, that you can't be harmed by things you can't experience. Because you're dead, you can't know that you're dead. Central to his argument is the notion that "death" and "I" are mutually exclusive and cannot co-exist: "Where I am, death is not; where death is, I am not." If you can accept these assumptions, you'll likely concede that death is nothing to fear. However, if you believe in an afterlife (i.e., the immortality of the soul), this "lights out" perspective will be of little relevance or comfort. Fortunately, other means of addressing death anxiety don't require acceptance of these Epicurean premises, many of which are contained in subsequent chapters.

Epicurus contends that death concerns are largely unconscious and must be inferred from disguised manifestations. These can include excessive religiosity, all-consuming accumulation of wealth and possessions, grasping for power and status, and unending pursuit of novel activities, all of which offer a counterfeit version of immortality. Because no activity, distraction, or material thing can satisfy our craving for eternal life, all such pursuits are intrinsically unsatisfying and unrewarding. Instead, Epicurus urges us to store and recall deeply etched memories of pleasant experiences. By drawing on such memories again and again, we'll not need the false satisfaction of endless hedonistic pursuits (Yalom, 2008).

Legend has it that Epicurus retained composure on his deathbed and died a peaceful death, recalling pleasurable conversations with friends and students, despite the searing pain of kidney stones. Consistent with his teachings, the last day of his life was described as "a truly happy day." Like Socrates, who held an entirely different view of death and the afterlife, Epicurus lived and died unafraid of death. Indeed, there are multiple roads to Rome.

Existential Bookends

> I do not fear death. I had been dead for billions and billions of years before I was born, and had not suffered the slightest inconvenience from it.—Mark Twain

Chapter 3. The Epicureans

Consider the dash that represents your life—the time between the year of your birth and the year of your death—"the brief crack of light between two eternities of darkness," as poetically described by Russian novelist Vladimir Nabokov (1989). Now, consider the time before your birth. Try to recall what it was like before you were born. Not how the world was—the purview of historians—but what it was like to be you before you existed. As you'll discover, it's impossible to imagine your prenatal existence, much less experience it. Finally, try to imagine your existence after your death. Similarly impossible, right? These two states of non-being are equally unfathomable.

Roman philosopher and poet Titus Lucretius Carus (aka Lucretius), an Epicurean of a later generation (99–55 BCE), observed a puzzling asymmetry in our attitudes toward our prenatal and posthumous nonexistence. Though we don't exist in either of these periods, we fear the later limit of life (death) but not the earlier limit of life (birth). This observation forms the basis for the *symmetry argument* against the fear of death, originally proposed in his epic poem *De Rerun Natura* (Lucretius, ca. 60–55 BCE/2007).

The argument posits that the time before your birth (pre-existence) and the time after your death (post-existence) are analogous states of non-being. Both entail the absence of you. Thus, given the symmetry between these two temporal limits of our existence (past and future), our attitudes toward our birth and our death should be equivalent. Since we don't consider not having existed for an eternity before our births to be a problem, neither should we consider not existing for an eternity after our deaths to be so dreadful. Likewise, since there's nothing inherently frightening in the past infinity of prenatal nonexistence, neither should we fear the future infinity of postmortem nonexistence. In short, it's no more reasonable to fear nonexistence after life than it is to fear nonexistence before life.

The formal reconstruction of the argument is as follows (Danaher, 2013):

1. The state of prenatal non-being is not bad for us.
2. Postmortem non-being is the same as prenatal non-being, in all important respects.

3. Therefore, death is not bad for us.
4. If something is not bad for us, then it is irrational to fear it.
5. Therefore, the fear of death is irrational.

Hence, Lucretius would have us "look back at the bygone ages of eternity that passed before we were born, and mark how utterly it counts to us as nothing. This is a mirror that Nature holds up to us, in which we may see the time that shall be after we are dead."

Stoic philosopher Seneca (ca. 65/1969) likewise opines that anyone who mourns the dead should also mourn those who have not yet been born: "Wouldn't a man seem to you the greatest of all fools if he wept because, for a thousand years previously, he had not been alive? He's just as great a fool if he weeps because he won't live for a thousand years to come." Fifteen centuries later, French Renaissance essayist Michel de Montaigne (ca. 1580/1993) echoes this sentiment in his essay *That to Study Philosophy is to Learn to Die*: "To lament that we shall not be alive a hundred years hence, is the same folly as to be sorry we were not alive a hundred years ago." Great minds think alike; great ideas are timeless.

Based on the symmetry argument, followers of Epicureanism—and the Stoics thereafter—maintained an indifference to death, often using the phrase *Non fui, fui, non sum, non curo* as an epitaph, commonly found on ancient tombstones of the Roman Empire. The bumper-sticker-worthy translation reads:

> I was not ... I was ... I am not ... I do not care.

Though, admittedly, death is the end of something born, it still stands that we're beings that have come into existence from nonexistence. The symmetry argument requires our awareness that before our birth extends a long span of time encompassing all of human history. Past events played out, only to be known to us by historians who recorded them. And in those histories, we were nowhere to be found—not as participants in historical events, or even as living inhabitants of this planet. The world was completely oblivious to us. After our transition back into nonexistence marked by death, history will still be made and recorded. And we won't be part of it.

It should be noted that this archaic philosophical argument is not just the purview of ancient philosophizers. Modern science guys are on board with symmetry, too. American astrophysicist, author, and science educator Neil deGrasse Tyson was just four blocks from the World Trade Center on September 11. In an interview on the DEAD Talks Podcast (Ferrigio, 2023), he explains how this shaped his perception of life and death and how death sits from a cosmic perspective. Echoing the Epicurean point of view, he asserts that he has no reason to believe that anything other than the decomposition of his body will happen after death. He then challenges the 34-year-old interviewer: "You're not asking yourself 'Where was I 40 years ago? I had to be somewhere.'" He argues that we don't lament the absence of existence before we're born, or even think about it. He concludes, "My absence of existence after I die is not any different from my absence of existence before I was born." A modern-day Lucretius.

The arguments of both Epicurus and Lucretius suggest that death itself is nothing to fear because we won't be around to experience it. But what if it's missing out on life that we fear? For Lucretius, our lust for life and our fear of death are one and the same, just framed differently. When we fret about not completing what we want to complete in life, or about not having enough time with our loved ones, we're fretting about death from the perspective of life (Maden, 2020). As Lucretius asserts, "It is this evil and excessive desire for life that makes us tremble with doubts and forebodings." He explains that our fear of death begets an unfocused craving for life that leaves us feeling indecisive about how to best use our time and perpetually unsatisfied with our lot, "our mouths always gaping open with a constant thirst for life."

For the Epicureans, the answer to death anxiety is to remember that death is nothing to us *and* that our incessant craving for something we can't have (i.e., more life than we're allotted) prevents us from appreciating the life we do have. If we can learn to embrace our mortality and resolve to spend our limited time well, we can stop lamenting—or trying to control—a fate we ultimately can't escape. The symmetry argument is simple, yet profound. In thinking of birth and death as twin experiences, as existential bookends, wouldn't it be possible to be less fearful of death? When we contemplate the vast scope of the universe, we recognize that the brief gap between our birth and our death is the only thing we'll ever experience. And that can be enough, as you'll soon discover.

The Epicurean view of death is, admittedly, a first-person, existential one. That is, it addresses only fear of the dissolution of oneself and concern that one could be aware that they're dead and be upset about it. Hence, these Epicurean arguments will be more useful for those who fear death itself, as opposed to the process of getting there (dying), the death of loved ones, or the prospect of leaving loved ones behind. Rest assured, there are plenty of remedies for these fears in the chapters ahead.

Chapter 4

The Stoics

Stoicism was a popular school of philosophy that flourished for around 500 years during its prime in ancient Greece and the Roman Empire. From its founding by Zeno of Citium in the year 300 BCE until Marcus Aurelius' death in 180 CE, Stoic philosophy played a pivotal role in Europe and boasts a large global following of zealous adherents to this day. For historical and cultural context, Stoicism—one of the Hellenistic schools of philosophy—overlapped with Epicureanism. In their day, they experienced a sort of sibling rivalry. The winner, as it turns out, is us. Stoicism was (and is) a practical philosophy, informed by its system of logic and understanding of human nature and the natural world. An "operating system" for life, Stoicism holds the promise of psychological resilience, the holy grail of mental health.

The most prominent and prolific thinkers and practitioners of the Stoic school (i.e., the "big three") were, in chronological order, the statesman Seneca the Younger (4 BCE–65 CE), the slave Epictetus (55–135), and Roman Emperor Marcus Aurelius (121–180). All three are notable for having practiced what they preached by using Stoic philosophy to navigate turmoil and uncertainties during their own lives and, ultimately, to face their deaths.

Though the scope of Stoicism is broad and includes logic, metaphysics, politics, and other social matters, the Stoics' greatest legacy is their ethics. As with most other schools of classical philosophy, the goal of life is *eudaimonia*, a Greek word often defined as "happiness" or "good-spiritedness," but better translated as "human flourishing." Stoicism's theory of metaphysics helps to explain its core tenets. God and the universe were viewed as one entity called the

Logos. All elements of the universe—planets, stars, humans, and animals—were regarded as passive matter, originating from the Logos and subject to the fate determined for them by this divine, rational entity. In Stoic thinking, fate and free will coexist.

The Stoics believed that humans possess a unique capacity for reason and, thus, prized rational thinking as the solution to many of life's challenges. They advocated acting on reliable information and contemplating situations fully, rather than reacting impulsively or emotionally. This thoughtful orientation enabled them to remain calm and indifferent to external events, no matter how difficult. The Stoics also held that certain destructive emotions, such as anger or fear, result from errors in judgment. As the universe was believed to be preordained by the divine Logos, the Stoics reasoned that it's irrational to worry about things that we can't control. Stoic philosophers didn't advocate expunging emotion altogether, but rather striving for inner peace through mental discipline.

At the outset, it's important to distinguish between *Stoicism* (uppercase) and *stoicism* (lowercase), as many of us have a lifetime of associations with the latter. As commonly understood, a stoic person copes with unpleasant emotions by suppressing or concealing them, maintaining a stiff upper lip. This arguably maladaptive style of managing emotions is unrelated to Stoicism, the ancient Greek school of philosophy. The Stoics experienced and expressed the same range of human emotions as the rest of us. What set them apart was their ability to regulate difficult emotions and to face challenges with composure. If you're skeptical about the mental health benefits of Stoic philosophy, it should be noted that it's the inspiration for—and foundation of—modern Cognitive Behavioral Therapy (CBT), the foremost evidence-based approach to a wide range of psychological suffering, including fear of death. We'll take a deep dive into CBT in Chapter 9.

Long before the self-help genre was invented, the Stoics equipped us with fundamental tools for the art of living—sometimes with brutal, no-bullshit candor and an instructional style akin to the Zen masters. Some of their counsel is not for the faint of heart, but always well-intended and often refreshing in its forthrightness. As I've read the Stoic philosophers, I've often uttered "Ouch!" under my breath. But after taking a beat, the sting of a Stoic truth bomb is invariably followed by "Ah yes, right."

Caveats aside, no school of thought in history has been more attuned to the haunting fear of death than Stoicism. As pragmatists, the Stoics viewed the world through a rational lens, consistent with the laws of nature. They understood death as a natural part of the cycle of life—a simple return to nature, the universal source of all things. Notably, this Stoic disposition aligns with modern Meaning Management Theory's "neutral acceptance" orientation toward death as natural, universal, and beyond our control (Menzies & Whittle, 2022).

Unlike some philosophical schools of thought, the Stoics didn't rely on belief in an afterlife to allay fears of death. They particularly rejected notions of heaven and hell. Like the Epicureans, they saw death as the end—an inevitable, final event for both body and soul. Because the Stoic philosophers were so matter-of-fact about death, there was no need to deny or avoid it. Rather, it was accepted and used as a reminder to make the best use of their time. Viewing death as a precondition for life, they meditated on death and dying daily—not out of a morbid preoccupation, but a desire to live fully. For the Stoics, embracing mortality is the key to living with life-affirming presence. The interdependence of life and death is a theme that resonates, again and again, throughout the pages of this book.

Based on their belief that it's fear of death—not death itself—that causes misery, the Stoics gifted us with several "rebuttals" to the fear of death, including formal logical arguments and thought experiments. I've compiled the most useful of these in this chapter, including the philosophies of Epictetus, Seneca, and Aurelius.

The Illusion of Control

> I cannot escape death, but at least I can escape the fear of it.—Epictetus

Marjorie, a self-described "control freak," started our therapy session like so many others: recounting catastrophe. She had planned a big event down to the last detail, obsessing over every element to the point of nightly insomnia. She made repeated phone calls to coordinate with the venue, triple-checked vendors, and micro-managed all who had any role in pulling this off. Not surprisingly, she alienated everyone involved with her obsessive "attention to detail." Marjorie anticipated everything that could go wrong and planned for each of these potential derailments. She had everything under control. Or did she? The planned event was her wedding. The unanticipated derailment was a global pandemic.

I was treating Marjorie for a severe, lifelong anxiety disorder, characterized by obsessive worry and compulsive behaviors designed to ward off disaster. Though she recognized that her excessive need for control was ruining her life and straining her relationships, it was the only thing that seemed to tamp down her anxiety. But her control was an illusion. Despite all the variables she managed to control, she constantly encountered things she couldn't control, or even anticipate. Like a global pandemic. As you can imagine, Marjorie was terrified of death—the ultimate thing she couldn't plan, anticipate, or control. When we weren't focusing on more immediate—or imminent—crises, her thanatophobia was a primary focus of our therapeutic work.

If your death anxiety is related to fears regarding loss of control, the noble slave-turned-philosopher Epictetus has something to offer you. Epictetus, one of Stoicism's most famous practitioners, was no stranger to hardships beyond his control. He was born in modern-day Turkey in 55 CE, a cripple and a slave to a wealthy statesman. Despite his rough start in life, he believed that by using our rational faculties, we can navigate through whatever life throws at us—or takes away from us. Like other Stoics, he sought to teach Stoicism as a practical philosophy for everyday life. His ideas formed the basis of the *dichotomy of control*, one of the core pillars of Stoic philosophy and practice. Epictetus (ca. 125/2004) introduces the dichotomy of control at the beginning of *Enchiridion* (*Handbook*), a short manual of Stoic precepts.

The Stoic dichotomy of control simply states that some things are within our control and others are not. It provides a framework for managing life's challenges by dividing them into two distinct categories: "things we can control" and "everything else." According to Epictetus, the only things within our complete control are our judgments (how we think about things) and our actions. Everything else in life—including health, wealth, other people's opinions, and the outcomes of our actions—depends to some extent on external circumstances. We can try to influence these things, but ultimately we don't have direct control over them. Once we've distinguished between things within our control and things beyond our control, Epictetus counsels us to focus on "controlling the controllables" and cultivating an attitude of detachment from everything else. If this ancient Stoic concept sounds familiar to you, "The Serenity Prayer" by theologian Reinhold Niebuhr, the cornerstone of the 12-step recovery model, offers a similar message: "God, grant me the serenity to accept the things I cannot change, courage to change the things I can, and wisdom to know the difference."

Easier said than done. In my clinical practice, I've observed that we typically make two errors of classification, with significant consequences for mental health. On the one hand, we try to control the things in life that we have no control over, such as other people (their beliefs, opinions, values, and actions), the past, the future, the weather, the economy, traffic, politics, time, bodily sensations, illness, aging, death, etc. When we try to control the uncontrollables, we have little to no impact and end up feeling powerless, frustrated, anxious, and bitter. It's easy to see how this illusion of control is linked to various forms of mental illness. For example, worry and generalized anxiety arise when we overthink aspects of the future (which we can't control). Depression is associated with rumination about the past (which we can't control). Social anxiety is incited by worrying too much about what other people think of us (which we can't control). Anger and frustration, even violence, result when we assume we can control others (LeBon, 2023). Conversely, in the second classification error, we surrender our agency and fail to take responsibility for things we *can* control, such as our beliefs, values, attitudes, and actions. Because we're not focusing our energy where we can have an impact, we remain stuck. This can result in a mentality of victimhood, helplessness, and a tendency to blame others and our circumstances for our suffering.

As an alternative to these two common pitfalls, the dichotomy of control enables us to use our time and energy more efficiently. It's helpful to consider control through the lens of *opportunity cost*, the forgone benefit that would have been derived from an option not chosen. Choosing to do one thing means we aren't able to do another. Spending our money on one thing means we can't use that money for something else. By focusing on things we can't control, we're diverting attention away from what we can control, thereby forfeiting our power and influence.

Control directly impacts our freedom, too. When we worry about things outside our control—up to and including death—we're letting those things be our master. Freedom comes from learning to accept the limitations of our control. When we practice separating what we can control from what we can't, suffering becomes optional. Can I do something about it? If not, then I let it go. If so, then I take action. Or I don't—that's still a choice.

If you reflect for a moment, you'll recognize that almost everything in life is beyond our control. But the one thing within our control is our mind—how we perceive, construe, interpret, and appraise external circumstances. Might we have control over the degree to which we're disturbed by things if we focus on our response to them rather than trying to change them? This is where Epictetus' most revolutionary concept comes in. He famously asserts that people aren't disturbed by the things that happen to them, but rather by their view of these things—an insight that inspired the development of modern-day Cognitive Behavioral Therapy (CBT). In a world where so many things are out of our control, this is excellent news! We may not be able to control external events, but we have discretion over how we respond to them. The notion that it's easier to change ourselves and our perceptions than to change the world around us has reverberated throughout the ages to this day. You might recognize some of these modern voices:

> If you don't like something, change it. If you can't change it, change your attitude.—Maya Angelou

> If you change the way you look at things, the things you look at change.—Wayne Dyer

> The primary cause of unhappiness is never the situation but your thoughts about it.—Eckhart Tolle

If you're skeptical about the power of this idea, or how it works in real life, let's try a thought experiment. Imagine that you're stuck in a traffic jam on the interstate. Cars appear to be backed up for miles, and nothing is moving. Since you're not going anywhere, you might as well observe the drivers in the cars around you. In the car on your left (Car A) is a man who's clearly fuming. His face is red, his arms are flailing about, his middle finger is extended, and he appears to be cursing his plight. At one point, he leans on his horn, as if to punish the traffic around him for being in his way. You can imagine that his blood pressure is through the roof. You next look at the driver in the car to your right (Car B). You see a man who appears to be annoyed, but busy. He's looking at a map, consulting his appointment book, and talking on his cell phone. You'd imagine he's problem-solving the inconvenience, perhaps notifying someone that he'll be late and making an alternative plan. You then look in your rear-view mirror to behold the man in the car behind you (Car C). You notice that he's singing and bopping, presumably to the radio, and taking the opportunity to eat a sandwich. He appears relaxed and not the least bit disturbed by the inconvenience. For the sake of the exercise, let's assume that each driver has somewhere to be at a particular time and is delayed by the traffic jam, so we can't attribute their divergent responses to divergent circumstances outside of the traffic jam.

If events themselves were the cause of misery, all three drivers would be responding in exactly the same way, right? After all, they're each experiencing the very same event. They're equally out of control over their circumstance—the traffic jam. They're equally delayed from getting where they need to be. But we see very different responses. How do we account for this? The answer lies in the thing that each driver has control over—how they perceive, think about, and talk to themselves about the situation. We can imagine their respective narratives:

> Driver A: This is a disaster. I'm going to be late. My day is ruined. How dare these drivers hold me up. I'm going to lean on my horn until traffic gets moving. If need be, I'll get out of my car and punch someone in the face.
>
> Driver B: This is unfortunate. I'm going to be late, but I can make alternative arrangements. Let me use this time to figure it out.

DRIVER C: Finally, a break! Alone in my car, free from my nagging boss at work and my screaming kids at home. I'll chill to some tunes and enjoy the sandwich I had no time to eat earlier.

Driver A was trying to control a situation beyond his control. Driver B was accepting the situation and managing it by controlling what he could. Driver C was reframing the situation as pleasurable and thereby in control of his response to it. None of them changed the traffic jam.

But what about things in life that are really, really bad? you might ask. Maybe I can manage a traffic jam or other minor inconvenience, but how much control do I have over my responses in the face of unspeakable tragedy? Perhaps there's no one better qualified to answer this than Holocaust survivor and existential psychiatrist Viktor Frankl. He endured three years as a prisoner in Nazi concentration camps, during which he lost his father, mother, brother, and wife. In his classic *Man's Search for Meaning*, a book chronicling his horrific experiences, Frankl (2006) writes,

> When we are no longer able to change a situation, we are challenged to change ourselves. Everything can be taken from a man but one thing: the last of the human freedoms—to choose one's attitude in any given set of circumstances, to choose one's own way.

His expansion on this idea is similarly profound: "Between stimulus and response there is a space. In that space is our power to choose our response. In our response lies our growth and our freedom." Though I first read Frankl's life-affirming, life-informing masterpiece decades ago, to this day when I'm stuck in a traffic jam—literal or metaphorical—I recall Dr. Frankl's words and make a choice. On a good day, I make a good choice.

But wait, there's more! This dichotomy of control thing isn't just situation-specific. Recent research suggests that its application impacts mental health and well-being overall. During Stoic Week 2022—an annual online event in which people from all over the world attempt to "live like a Stoic" for seven days—over 2,000 participants were asked to rate how much they identified with two statements relating to the different parts of the dichotomy of control: "I control the controllables" and "I let go of things that I can't control."

They also completed questionnaires to assess their life satisfaction, flourishing, and emotions. Both parts of the dichotomy of control were found to have significant positive correlations with all measures of well-being. Specifically, "controlling the controllables" had an extremely high correlation with flourishing, while "letting go of things I can't control" had a significant association with the balance of positive over negative emotions (LeBon, 2022).

Having established the philosophical and empirical bases of the dichotomy of control, let's apply the concept to your fear of death—the reason you're here, after all. Nothing is more uncontrollable than death. Of all matters falling into the "out of our control" category, death is the ultimate one. Except for suicide, we mortals possess little to no control over when, where, or how we die. While we may be able to delay death through healthy lifestyle habits and avoidance of danger, it will ultimately find us whether we're ready or not. Therefore, for the Stoics, death is not something to fear, avoid, lament, or hate. Rather, it's something to be accepted as part of the natural order of life.

Though death is inevitable (i.e., beyond our control), our *view* of death is our responsibility, and we can learn to accept it as neither intrinsically good nor bad; it just is. Death itself has no attributes, save the ones we assign it. Death, like tofu, is neutral until we marinate it in our own juices. In *Enchiridion*, Epictetus expands on this notion that there's nothing *inherently* horrible or terrifying about death: "Death is nothing dreadful (or else it would have appeared dreadful to Socrates), but instead the judgment about death that it is dreadful—that is what is dreadful."

The dichotomy of control is particularly useful when we can't change something (our mortality) but wish to limit its impact on our well-being (our anxiety). Our fear of death has evolved from the culturally instilled and reinforced impression that the end of life must be perceived as terrifying and tragic. But these are cultural overlays, not reality. So ask yourself, How am I looking at death now? What ideas, images, assumptions, and preconceptions do I hold that make it so fearful? Could I look at it differently? More objectively? Since our impression of death resides only in our imagination, we can reimagine death. Managing our perception of death is our strongest ally in overcoming death's terror—the final frontier of controlling what we have control over. The dichotomy of control, though potent, isn't designed to suppress all negative emotions about mortality. Rather, it's about changing entrenched thought patterns from an all-encompassing negative disposition toward death to a more balanced perspective.

A welcome benefit of applying the dichotomy of control to fear of death is its positive impact on all other fears. Seeking indifference to "the big one" helps alleviate anxiety over life's inevitable uncontrollables in general. If we can make peace with the worst thing that can happen to us or our loved ones, all other anxieties fall into perspective. As death is the bottom line of all fear, if we can conquer the fear of death, there's nothing else to fear. As French philosopher Albert Camus observes, "There is only one liberty, to come to terms with death, thereafter anything is possible."

An undeniable reality of life is that "shit happens." Mostly shit that's out of our control. We'll get sick, the weather will ruin our plans for the day, a global pandemic will upend our lives for years. And, in the end, we'll die. Learning to take charge of our perceptions of and responses to these inevitabilities is, perhaps, the greatest investment we can make in increasing our resiliency and life satisfaction. As a means to this end, embracing the dichotomy of control and practicing it daily can change how we deal with life, suffering, and mortality.

Life on Loan

> We must remember that nothing in this world really belongs to us. At best, we are merely borrowers.—Christopher Isherwood, American novelist and playwright

Imagine you've adopted a pet—a dog, let's say. After much deliberation, you finally choose a name: Brutus. You feed him, train him, walk him, sleep with him. And, despite a few ruined pairs of shoes and accidents on the carpet, you fall in love. You're now attached to Brutus. Brutus is yours; he belongs to you. You are the owner of Brutus. Imagine that some months pass and your beloved Brutus, while doing dog things, gets into something he shouldn't and ingests a toxic substance. You rush him to the vet but it's too late. Brutus is dead. You've lost your precious boy. Of course, you're devastated, grief-stricken.

Now imagine that you foster a dog from a local shelter. The dog already has a name: Bentley. The agreement is that you'll care for Bentley until he finds his forever home. The time this will take is, of course, indeterminate. You feed him, train him, walk him, sleep with him. And, despite a few ruined pairs of shoes and accidents on the carpet, you fall in love. You're now attached to Bentley. But he's not yours; he belongs to the shelter. You are the foster parent of Bentley, not the owner. Imagine that some months pass and an adoption agreement has been signed. You must now take Bentley back to the shelter where his forever parent will pick him up and take him to his forever home. Bentley has been returned. How do you feel? You are, no doubt, sad. You will miss Bentley. But are you devastated? Grief-stricken? Probably not. Because you understood from the start that Bentley was only with you for a time, that he did not belong to you. You may even feel grateful to have known Bentley and been entrusted with his care for a short time.

What if we adopted (pun intended) this orientation to our own lives and the lives of those we love? What if, one day, our life—and theirs—was "returned" instead of "lost"? According to Buddhist thinkers, attachment is the cause of suffering. The Stoics likewise identify this challenge, though framed somewhat differently. So much of the difficulty we have with death—our own or others'—is the prospect of loss. But to dread losing something, we must conceive of it as belonging to us. As Epictetus (ca. 108/2008) wisely points out, "A man only loses what he has ... Loss and sorrow are only possible with respect to things we own."

According to the Stoics, nothing belongs to us; everything in life is borrowed. Think about this for a moment. Where have all the best things in your life come from? Did you create them from scratch? Were you born with them? The truth is, we came into this life with nothing and we will leave with nothing. Everything we have in between—possessions, achievements, relationships—is on loan, for our enjoyment during our brief stay. All these things are given to us by the universe, fortune, a divine being, or whatever else we may believe. Thus, when we lose someone, they're returned to the giver, divine or otherwise. We, too, are ultimately handed back over into the hands of the Logos, according to the Stoics. This is one of the ways that the Stoics maintained emotional equilibrium when things went wrong for them. They understood that everything in life is transient; they were always prepared to "give back," to "return." Epictetus (ca. 125/2004) states this disposition bluntly in *Enchiridion*:

> Under no circumstances ever say "I have lost something," only "I returned it." Did a child of yours die? No, it was returned. Your wife died? No, she was returned. "My land was confiscated." No, it too was returned.
> "But the person who took it was a thief."
> Why concern yourself with the means by which the original giver effects its return? As long as he entrusts it to you, look after it as something yours to enjoy only for a time—the way a traveler regards a hotel.

Ouch. This may be one of the hardest, harshest Stoic lessons to accept. How callous to think of a dead child as "returned." This certainly does nothing to disabuse the aforementioned misconception that plagues Stoicism: that Stoics are emotionless and, well, stoic. Epictetus is certainly not suggesting that we think of a spouse or a child in the same way as a houseplant. There's no doubt that we will grieve when we lose a loved one, a normal human response. But, given the inevitability of death, it shouldn't come as a complete surprise. Epictetus simply reminds us of the impermanence of everything around us, including our loved ones. If we deeply understand that life is transient and ever-changing and that everything we enjoy is a gift from the universe, we will no longer suffer in the same way when things are taken from us.

Epictetus also warns us not to concern ourselves with *how* things get returned. Material things get lost, broken, stolen, or outlive their usefulness. Relationships, too, get returned in various ways. People move away, grow apart, and die; relationships run their course. It behooves us to accept that this is a natural, inevitable process—that one day, everything we know and care about will be gone. Even you, someday, will disappear without a trace. By adopting a "just passing through" mindset, we can enjoy life's blessings like a weary traveler would enjoy a brief stay in a hotel. Remember, we're not taking up permanent residence here. We're renting, leasing, or borrowing—whatever language makes the most sense to you. Ownership—*in* life and *of* life—is an illusion. Sort of like control.

Epictetus is known to have struggled with attachment in his own life. You may recall that he was born into slavery but worked his way out of poverty to enjoy the trappings of a good life. With his hard-earned money, he purchased an expensive brass lamp which he kept burning at all times. One night, he heard a noise and rushed downstairs to find that a thief had stolen his prized lamp. He felt shocked and violated at having this hard-won possession taken from him. But, being Epictetus, he caught himself and vowed to get a cheaper, less attractive lamp made of clay. Legend has it that he kept that clay lamp for the rest of his life, a reminder to avoid attachment to material things that are actually on loan.

The notion of impermanence may be relatively easy to grasp when it comes to our material possessions, but what about the prospect of losing the people we love, whether due to death, abandonment, or other circumstances? In anticipation of the seemingly unbearable loss of loved ones, how do we ground ourselves in the fact that even the most beautiful, soul-satisfying things in life are merely on loan, granted to us only for the time being? The Stoic answer lies in training ourselves to accept, even embrace, the temporality of all things—including the relationships we cherish most and wish would last forever. Impermanence makes everything more valuable. If we can remember this in the face of great loss—or anticipation thereof—we will be left with the irrevocable gladness that we had it at all, for the time we did. This bittersweet feeling, the Stoics argue, is the alternative to paralyzing devastation in the face of loss. Wouldn't you rather experience grief + gratitude, instead of pure, undiluted grief?

In *Discourses*, a series of informal lectures, Epictetus (ca. 108/2008) offers a meditation on loosening the grip of grief in parting permanently from someone we've loved:

> Do you also remind yourself in like manner, that he whom you love is mortal, and that what you love is nothing of your own: it has been given to you for the present, not that it should not be taken from you, nor has it been given to you for all time, but as a fig is given to you or

a bunch of grapes at the appointed season of the year. But if you wish for these things in winter, you are a fool. So if you wish for your son or friend when it is not allowed to you, you must know that you are wishing for a fig in winter. For such as winter is to a fig, such is every event which happens from the universe to the things which are taken away according to its nature.

A fig in winter. What a metaphor. For those uninitiated to the delight of figs, they're a fruit native to the Mediterranean, in season just twice a year (in June, and again in August). With this metaphor, Epictetus warns us of two follies: first, of craving figs in the winter when they're not available; second, of failing to have our fill of them when they're around. This metaphor applies to everything in life, from our loved ones to everything material we believe we possess. To everything, there is a season—figs and all.

What of our own life? That, too, is only borrowed and can be reclaimed in an instant, without any warning, without our permission. We don't know how long we are given to keep it, and once our lease is up, we've got to hand it over. All we know is that it's not up to us to decide. We can only decide how we want to live right now. Paradoxically, the more we embrace life in its finitude, the less frightened we'll feel about giving it up when the time comes. When we forget this, we take life for granted. Prepare to age and decline? Maybe later, but we're healthy now. Prepare to die? Too far off. But as you're discovering, denial, avoidance, and postponement only fuel fear.

Hence, the Stoics would have us look at things the way they are, and not indulge in wishful thinking about how we'd like them to be. They would have us surrender our emotional attachment to things that are beyond our power to control. Brutal realities, if reconciled now, can reduce unnecessary suffering. Though uncomfortable, facing the impermanence of life is an investment in peace. Don't assume that figs will always be in season. Be ever mindful that everything has its time, and that the time allotted is finite. Everything is loaned, not owned. Everything is eventually returned, not lost. Life itself included.

Death Is Happening Now

> This is our big mistake: To think we look forward to death. Most of death is already gone. Whatever time has passed is owned by death. —Seneca

My financial advisor looked up from her computer and asked me, "How many more years do you expect to live?" The question took me aback, as I was barely 60. But, of course, all of her calculations were to be based on my anticipated "expiration date." Would my retirement savings need to last 10 years? 20 years? 30? Naturally, I went down a rabbit hole in quest of the most accurate answer to her question. I must have filled out a dozen life expectancy calculators and consulted just as many actuarial tables before I realized the futility of the exercise. We would have to plan in the face of great uncertainty.

As I contemplated mortality and spoke about it with aging friends and colleagues, I became aware that we tend to think of our lifespan as an allotment of sorts. Though unknown, we believe we're granted a certain number of years to live out before we die. If we die before our anticipated "quota" runs out, we feel robbed of something we believe we were owed. A life is "cut short" when the allotted years aren't realized. In these cases, we speak of "untimely" or "premature" death. If we live beyond our expected span, we're "living on borrowed time" or "cheating death." And though we can acknowledge that the lifespan we imagine (or calculate) was never actually promised, we retain the notion that we're granted a certain number of years, usually based on statistical probabilities. Within this framework, we think in terms of how many years we might have left, as if our life is a countdown to death. Like the bag of lettuce languishing in my produce drawer, I note its expiration date (soon!) and make a salad for dinner.

Unless we're very old or suffering from a life-limiting illness, we tend to view death as something that lies in the distant future. Even those of us who choose not to live in denial of our mortality can be guilty of this. We also tend to think of death as a single, discreet event that will happen to us eventually. It's a stationary point in time, and we're moving toward it slowly or quickly, depending on our age and health.

Seneca the Younger, a Roman Stoic philosopher and tutor to despot Emperor Nero, argues that this is the wrong way to think about it. Instead of thinking of death as a one-time, big-time horrible event in the future, he counsels us to think of death as a process that's happening to us right now. We're dying every day, every minute, every second. Even as you read these words, time is passing that you'll never get back. (Well spent, I hope.) The time that has passed, Seneca says, belongs to death. Our final day on Earth is, essentially, the completion of a process that has been unfolding for our entire lives. Without realizing it, the day we're born is the day we start dying. As Seneca (ca. 65/1969) elaborates in *Letters from a Stoic*:

> We die every day. For every day a little of our life is taken from us; even when we are growing, our life is on the wane. We lose our childhood, then our boyhood, and then our youth. Counting even yesterday, all past time is lost time; the very day which we are now spending is shared between ourselves and death. It is not the last drop that empties the water-clock, but all that which previously has flowed out; similarly, the final hour when we cease to exist does not of itself bring death; it merely of itself completes the death-process. We reach death at that moment, but we have been a long time on the way.

Centuries later, American novelist John Updike (1989)—a mind closer to our own time—echoes this sentiment when he writes, "Each day, we wake slightly altered, and the person we were yesterday is dead, so why, one could say, be afraid of death, when death comes all the time?"

What are the implications of thinking of death in this way? If we understand that we're in the *process* of dying—every minute, every second—and that the years we've lived are "already in the hands of death," we're compelled to live in the present, to be mindful of each moment we're surrendering to death. Are we not, then, also compelled to slow down? To not rush through this moment, but exist in it? If death is (eventually, inevitably) on the other side of whatever we're doing, what's the rush? It's death we're rushing toward. And we're doing so at the expense of the present moment.

Another implication of the notion that death is happening now, no less important, is our management of the time we have. Seneca observes that we go through life as if we're immortal. We take time for granted, as if unlimited. We waste time. But if death doesn't lie off in the distance but is with us right now, we must put nothing off, leave nothing unfinished. We must seize the time that still belongs to us before, in the next moment, giving it over to death. In *Moral Letters to Lucilius*, a collection of 124 letters to his friend, Seneca (ca. 65/1969) speaks of this urgency:

> Let us prepare our minds as if we'd come to the very end of life. Let us postpone nothing. Let us balance life's books each day... The one who puts the finishing touches on their life each day is never short of time.

Seneca addresses the false notion of lifespan as an allotment in another letter to his young friend: "You are younger than I, but what does it matter? Years are not given out by quota. There's no way to know the point where death lies waiting for you, so you must wait for death at every point." In *On Consolation to Marcia*, another set of letters, Seneca (ca. 40–45/2017) reiterates this notion of Stoic determinism. He disputes the idea that we are due a certain number of years, as death is happening at every phase of life:

> To each man a varying length of days has been assigned: no one dies before his time, because he was not destined to live any longer than he did... We all fall into this mistake of supposing that it is only old men, already in the decline of life, who are drawing near to death, whereas our first infancy, our youth, indeed every time of life leads thither.

From the perspective of the Stoic Logos, the cosmic web of cause and effect, there's no such thing as too early or too late. Things happen when they happen. Death, too. This abstract construct can have enormous practical impact if we internalize it and act accordingly: Don't waste time. You have what you have. You just don't know how much.

When contemplating Seneca's concept of death, I find a bank account analogy useful. Let's say that you open a bank account and deposit $100. There will never be any future deposits; what you spend can never be replenished. But you have access to your balance, so, at any given time, you know exactly how much money you have left. As you write checks or use your debit card, you can always see the impact on your balance. You can spend accordingly. You can budget.

You simply spend down what you know you have. When you run out, you're out. Now let's imagine the same scenario, but with the provision that someone has opened the account on your behalf and you don't know the amount of the initial deposit. Nor is there any way to check the balance. So you spend, not ever knowing how much you have left.

The first scenario is the "quota" scenario. Based on statistical probabilities regarding life expectancy, you can calculate the difference between your current age and your presumed expiration date. You have an idea of your "balance," so at any age, you think in terms of how much (time) you have left. You're moving toward a 0 balance (death) at some point in the future. The second scenario is analogous to Seneca's thinking—and much more realistic. At birth, you don't know how much was deposited to your account (your actual lifespan). And what's more, along the way, you never know your actual balance (how much time you have left). As you spend (live), does it not make more sense to think of your account in terms of what you've already spent, and what you're spending in the moment, as opposed to your balance, which you can't know? Wouldn't you spend more intentionally, aware of your account's limited, non-renewable resources? As Seneca (ca. 49/2005) points out, it's not just the finite nature of life we must remain mindful of; it's the unknown span of our existence. Indeed, he says, "It is easy to organize an amount, however small, which is assured; we have to be more careful in preserving what will cease at an unknown point."

Thinking of life as a countdown to death is a terrifying prospect, no doubt. But Seneca offers us an alternative. Might your fear of death be tempered by the realization that it's not looming, but already happening? Might this awareness compel you to live more presently and mindfully?

Life Is Short. Or Is It?

> Our fear of death is like our fear that summer will be short, but when we have had our swig of pleasure, our fill of fruit, and our swelter of heat, we say we have had our day.—Ralph Waldo Emerson

Have you ever noticed the profound wisdom imparted by bumper stickers? Granted, many are just ridiculous—"Honk if you'd rather be fishing," for example—but every now and then, I roll up on a gem. I once saw a bumper sticker that read "Life is too long … to live like this." A few years later, while reading Paulo Coelho, I came across this elaborate sentiment: "Life is too short, or too long, for me to allow myself the luxury of living it so badly." Ah, I thought. Thirty years later, I'm still pondering this intriguing alternative to the customary, oft-expressed aphorism "Life is short."

But enough of my musings. Back to you. Raise your hand if you don't want to die. Bear in mind that if you never die, you'll live forever. Now think again. Would you really want to live forever? If not, how long would you like your life to last? 10,000 years? 5,000 years? 500 years? Granted, you might always want "more," but forevermore? How much life is "enough"? I invite you to think deeply about the dystopian prospect of immortality, or even extreme longevity. What would you do with so much time? What form or direction would your life take with an unlimited span to evolve? And what meaning would it have, if unending? We fear death, we complain that life is too short, but have we considered the alternative? As Anglo-American author Susan Ertz astutely observes, "Millions long for immortality who don't know what to do with themselves on a rainy Sunday afternoon."

Nonetheless, throughout the ages, humans have quested for immortality. But is the life we're granted really "too short"? Perhaps life is just about the right length as it is. We have only to ponder corporeal immortality to realize that there's a reason for finitude, that it makes sense. In his book *Life is Short: An Appropriately Brief Guide to Making it More Meaningful* Dean Rickles (2022), professor and director of the Sydney Center for Time, examines the horrific prospect of life eternal and argues that meaning comes from limit. Likewise, Sam Dresser (2020) of *Aeon Media* highlights the benefits of temporality:

> Without death, life would be nothing but a dire repetition, pointless and endless. Immeasurably long lives would eventually deflate into the most banal tedium. Millennia upon millennia upon millennia would have to be lived out and, even then, there would be an eternity to go. Eventually, the most sublime and wondrous experiences possible would become punishing in their drab familiarity.

The Stoics maintained that life is sufficiently long if lived well. In his essay *De Brevitate Vitae* (*On the Shortness of Life*), Seneca (ca. 49/2005) writes, "It is not that we have a short time to live, but that we waste a lot of it. Life is long enough, and a sufficiently generous amount has been given to us for the highest achievements if it were all well invested." To put Seneca's thoughts on lifespan in historical context, it's notable that the average life expectancy in the Roman Empire of his time was just over 20 years. Closer to home, the average life expectancy in the United States was just 45 years as recently as 150 years ago (Menzies & Whittle, 2022). The shortness of life is relative.

Regardless of lifespan, Seneca was unequivocal in his conviction that it's not to be wasted. He certainly had his own ideas about pursuits that he considered wasteful. What are yours? What are the things you wouldn't spend time on if you thought you had only six months to live? The answer to this is, of course, quite personal. And not as simple as the default "mindless scrolling through social media" that many of us would identify. For some, it's time spent people-pleasing, trying to gain the approval of others. For others, it may be the long hours spent at the office—perhaps in neglect of relationships—in pursuit of wealth, status, or possessions. For still others, it's hours spent fussing over their appearance.

Think of the endless distractions and interruptions that compete for our time and attention each day: phone calls, emails, pointless meetings, video games, television, apps, obligatory events. Regardless of the particulars of your indiscriminate use of time—no judgment—the Stoics remind us how quickly our stores can be depleted if we're careless. And they didn't even have smartphones. People on death's threshold—our best teachers—echo this sentiment. In *My Last Days*, an uplifting documentary series on end of life, creator Justin Baldoni (2016) notes that not a single subject dying of terminal illness said, "Damn, I wish I had worked more." Or spent more time online. Or gossiping. Or comparing themselves to others. The Stoics counsel us to resist these and instead prioritize what we truly value.

People can be depleting, too. Booker T. Washington observes that "the number of people who stand ready to consume one's time, to no purpose, is almost countless." If you've ever encountered a "social vampire," you know this to be true. And let's not forget about the time-suck, soul-suck of small talk, a personal pet peeve of mine. Reflecting on the death of a friend, lifestyle guru Tim Ferriss observes that "too often, we spend time focusing on the trivial with people who contribute nothing but their own self-interest." Hence, the Stoics diligently guarded their personal time, space, and thoughts from trespassers and needy neighbors, presaging the modern concept of "boundaries." Seneca (ca. 49/2005) points out an interesting paradox: "In guarding their fortune men are often close-fisted, yet, when it comes to the matter of wasting time, in the case of the one thing in which it is right to be miserly, they show themselves most extravagant." He's saying that we enforce our boundaries selectively: We protect our physical property, but not our time.

When we reflect on how much of our time is misspent or spent thoughtlessly, we may rationalize that this or that expenditure is just an hour in a day or a day in a week. But as Annie Dillard, prolific American author, points out, "How we spend our days is, of course, how we spend our lives. What we do with this hour, and that one, is what we are doing." Charles Darwin, evolutionary biologist and keen observer of human behavior, is known to have said, "A man who dares to waste one hour of time has not discovered the value of life." Who can argue with Dillard and Darwin?

If we complain that life is too short, why do we watch so much television? Why do we spend so much time on our devices? When we reflect on how we spend our time, it doesn't appear that lack of time is the problem. On the contrary, it seems that life is already too long—so long that we become complacent and fritter it away. If time is our most valuable resource, why, then, do we find ourselves wasting it? First, according to Seneca, we squander so much of our time because we forget it's limited. He scolds:

> You are living as if destined to live forever; your own frailty never occurs to you; you don't notice how much time has already passed, but squander it as though you had a full and overflowing supply—though all the while that very day which you are devoting to somebody or something may be your last. You act like mortals in all that you fear, and like immortals in all that you desire.

Seneca points out that the things we chase and trade on in our day-to-day lives—money, possessions, success, status, approval—would all, in the end, be gladly exchanged for a little more time. And yet, we think time is ours to waste, speaking of "time to kill," or "dead time" between projects. The irony!

A second way we *make* life short is by spending our daily lives looking forward to a future that doesn't exist. How often have you heard yourself say (or think), "When the kids are off to college ... when I retire ... when I finish this project ... I'll finally have time for myself"? Always looking ahead to the next thing, we live in restless anticipation of what comes later. But what guarantee do we have of a "later"? What sense does it make to aim to begin life at a point that may never arrive? Being preoccupied with the future steals us away from finding value in the present. The present is merely something to get through on the way to something better. And when the anxiously anticipated event does come, our enjoyment of it is eclipsed by preoccupation with the next thing, and the next. As Seneca points out, we "lose the day in waiting for the night, and the night in fearing the dawn." Instead, he counsels us to "live immediately." Or, in the words of my (second) favorite bumper sticker: "Don't postpone joy!"

Finally, we contribute to our angst over the shortness of life by giving our lives to acquisition and ambition. How often have you heard yourself say (or think), "Once I acquire this ... or achieve that ... I'll be happy"? Of course, this way of thinking plays into the second error: We put off our happiness or fulfillment to a later date, attaching it to a thing or circumstance beyond our immediate control. The problem with ambition, Seneca contends, is that what we strive so hard to achieve will never be enough, once we achieve it. Ambition begets ambition. The same can be said of acquisition. The more we have, the more we want, and the less content we are with what we have. And whether success or possessions, once attained, we have to worry about retention. In this vicious cycle of fleeting highs and endless desires, says Seneca, "there will always be causes for anxiety, whether due to prosperity or to wretchedness. Life will be driven on through a succession of preoccupations: we shall always long for leisure, but never enjoy it."

So how do we cope with the (apparent) shortness of life? If we fear death because of our misguided perception that life is too short, how can we make it less so? Seneca's lessons from *De Brevitate Vitae*, though written two millennia ago, are relevant to the concerns we struggle with today. He urges us to take stock of how we've lived so far and account for the time that's been truly lived, instead of filled with unworthy preoccupations and distractions. Above all, we must recognize that time is our most precious, finite, non-renewable resource and avoid wasting it at all costs. Sure, we understand this intellectually, but how many of us can say that we truly live? Seneca writes, "If each of us could have the tally of his future years set before him, as we can of our past years, how alarmed would be those who saw only a few years ahead, and how carefully would they use them!" Fortunately, we don't have to wait until death approaches to recognize the value of time and spend it wisely. Present awareness of our finitude enables us to cherish the time that we have. The *scarcity principle* is relevant here: Like toilet paper in a pandemic, the less we have of something, the more we value it. As for life itself, meaning derives from limit.

Seneca (ca. 40–45/2017) further argues that mere elapsed time is not a good measure of a life's worth: "Begin to reckon his age, not by years, but by virtues: he lived long enough." He chides us to focus on the quality, not quantity, of life, lest we be like a boat that has never left the harbor:

> You must not think a man has lived long because he has white hair and wrinkles: he has not lived long, just existed long. For suppose you should think that a man had had a long voyage who had been caught in a raging storm as he left harbor, and carried hither and thither and driven round and round in a circle by the rage of opposing winds? He did not have a long voyage, just a long tossing about [Seneca, ca. 49/2005].

French Renaissance essayist Michel de Montaigne (ca. 1580/1993) echoes this sentiment that time and value aren't correlated: "Wherever your life ends, it is all there. The utility of living consists not in the length of days, but in the use of time; a man may have lived long, and yet lived but a little." Stoic philosopher Marcus Aurelius (ca. 161–180/2003) likewise points out that longevity is, essentially, inconsequential:

> Even if you're going to live three thousand more years, or ten times that, remember: you cannot lose another life than the one you're living now, or live another one than the one you're losing. When the longest- and shortest-lived of us dies, their loss is precisely equal.

So, counterintuitively, the answer to "life is too short" is not to try to prolong it. For Seneca, "Life cannot be free from worry for any man who thinks too much about extending it." Besides, as our Epicurean friend Lucretius (ca. 60–55 BCE) bluntly points out, by prolonging life we subtract nothing from the time we'll be dead:

> No matter how many generations you live through, the same eternal death is still waiting, and someone who ends life as the sun goes down today will have just as long a period of nonexistence as one who died many months and years before.

If you struggle with the prospect of dying "too soon," the best way to face up to the fleeting nature of life is not to lament its shortness but rather to live it fully and purposefully, to spend your limited time wisely, to do everything you're here to do. Life is only too short if you waste it. Make sure that when you die, no matter your age, you've lived "enough."

You Could Leave Life Right Now

> If you live each day as if it was your last, someday you'll most certainly be right.—Steve Jobs

Have you ever pondered what you would do if, tomorrow, you were diagnosed with a terminal illness? This thought experiment invites your consideration of how you might live your life differently if you were suddenly given just a few months to live. You've undoubtedly heard the cliché "Live each day as if it were your last," to the point of eye-roll familiarity. This notion, like so many others we encounter in popular culture, is the legacy of the Stoics—Marcus Aurelius, in particular.

The last great ancient Stoic we know of, Aurelius served as the Emperor of Rome for two decades, from 161 CE to his death in 180.

Considered the last of the "Five Good Emperors," his reign was plagued with famines, invasions, a coup, and near-continual warfare. Like his Stoic predecessors, his philosophy was well-tested by life's hardships. And he, like the others, walked the talk. His collection of personal reflections, known as *Meditations*, is considered one of philosophy's most famous and enduring texts, a perennial bestseller. The inspiration for these journals came from Epictetus' *Discourses*, previously introduced, which heavily influenced Aurelius as he studied philosophy in his formative years.

In *Meditations*, Aurelius (ca. 161–180/2003) addresses the issue of mortality, and how to best come to terms with our limited time on Earth. He starkly reminds us: "You could leave life right now. Let that determine what you do and say and think." The Emperor didn't mince words. What did Aurelius intend with this dire pronouncement? Was he suggesting we live it up and throw caution to the wind? Eat, drink, and be merry? To the contrary, he was suggesting that we live life more intentionally, not carelessly. He was offering an alternative to the complacency of living our lives as if they'll go on forever, echoing Seneca's exhortation to avoid wasting time as if we have an unending supply and to "postpone nothing." The point is urgency. If I died right now, what have I left undone? Unsaid? Have I lived in accordance with my values? The Stoics understood there's nothing like awareness of our temporality to sharpen our focus.

The message I take away from Aurelius is twofold: Live life on your own terms and leave nothing on the table. Fear of death is often the result of regret regarding these two matters. If there's something that bothers you, do something about it. If you have unfinished business, take care of it. If you have something you need to say, say it. If there's someone you need to speak to, make the call. Don't labor away in a deeply dissatisfying job, or stay in an irretrievably broken relationship. Take action now to avoid regret in the end.

For the Stoics, the prospect of death compels us to live in alignment with our priorities and values. But how do we deal with our fear of it? Aurelius addresses this later in his *Meditations*: "Think of yourself as dead. You have lived your life. Now, take what's left, and live it properly" and then, "Stop whatever you're doing for a moment and ask yourself: Am I afraid of death because I won't be able to do this anymore?" To me, this question is mic-drop revolutionary. As you confront your fear of death, ask yourself what it is about life that you're so desperate to cling to. What is the *this* you're doing that you're so afraid of parting with? Is the fear of losing it—whatever it is—an obstacle to peaceful living? When death anxiety creeps in, consider whatever you're doing at the moment and ask, "Am I afraid because I won't be able to do this thing anymore?" By repeatedly examining what you're so afraid of losing, you'll realize that there's really nothing to fear. Try it right now, if you will. It's a safe bet that what you're doing at the moment is reading. Yes? Ask yourself, "Am I afraid of death because I won't be able to read anymore?" If so, need I be so fearful of letting go of this activity? Sad, yes. Fearful, perhaps not.

In urging us to imagine that we're dead, Aurelius, like his Stoic colleagues, implicitly addresses our fraught relationship with time. We're constantly racing against the clock, trying to fit everything in. Life can seem like an endless to-do list. In "taking what's left and living properly," all we have is the present. There's a vibrancy to the present moment when it's free from the weight of the remembered past and the anxiety of the imagined future. Returning to Aurelius' challenge to remember that "you could leave life right now," how might that inform the ways you prioritize your time, thoughts, and actions? Too many people realize the preciousness of time only at the end of their lives. The Stoics provide us with tools for escaping this pitfall. Intentional avoidance of regret is one of the most powerful means to palliate the fear of death and make peace with mortality.

The Power of Negative Thinking

> If you wish to put off all worry, assume that what you fear may happen is certainly going to happen.—Alain De Botton, *The Consolation of Philosophy*

How many times have you been told to "think positive" when fretting about something bad that might happen? This advice was famously dispensed by Norman Vincent Peale, author of *The Power of Positive Thinking*, over seven decades ago. Our modern culture—informed by pop psychology—is infused with "positivity" messaging and appeals to "look on the bright side." Positive affirmations abound. A Google search or stroll through the self-help section of any bookstore reveal the pervasiveness of this solution to all manner of physical, psychological, and spiritual woes. Cancer diagnosis? Be positive! Depression? Be positive! "Just be positive" is purported to be the panacea for all ills.

How has this advice worked for you when faced with challenging life circumstances? And how has it landed with you when you're suffering? Am I the only one who finds "think positively" to be positively annoying? Though I'm certainly not summarily dismissing it as a coping strategy, it has its limitations. And, as you'll soon learn, not everyone can do it.

Of course, we can count on Stoic philosophers to recommend a different approach—one that turns "the power of positive thinking" on its head. The Stoics devised a practice of *premeditatio malorum*, a Latin phrase roughly translated as "premeditation of evils," or, in modern terms, "negative visualization." One of the most fundamental and powerful exercises in the Stoics' toolbox, premeditatio malorum is a meditative practice that involves visualizing all of the things that can go wrong in the future. Wait, what? But I do that already. Bear with me here.

The Stoics, in their wisdom, recognized that misfortune can befall us at any moment and that the most unbearable things in life are often those that we never expected, that catch us off guard. Reflect on this for a moment to see if it rings true for you. That breakup you never saw coming, the sudden death of a loved one, the job layoff that blindsided you, the unexpected flat tire on your way to an important interview—these are the things that hit the hardest, right? When we expect only good things to happen to us ("positive thinking"), even the smallest misfortune has the power to derail us. However, as British novelist Mary Renault points out, "There is only one kind of shock worse than the totally unexpected: The expected for which one has refused to prepare."

The Stoics reasoned that by pre-meditating worst-case scenarios, they could brace themselves against the harsh realities of life and be better prepared to face them calmly and rationally. Hence, premeditatio malorum was used as a tool to manage anxiety over what might happen, and to fortify against the blow of unanticipated misfortune. So the Stoics went around imagining that the shit would hit the fan so that they'd be prepared to stay cool when the shit eventually hit the fan. Genius!

The practice of premeditatio malorum involves deliberately and systematically anticipating—and preparing for—future hardships before they happen. The steps are simple. First, you imagine (visualize) some negative contingency that could happen in life—anything from a minor disturbance, misfortune, or inconvenience (e.g., missing your flight) to a major catastrophe (e.g., death of a loved one). For any scenario, you ask yourself, "What could go wrong? What's the worst that can happen?" and then visualize it happening. Next, you allow yourself to briefly feel the emotions associated with that distressing event. Finally, you analyze the situation and ask yourself, "How could I cope with such a situation? Is there anything I can do in advance to prevent it, avoid it, or mitigate the outcome?"

The goal of anticipating misfortune is threefold: to preempt the element of surprise, strategically plan for it ahead of time, and respond calmly and effectively if/when it befalls. It is, essentially, a risk management tool to prepare ourselves for difficult times ahead, which often turn out not to be nearly as horrible as we imagined. I'm reminded of Mark Twain's wry quip: "I've had a lot of worries in my life, most of which never happened," an echo of Seneca's contention two thousand years previous: "We suffer more often in imagination than in reality."

The key idea of premeditatio malorum is very similar to the modern-day adage, popularized by poet and activist Maya Angelou: "Hoping for the best, prepared for the worst, and unsurprised by anything in between." You may also recognize this ancient Stoic strategy as a precursor to modern Cognitive Behavioral *imaginal exposure therapy* (Chapter 9), which has been proven to decrease anxiety, including death anxiety. Albert Ellis, the father of Rational-Emotive Behavior Therapy, likewise appropriated this Stoic practice of imagining the worst-case scenarios, not the best-case, in managing anxiety about the future. He reasoned that if we can face and come to terms with the worst that can happen, we learn that we can withstand it. Consider this (in)famous example of an Ellis intervention to overcome fear of embarrassment in people with social anxiety. (Cringe warning.) You enter a packed elevator and, instead of turning around to face the front as social protocol dictates, you stand facing the occupants for as many floors as you can tolerate. To make the exercise even better/worse, you call out the floors as the elevator moves through them. I've done this experiment and lived to tell about it. Though excruciating, nothing horrible happened. I wasn't attacked. I didn't "die" of embarrassment. The result? Any other imaginable social situation will forever be less awkward. It even reduced my fear of public speaking.

Seneca himself practiced radical premeditatio malorum in his daily life. He was known to review his plans for the week and imagine everything that might go wrong. For example, if he was planning a trip, he considered that there could be a storm on the morning of his departure, the captain could fall ill, or pirates could attack the ship. With this mentality, he was prepared for any disruption. For him, "Nothing happens to the wise man against his expectation." Seneca likewise applied premeditatio malorum to his worldly possessions. Though he was quite wealthy, one of the richest men in Rome, he was prepared to lose everything if something happened to deprive him of his possessions.

Other Stoics speak of applying the practice to people-ing: "When you wake up in the morning, tell yourself: The people I deal with today will be meddling, ungrateful, arrogant, dishonest, jealous and surly" (Aurelius, ca. 161–180/2003), and "When going to the swimming pool, reflect on what may happen at the pool: some will splash the water, some will push against one another, others will abuse one another, and others will steal. Thusly you have mentally prepared yourself to undertake the act" (Epictetus, ca. 125/2004). I hope you find these ancient, yet timeless, commentaries on humankind as amusing—and on point—as I do.

Okay, so the Stoics had boat mishaps, bankruptcy, and bullies covered, but what about death, the ultimate adversity? This is where premeditatio malorum is a particularly effective tool. With regard to mortality, this practice serves as a form of preparation for the reality that you and your loved ones will die. It is, essentially, rehearsal for the most feared events. Hence, the Stoics made it a habit of contemplating the loss of the people they held most dear, as well as premeditating their own deaths.

Seneca was an ardent proponent of premeditatio malorum in dealing with such losses. In a letter of consolation to his friend over the death of her son—*On Consolation to Marcia*—Seneca (ca. 40–45/2017) warns that we should always be prepared for the unknown and take nothing for granted:

> That person has lost their children: you too, can lose yours; that person received sentence of death: your innocence too, stands under the hammer. This is the fallacy that takes us in and makes us weak while we suffer misfortunes that we never foresaw that we could suffer. The person who has anticipated the coming of troubles takes away their power when they arrive.

In 41 CE, Seneca was sentenced to exile on the Mediterranean island of Corsica for an alleged affair with the sister of Claudius, the Roman emperor. There was no one more devastated than his mother, Helvia. Sometime in the next eighteen months, he penned one of his most extraordinary works—*Of Consolation to Helvia*—in which he spoke of the power of inoculating oneself against misfortune.

Undoubtedly, the ultimate application of premeditatio malorum is the anticipation of our own death. Seneca (ca. 65/1969) asserts, "It takes the whole of life to learn how to live, and what will perhaps make you wonder more, it takes the whole of life to learn how to die." In *Letters from a Stoic*, he elaborates:

> Rehearse death. To say this is to tell a person to rehearse his freedom. A person who has learned how to die has unlearned how to be a slave. There is but one chain holding us in fetters, and that is our love of life. There is no need to cast this love out altogether, but it does need to be lessened somewhat so that, in the event of circumstances ever demanding this, nothing may stand in the way of our being prepared to do at once what we must do at some time or other.

Seneca is certainly not saying that it's wrong to love life. Rather, he's suggesting that we learn to hold it more lightly, that we may relinquish it with greater ease when the time comes.

Like other Stoic philosophers of his time, Seneca lived by his philosophy. Though his life was full of tragedy, he was known to comfort his friends and family when misfortune befell him, rather than reacting emotionally himself. His canon of consolation letters—*On Consolation to Marcia, Of Consolation to Helvia, On Consolation to Polybius*—is, perhaps, his crowning achievement. Seneca was a model of Stoic equanimity in the face of extreme adversity, up to and including his forced suicide at the hands of the cruel and paranoid Emperor Nero. Through the ordeal (slashing his wrists *and* ingesting poison), he accepted what fate had in store. Having envisioned his own death countless times, he was prepared.

The practice of premeditatio malorum has survived two millennia. William Irvine (2008), contemporary Stoic philosopher, was the first to call this ancient Stoic practice "negative visualization" in *A Guide to the Good Life: The Ancient Art of Stoic Joy*:

> The Stoics recommended that we spend time imagining that we have lost the things we value—that our wife has left us, our car was stolen, or we lost our job. Doing this, the Stoics thought, will make us value our wife, our car, and our job more than we otherwise would. This technique—let us refer to it as negative visualization—was employed by the Stoics at least as far back as Chrysippus. It is, I think, the single most valuable technique in the Stoics' psychological tool kit.

Now, before you start catastrophizing about being abandoned, carless, and unemployed, it's important to make a distinction between premeditatio malorum and anxiously fretting, or even obsessing, about what might happen. Negative visualization is an intellectual exercise—a brief, practical, and solution-oriented approach—not a perpetual worry-fest. There's a tremendous difference between anticipatory anxiety caused by "what-if-ing" about the future (i.e., "suffering more in imagination than reality") and proactively readying ourselves for whatever life throws at us. The whole point of negative visualization is to preempt worry and to gain peace of mind, the Stoic ideal.

Despite these important distinctions, premeditatio malorum is often misunderstood in modern times. It's tempting to see this Stoic strategy as pessimistic, a downer—and likely to make us feel worse. After all, negative visualization is so ... negative. What about positive visualization? Isn't that more ... positive? More better? Consider this: Adversity in life is inevitable. Loss is inevitable. Death is inevitable. If we only allow ourselves to anticipate the future positively, we will likely be ill-prepared when something unpleasant happens. Not if, but when. Addressing life's challenges with positive affirmations may seem intuitive, but this positivity strategy is more pleasant than it is potent. It just doesn't hold up "when the going gets tough."

A dramatic example of the failure of optimism when the going gets *really* tough is the *Stockdale Paradox*. In his book *Good to Great*, Jim Collins (2001) introduces the concept, named for Admiral Jim Stockdale, the highest-ranking U.S. military officer in the "Hanoi Hilton" prisoner-of-war camp during the height of the Vietnam War. Tortured repeatedly during his eight-year imprisonment, Stockdale lived out the war with no set release date and no certainty as to whether he would even survive to see his family again. In an interview with Stockdale, Collins asks him, "Who didn't make it out?" to which Stockdale replies, "Oh, that's easy. The optimists." The optimists were the ones who believed that they'd make it out by Christmas ... then Easter ... then Thanksgiving. As each holiday came and went without release, their hearts were broken, over and over, to the point of death. Stockdale explains that he had to unflinchingly accept the reality of his situation: that he might never get out, that he would be tortured, that he was not in control, and that he had so much unknown pain and suffering ahead. Stockdale happened to be a student of Stoic philosophy and possessed the mental discipline to confront the most brutal facts of his current reality, the key to his survival of unspeakable hardship.

Accounts of Holocaust survivors likewise suggest that this optimism paradox holds true. The most broken prisoners of concentration camps were those who believed they would be rescued. From the Stoic perspective, they would have been better off imagining that they wouldn't be rescued, directly confronting the reality of their situation without relying on hope. But what's wrong with hope? It's so counterintuitive to think that hope amidst hardship is counterproductive. We've all been indoctrinated to "never give up hope" when times are hard. But the Stoics weren't fans of hope, seeing it as a form of wishful thinking and denial of reality. Seneca (ca. 65/1969) famously declares, "Cease to hope and you will cease to fear." He's saying that hope and fear are two sides of the same coin—we can't have one without the other. To have hope is to have fear that our hope won't be realized. For him, peace of mind comes from relinquishing hope. Paradoxically, giving up hope allows us to live squarely in the present, rather than the future, where hope resides. The coin of hope also has another dark side: hopelessness. We can't hope without the possibility of hopelessness, perhaps the most dire of human conditions. By relinquishing hope, we also relinquish the prospect of hopelessness.

Epictetus' dichotomy of control is relevant here. If we're anxious about the future, it's because we wish things to turn out a certain way, rather than accepting that they will turn out as they will. The illusion of control—believing that we can control things that aren't within our control—is related to the hope/fear coin. Epictetus (ca. 108/2008) makes this point in *Discourses*: "When I see a man anxious, I say, What does this man want? If he did not want something which is not in his power, how could he be anxious?"

And so, for the Stoics, peace of mind (i.e., freedom from anxiety) is predicated on thinking negatively, preparing for the worst, and relinquishing hope. Did these wacky ancient philosophers have it all wrong? Have contemporary thinkers replaced these mistaken and outmoded notions with something more intuitively resonant? Less countercultural? More ... positive? To the contrary, they've doubled down.

In *The Antidote: Happiness for People Who Can't Stand Positive Thinking*, contemporary British author and journalist Oliver Burkeman (2012) makes the case for an alternative to the "think positive" strategy and suggests that a counterintuitive approach—"the negative path to happiness"—is more durable. He contends that it's our constant effort to eliminate the negative and emphasize the positive that's causing us to feel anxious, insecure, and unhappy. As he sees it, "Confronting the worst-case scenario saps it of much of its anxiety-inducing power. Happiness reached via positive thinking can be fleeting and brittle; negative visualization generates a vastly more dependable calm."

In his book *How to Think Like a Roman Emperor*, Stoicism

scholar and cognitive behavioral psychotherapist Donald Robertson (2019) explains why "negative thinking" could be more helpful than the well-known "positive thinking": "Recent psychological research tends to show that people who are able to accept unpleasant thoughts and feelings, without being overwhelmed by them, are more resilient than people who try to distract themselves or avoid such experiences, through strategies such as positive thinking."

Interestingly, it seems that some people are naturally inclined to think negatively. Psychologist Julie Norem (1986) estimates that about one-third of Americans instinctively adopt this orientation, which she terms *defensive pessimism*—a cognitive strategy employed to manage anxiety generated in anticipation of stressful events. Positive thinking, by contrast, is the effort to convince yourself that things will turn out fine, which can reinforce the belief that it would be absolutely terrible if they didn't.

A research study published in the *Journal of Abnormal Psychology* suggests that people who are biologically predisposed to engage in negative visualization tend to feel good about their lives and circumstances (Moser et al., 2014). This study was the first to provide evidence that positive and negative thinking is hardwired in the brain. Moser, the lead author, concludes: "You can't just tell your friend to think positively or to not worry—that's probably not going to help them. So you need to take another tack and perhaps ask them to think about the problem in a different way, to use different strategies." Like premeditatio malorum, for example.

Though negative visualization is primarily about preparation and fortification, a delightful side-effect of its application is appreciation. When imagining how things can be worse than they are, it's a tremendous relief when they aren't at the moment. If death is the worst you can premeditate, awareness of your *current* aliveness is just awesome.

In closing out this chapter on Stoic wisdom for making peace with mortality, I leave you with these inspirational mantra-esque takeaways, suitable for posting on your bathroom mirror:

Chapter 4. The Stoics

> Control is an illusion.
> Nothing belongs to you.
> You're dying right now.
> Life is plenty long.
> Don't waste time.
> Anticipate disaster.

You're welcome!

Chapter 5

The (Pre)Existentialists

Though the formal existentialist movement of Western philosophy didn't occur until the 20th century, two revolutionary thinkers—a French Renaissance essayist and a 19th-century German philosopher—presaged the movement and made important contributions to our understanding of the human condition, especially concerning mortality. Though they lived three centuries apart, they shared skepticism toward the dogma of conventional belief systems (particularly religion and metaphysics) and celebration of the transience of life. Both conceived of death as inextricably intertwined with life, "an ongoing process accompanying the human being along the entire life path, the recognition of which constitutes the basis of a common philosophical illumination leading to freedom, happiness, and wisdom" (Baruchello, 2002). Without further ado, the wisdom of two existentialists before their time.

Montaigne's Smack Upside the Head

> Men's courses will foreshadow certain ends, to which, if persevered in, they must lead, said Scrooge. But if the courses be departed from, the ends will change. Say it is thus with what you show me!—Charles Dickens, *A Christmas Carol*

In 1570, a young French nobleman was riding "an undemanding but not very reliable horse" through the woods near his Dordogne estate. It was a leisurely outing, a break from his considerable political and familial duties. Some of his workers accompanied him on horseback, one of whom decided to show off by galloping to the front of the line. He misjudged the width of the path and, unable to stop in time, violently collided with the nobleman's horse from behind, causing him to fly up into the air and come crashing to the ground. As he lay unconscious, his companions, believing him to be dead, attempted to carry his inert body back home to his wife. *Quel tragique*! But wait ...

The "dead" nobleman was Michel de Montaigne (1533–1592), who fully recovered and went on to become one of the most influential writers of the French Renaissance. Celebrated as the father of the school of philosophy called Skepticism, he was best known for pioneering the essay as a literary genre. In his masterwork *Essais* (literally translated as "attempts" or "trials"), a three-volume collection of 107 essays, Montaigne (ca. 1580/1993) chronicles his fall and near-death experience in broken streams of consciousness.

During his journey home, Montaigne began to revive, "but only little by little and over so long a stretch of time that my first sensations were closer to death than to life." Though he recalls his wife running toward him, "the fact is that I was not there at all," he later wrote. He had "traveled far away," and the things he saw—his writhing body, his screams—were "idle thoughts, in the clouds, set in motion by the sensations of the eyes and ears; they did not come from within me." He reported feeling neither pain nor "commotion," though he was, in reality, vomiting up clumps of clotted blood and fighting for every breath. "It seemed to me that my life was hanging only by the tip of my lips; I closed my eyes in order, it seemed to me, to help push life out, and took pleasure in growing languid and letting myself go." There was no struggle or resistance. Over the next few hours, Montaigne's thoughts "floated on the surface of my soul ... not merely free from unpleasantness but tinged with that gentle feeling which is felt by those who let themselves glide into sleep." For that blessed interval, the pain of his body "did not belong to us." He refused all medicines, certain that he was destined to slip away. According to him, it would be "a very happy death."

Montaigne recovered from his accident and lived another 22 years, but his brush with death was never far from his mind. Of his *Essais*, he says, "I am myself the matter of this book." The inclusion of his riding accident suggests its significance as a turning point in his life. A year after his fall, he withdrew from the world for a life of reading, thinking, and writing. Until his death, he spent most of his days philosophizing in the stone tower adjacent to his house. We are the fortunate beneficiaries.

Had he not been knocked off his horse, Montaigne might not have produced his immense and influential collection of essays. His near-death experience yielded a clarity of purpose, a sense of heightened resolve. How ironic that a blow to the head resulted in such lucidity, such insight into a more expansive, reflective understanding of the mind and the world—an enlarged consciousness. Montaigne's life-altering experience reminds us of the Biblical conversion of Saul who, likewise, "fell to the ground" in the face of blinding spiritual revelation. Thus, Saul became Paul, someone altogether new. Like Montaigne, it took a smack upside the head to rock his world and render him utterly transformed. For the fictional character Ebenezer Scrooge in Dickens's *A Christmas Carol*, it took three ghostly visitations to effect redemption. Existential psychiatrist Irvin Yalom (2008) refers to these jolts as "awakening experiences" or "existential shock therapy," with the potential to catalyze profound growth and change.

Montaigne's fall changed not only the course of his life, but also his relationship with death. He previously suffered from a debilitating fear of death, having lost his father, brother, best friend, and five infant daughters. The perpetual slaughters of the religious wars of his time undoubtedly fueled his fear. But, in the aftermath of his fall, death no longer seemed like a feared stranger, but rather "a friendly face." In dying, he now realized, "You do not encounter death at all, for you are gone before it gets there. You die in the same way that you fall asleep: by drifting away." Of the gentleness of death, he later wrote, "If you don't know how to die, don't worry; Nature will tell you what to do on the spot, fully and adequately. She will do this job perfectly for you; don't bother your head about it." After a lifelong fear of death, Montaigne discovered that death was not so terrifying after all. For the rest of his days, the life-affirming embrace of mortality would be a recurring theme.

The notion that dying is more of a glide than a struggle is echoed in the concluding lines of Leo Tolstoy's (1886/2008) masterpiece on dying: *The Death of Ivan Ilych*. Knowing that he was dying, Ivan Ilych experienced abject terror at the prospect, despite being in excruciating pain. And yet, in his final moments, he felt the pains that had been oppressing him "all dropping away at once from two sides, from ten sides, and from all sides," ultimately freeing him. In the end, he exclaimed, "So this is what it is! What joy!" These accounts—biographical and fictional—suggest that dying isn't as horrible as we imagine. Though it may look like suffering from the outside, this may not at all be the experience of the dying. As we'll explore in Chapter 13, hospice workers who have witnessed thousands of deaths report that there's mercy built into the nature of dying, that death takes care of us in the end. Montaigne's reassuring words bear out.

Montaigne has hard-earned, smack-upside-the-head, wisdom to offer those who struggle with death's terror. Rather than indulging the fear of death with denial and avoidance, he calls for facing it head-on, with awareness and intention. He famously declares that the best way to prepare for death is to think about it constantly. This echoes the Stoic meditative practice and, as you'll soon learn, an approach common to Eastern spirituality. To be ready to die, we must acquaint ourselves with life's conclusion. In his essay *That to Study Philosophy is to Learn to Die*, Montaigne (ca. 1580/1993) speaks of the need to face our mortality without fear by premeditating or "rehearsing" death:

> Let us learn bravely to stand our ground, and fight him. And to begin to deprive him of the greatest advantage he has over us, let us take a way quite contrary to the common course. Let us disarm him of his novelty and strangeness, let us converse and be familiar with him, and have nothing so frequent in our thoughts as death. Upon all occasions represent him to our imagination in his every shape; at the stumbling of a horse, at the falling of a tile, at the least prick with a pin, let us presently consider, and say to ourselves, "Well, and what if it had been death itself?" and, thereupon, let us encourage and fortify ourselves. Let us evermore, amidst our jollity and feasting, set the remembrance of our frail condition before our eyes, never suffering ourselves to be so far transported with our delights, but that we have some intervals of reflecting upon, and considering how many several ways this jollity of ours tends to death, and with how many dangers it threatens it. Where death waits for us is uncertain; let us look for him everywhere.

> The premeditation of death is the premeditation of liberty; he who has learned to die has unlearned to serve. There is nothing evil in life for him who rightly comprehends that the privation of life is no evil: to know how to die delivers us from all subjection and constraint.

You may recognize the Stoic theme here: Learning to die is a prerequisite to learning to live and a path to freedom. It's not death itself, but the terror of annihilation, that keeps us enslaved. Montaigne concludes: "All the wisdom and reasoning in the world boils down finally to this point: to teach us not to be afraid to die."

Montaigne's story is as old as time: Brush with death, take stock, emerge transformed. Fortunately, you don't need a close encounter with extinction to reckon with your mortality.

Nietzsche's Existential Groundhog Day

> Love the life you live. Live the life you love.—Bob Marley, Jamaican reggae musician

What if you had your life to live over—not with the benefit of hindsight, but exactly as you lived it the first time? This was the thought-provoking question posed by German existential philosopher and cultural critic Friedrich Nietzsche (1844–1900). Inspired by the writings of Montaigne three centuries earlier, he grappled with the big issues of human existence, especially mortality. A radical dude, Nietzsche was (in)famous for his uncompromising criticism of traditional European morality and religion, and of conventional philosophical ideas. It's not surprising, then, that his concept of *eternal return* (also called *eternal recurrence*), is nothing short of mind-blowing.

Eternal return is a philosophical thought experiment in which time repeats itself in an infinite loop: The same events continue to occur in exactly the same way, over and over again, for eternity. A sort of existential *Groundhog Day*. Nietzsche reported that this idea came to him suddenly in August 1881 while he was on one of his epiphanic hikes through the Swiss Alps. After introducing the concept at the end of *The Gay Science*, he made it one of the fundamental concepts of his next work, *Thus Spoke Zarathustra*. The notion of eternal return is best defined by one passage in *The Gay Science*, entitled "The Greatest Weight":

> What, if some day or night a demon were to steal after you into your loneliest loneliness and say to you: "This life as you now live it and have lived it, you will have to live once more and innumerable times more; and there will be nothing new in it, but every pain and every joy and every thought and sigh and everything unutterably small or great in your life will have to return to you, all in the same succession and sequence—even this spider and this moonlight between the trees, and even this moment and I myself. The eternal hourglass of existence is turned upside down again and again, and you with it, speck of dust!" [Nietzsche, 1882/2001]

Nietzsche follows this graphic depiction of infinite repetition with a challenge: "Would you not throw yourself down and gnash your teeth and curse the demon who spoke thus? Or have you once experienced a tremendous moment when you would have answered him: 'You are a god and never have I heard anything more divine.'" In other words, if you were to discover that every moment of your life was to recur in sequence over and over for all eternity, how would you react? Does the idea of living your identical life on infinite repeat—whether 25 or 85 years thus far—feel like a divine gift or a wretched curse? For Nietzsche, the prospect of endlessly (re)experiencing every detail of our lives will delight us, crush us, or mobilize us.

The eternal return thought experiment is, essentially, a brutal assessment of one's relationship with one's life. It asks, "How well disposed would a person have to become to himself and to life to crave nothing more fervently than the infinite repetition, without alteration, of each and every moment?" (Nietzsche, 1885/2005). Presumably, most of us would find such a thought intolerable. We'd prefer the unending repeat of our lives in an *edited* version, excluding all of life's pain, suffering, disappointments, and regrets. But the point of eternal recurrence is that the entire life is disavowed or affirmed, not merely this instant or that. Hence, the thought experiment is a litmus test of a life in its totality, as currently lived. It's designed to highlight areas where we might be getting a bit careless, or living mindlessly. It illuminates the wasteful or cringe-worthy moments we'd prefer not to repeat. Though we can't possibly live every day as if it's our last—or worthy of repetition—might we not be more intentional about how we spend some part of each day?

At the heart of Nietzsche's thought experiment is the notion that we're responsible for how we live our lives. This is not to say that we're in complete control of them—we know better. But we must accept the consequences, good or bad, of our willful actions. The specter of infinite recurrence compels us to choose our actions wisely. If our choices are to be replayed endlessly, they'd better be good ones. For Nietzsche, good choices aren't those dictated by morality, religion, or convention. Rather, good choices are those that affirm our true, authentic selves—those we can live with in hypothetical perpetuity.

Nietzsche's concept of eternal return is inseparable from his oft' repeated phrase *amor fati*, or "love of one's fate." The idea here is to choose a fate worth loving—one you wouldn't mind repeating. His exhortation to "consummate your life" means to realize your potential, live fully, "become who you are," and—here's the punch line—die without regret. The importance of living authentically is consistent with the findings of Australian hospice nurse Bronnie Ware (2019) who published a book on the top five regrets of those facing imminent death. The most common regret of all was, "I wish I'd had the courage to live a life true to myself, not the life others expected of me."

What does all of this have to do with your fear of death? Your relationship with death is inextricably connected to how you live your life. It's axiomatic that regret is correlated with fear of death, and a life well lived (amor fati) is correlated with acceptance of mortality. Returning to the thought experiment, knowing for the rest of your life that everything that happened would happen again might change how you regard each of your experiences. Reasoning this through, it seems it would make a difference *when* the demon appears to you bearing the news of your eternal recurrence. If at the very end of life, whether the news is met with horror or elation, it's too late to make a difference in how you live your life, already lived. The whole of your preceding life would be unaffected. However, any time before that (such as now!), it would color your attitude toward experiences for the rest of your days and, perhaps, make a difference in all of your life choices. If you're aware that every moment is a permanent possession, you might consciously try to construct a life that, from now on, you wouldn't mind reliving. At the very least, you'd live more mindfully.

It's unknown whether Nietzsche believed in the literal truth of eternal return, or intended it merely as an allegorical, hypothetical thought experiment. Regardless, the idea can be used as an impetus to calibrate our lives. Think of your own life, the life you're creating now. What story would you want to live over and over again? An apt corollary to "live each day as if it's your last" is "live each day as if it's eternal." Resolving to live a life worth repeating is a powerful counter to the prospect of mortality.

Part III

Spiritual Approaches

In contrast to the previous philosophical approaches which rely on applied logic and reason to address the fear of death, spiritual approaches explore the transcendent and metaphysical dimensions of human experience. Spiritual approaches to mortality are often associated with religious traditions, beliefs, and practices, but they can also be independent of—and even eschew—organized religion. Though spiritual or supernatural approaches (to anything) are often considered to be irrational, unscientific, or "woo-woo," many people find them to be the only reliable source of comfort in facing their mortality. This is why every hospice team includes a chaplain. It's assumed that there's a numinous element to dying, along with the more obvious physical, psychological, and social aspects.

In college, I took a comparative religion course—a survey of all the major world religions, and many of the more obscure ones. My late father was "a man of the cloth," and I was determined to take a critical look at my indoctrination. My still-impressionable mind came away from exposure to this dizzying array of religious options with a conclusion that has persisted to this day: All organized religions include a destination (where you go after you die) and a roadmap (the way you get there). It was hard for me to imagine that there was a "right" way and that everyone who chose a different path was doomed to eternal damnation. At the risk of irreverence (sorry, Dad), comparative religions seemed like a "choose your own adventure" prospect. Or, an adventure chosen for you, based on geographical, cultural, and familial considerations.

I've since become interested in the *why* of religion—a much more satisfying pursuit than the *what* that had so confounded me—and in exploring the individual, interpersonal, and sociocultural functions served by religion. Undeniably, religion plays a significant role in managing fears regarding mortality. Though Karl Marx intended something a bit different when he declared religion "the opiate of the masses," it's clear that religion offers—by design—a universal, pre-packaged panacea for existential angst.

CHAPTER 6

The Afterlife
World Religions

> Belief in the supernatural is another powerful route to overcoming the very natural desire to stay alive.—Malcolm Potts, *Sex and War*

Uncertainty regarding what happens after death is a common basis of death anxiety. This concern is often associated with religious—or non-religious—beliefs regarding the afterlife. What do you believe? Gallup has been asking this question of American citizens since 1999, though a bit more specifically. Had you participated in the July 2023 Gallup poll, you would have been asked which of the following comes closest to describing your beliefs—you are religious, spiritual but not religious, or neither. How would you respond? Nearly half of Americans (47%) describe themselves as religious, 33 percent self-identify as spiritual but not religious, 18 percent respond that they're neither, and 2 percent volunteer that they're "both." Notably, the percentage of respondents who say they're religious, spiritual, or both (82%) is down from 87 percent in 2002, and 90 percent in 1999 (Jones, 2023). Despite this precipitous decline in religiosity and spirituality among American citizens, religion isn't going anywhere. It's generally considered a ubiquitous force in human culture and the oldest, most enduring solution to the problem of mortality. According to existential psychiatrist Irvin Yalom (2008), "Death anxiety is the mother of all religions, which, in one way or another, attempt to temper the anguish of our finitude."

Despite their diversity, the major world religions share several common features: belief in a supernatural higher power, a creation story, and, most relevant for our purposes, an afterlife narrative. A brief overview of "the big six," in order of number of adherents worldwide, will facilitate our understanding of how various belief systems might impact death anxiety—for better or worse.

Christianity. The Christian faith promises eternal life in heaven with God through faith in Jesus Christ and belief in His resurrection. Hell, a cautionary destination, is a place of eternal punishment for non-believers. For Christians, afterlife disposition is based on faith and actions, as set forth in *The Holy Bible*, the inspired Word of God.

Islam. Muslims believe individuals are held accountable for their deeds, which determine their fate in the afterlife. Per *The Quran* (holy book of Islam), a day of judgment or reckoning occurs after death, and the righteous are rewarded with eternal bliss in paradise (*Jannah*), while those unfaithful to Allah are punished in hell (*Jahannam*). Islam shares a dualistic version of the afterlife with Christianity.

Hinduism. The Hindu concept of the afterlife centers around the cycle of reincarnation, the soul's rebirth into a new body based on past actions (*karma*). The ultimate goal is to attain *moksha*, the soul's liberation from the cycle of reincarnation, and merger with the divine.

Buddhism. The Buddhist concept of the afterlife is rooted in *samsara*, the cycle of birth, death, and rebirth—a version of reincarnation. By following the Eightfold Path, Buddhists seek to attain enlightenment and break free from this cycle, thereby reaching *nirvana*, a state of liberation from suffering.

Sikhism. Sikhs also believe in the cycle of birth and death, reincarnation, and karma. By leading a virtuous life, guided by the teachings of the *Guru Granth Sahib* (the Sikh holy scripture), they seek to escape the cycle of rebirth and merge with God (*Waheguru*).

Judaism. Though Jewish beliefs regarding the afterlife vary and are less central or well-defined as in other religious traditions, the primary afterlife construct is *Olam Ha-Ba* (The World to Come). Judaism generally focuses on the importance of a righteous earthly life, ethical conduct, and the value of good deeds, as outlined in the *Torah*.

This brief (and greatly simplified) overview demonstrates that all major world religions offer some version of life after death. That is, they believe in the immortality of the soul—the essence of a person (variously referred to as soul, mind, spirit, consciousness, energy, or awareness)—which transcends the body at death. These faith traditions all hold that the soul leaves the body and moves on to another existence—an ascent to paradise or descent to hell, a rebirth into another body, or a merger with a divine, eternal being. Traditional Christianity, Islam, and Judaism envision a resurrection of a spiritual body at the time of judgment. Across all religions, the physical body is merely a temporary shell, shed at death, and separate from the immortal soul. This spiritual perspective directly contrasts the materialist view of the Epicurean and Stoic schools of philosophy.

In surveying the major world religions, we see another common thread: terms and conditions. Admission into these enviable versions of the afterlife depends on how you've lived your life on Earth. In most cases, the soul is judged and dispatched to some eternal place, such as heaven or hell, accordingly. This "reap what you sow" mentality is so pervasive, it can be argued that society is predicated on belief in an afterlife. The notion that virtue is rewarded and sin (however defined) is punished in the end—carrot and stick—is part of the social contract. It serves to keep people in line.

Religious doctrine spells out exactly what's required to optimize one's postmortem fate. For some religions, the price of admission to a desirable afterlife is faith or belief in a higher power, an entity, or a creed. For others, good works, or being an honorable, righteous person, are the ticket. Some religions require both. An historical example of a blatantly transactional religious contract occurred in Medieval Europe. Christians were compelled to buy *indulgences* from priests in exchange for absolution from their sins and a fast track through purgatory. For example, you'd make a "donation," pray for a certain monarch, or go on a pilgrimage and get a receipt or *letter of indulgence*. This practice persisted until 1517 when Martin Luther posted his 95 theses, declaring, "We don't need no stinkin' indulgences," signaling the start of the Protestant Reformation. The exploitative middle man was eliminated, and purchasing indulgences was replaced with working hard and living a good life as pathways to heaven. Salvation could no longer be bought, at least not with cash.

Regardless of the currency, organized religion comes with an expectation of eternal reward or punishment based on what you believe and how you act in this life. Your fate is conditional. When it comes to death anxiety, this can cut both ways. On the one hand, there's something comforting about the idea that your salvation is in your own hands—that, essentially, you're in control of your ultimate destiny. You do the things, you get the eternal reward. As long as you know the rules, you can choose to comply. On the other hand, the notion of a conditional afterlife can trigger more confusion, uncertainty, and fear about what happens after death.

For my patients who struggle with this fear, they question whether they've chosen the "right" belief system. What if they're wrong? They also struggle with mixed and conflicting messaging—even within one religion, denomination, or congregation—depending on how orthodox the teaching, or what version of the terms and conditions have been adopted. I hear them express the fear that, despite their best efforts, they'll somehow miss the mark and burn in their particular religion's version of hell. Fear of punishment in the afterlife is a common basis of death anxiety. This fear is often manifest in perpetual tension between faith and doubt. Is my faith strong enough—both to assuage my fear of death now and to ensure a favorable outcome later? Am I devout enough to be in good standing regarding my eternal prospects? These questions burn as brightly in the minds of those who fear their postmortem disposition as the imagined flames of hell.

If religion is designed to be an antidote to the fear and uncertainty inherent in awareness of mortality, how is it that this salve can end up exacerbating the very pain it's designed to soothe? To better understand this, let's revisit the study that examined the relationship between religiosity and fear of death, introduced in Chapter 2. This meta-analysis, published in *Religion, Brain and Behavior*, combined the data of 100 high-quality international studies and concluded that the relationship between religiosity and fear of death is quite weak, certainly not linear. According to Jong (2021), "If the fear of death motivates religiosity, it does so subtly, weakly, and sporadically."

In contradiction to the age-old, intuitive notion that religion—belief in an afterlife, in particular—serves to protect against death anxiety, the inverse-U pattern seems to better reflect reality. That is, those least afraid of death are the very religious and the non-believers. It may be that the devoutly religious are secure in their convictions regarding their eternal reward and that the atheists simply reject notions of heaven and hell and, therefore, aren't worried about it. Or, it could be that people who aren't afraid of death aren't compelled to seek religion in the first place. This is correlational research, so we can't assume causality. But what about those poor moderately religious folks who are most afraid of death, the ones in the middle of the inverse-U for whom religion isn't affording much comfort in the face of mortality? I propose that they seek religion to manage their pre-existing fear of death and embrace the notion of an afterlife with attendant terms and conditions. Their death anxiety then manifests in concerns regarding the conditionality of their ultimate disposition. In the face of confusion and uncertainty stemming from conflicting afterlife narratives and doubts about the status of their immortal soul, death anxiety is exacerbated. If we're to believe the science regarding the impact of religion on fear of death, it behooves us to be "all in" or "all out." But it's not quite that simple.

What about non-believers—those who self-identify as atheist, agnostic, nonreligious, secular, or secular humanist? A brief overview of these alternative worldviews will round out our understanding of the diversity of beliefs about life after death.

Atheism. Atheism is the absence of belief in any deity or supernatural being. Atheists generally adopt a materialist view of death as the cessation of consciousness and existence. They reject the notion of a soul that continues beyond death and lives on in an afterlife.

Agnosticism. Like atheists, agnostics don't identify with a particular religious belief system. Rather than accept or reject notions of deities or the afterlife, they suspend judgment about these religious constructs as unknown and unknowable. They tend to be skeptical of religious certainties. Unlike atheists or religious people, they view the afterlife as a mystery.

Secular Humanism. Secular humanists reject supernatural beliefs as "religious mythology," and tend to be agnostic regarding an afterlife. Their worldview is more concerned with human values, reason, ethics, and compassion in present life on Earth. They believe that humanity is capable of self-fulfillment, meaning, and morality without belief in God.

Whether adherence to a particular religious construct or a non-religious spiritual or philosophical belief system, we see a vast spectrum of beliefs and non-beliefs, with varying implications for death anxiety. Statistically, though, organized religion occupies center stage.

With an understanding of how religions generally work, let's examine their role in managing existential concerns through the lens of Terror Management Theory (TMT), previously introduced. As you recall, denying the reality of one's finite existence is a primary defense against death anxiety. This manifests in two forms: pursuit of literal immortality (belief in an afterlife) and symbolic immortality (belonging to a valued social system). According to TMT, organized religion checks both of these boxes. Specifically, religion offers the following buffers against the existential threat of mortality:

Answers. By providing answers and explanations for the many mysteries of life, death, and everything in between, religion offers a framework for understanding the meaning and purpose of existence. Adhering to a particular religious worldview provides a sense of belonging to something larger than oneself, and a sense of significance and continuity beyond physical existence.

Immortality. Religion offers comfort in the belief that death is not the end, but rather a transition to another state of being. For those of immutable faith, belief in an afterlife and the promise of immortality relieves anxiety regarding their mortal finitude.

Rules. Religion sets forth how one should live, whether in the form of rules (shalts and shalt-nots), or general guiding principles of morality and ethics. When one's eternal fate rides on following the rules, having an externally imposed moral compass can be a great comfort. For many, the more black and white the better.

Certainty. Religion can bring certainty and clarity to those intolerant of ambiguity. Many people manage uncertainty by constructing or adopting complex narratives about how they came to be (creation stories) and what will happen next (afterlife narratives). Religion fills the void of uncertainty by providing these narratives.

Community. Religious affiliation is like belonging to a club of like-minded individuals who share common beliefs and values. Congregations offer ready-made community and meet the needs of belonging, support, and social connection—all buffers against the fear of death.

Rituals. Religious rituals, ceremonies, and practices provide a structured framework for managing mortality. Communal participation in prayer or meditation and symbolic acts, such as religious sacraments, can be tremendous sources of comfort, meaning, and connection in the face of dying, death, and grief. The role of rituals in managing death anxiety will be explored at length in Chapter 7.

Within the TMT framework, we see that religion is a highly attractive "immortality project," as well as serving many psychosocial functions. Numerous research studies demonstrate that reminders of our mortality (mortality salience) can lead to an increase in religious beliefs and practices, as well as a greater adherence to cultural values and traditions. Indeed, theorists from Freud to Becker have long posited that fear of death is among the chief causes of religious belief. Though this "anxiety-begat-religion" theory is hotly debated to this day, a more relevant question is, "Does it work?" This is a question that can only be meaningfully answered by each individual who looks to religion to alleviate suffering from awareness of their finitude. Though religiosity doesn't appear to correlate strongly or reliably with relief from death anxiety, religion can't be discounted as one of many answers to the problem of mortality and, for some, the only answer.

It's important to note that belief in an afterlife—whatever fear-mediating benefit it confers—isn't necessarily predicated on religiosity, or even spirituality. The vast majority of cultures, if not all, have developed some sort of construct for what happens to consciousness after death. Despite great diversity in the details, notions of an afterlife are nearly universal. Archeological and anthropological investigations of ancient funerary rituals reveal that homo sapiens from every culture and corner of the globe buried their dead in shallow graves with items they might need in the afterlife, including food, weapons, tools, and various other personal belongings. As these items would have been considered useful to the living, even of great value, we can only infer that these prehistoric peoples believed that death was not the end, that some element of a person survived the dying experience, and that these utilitarian items would be needed by the deceased in the next chapter of their spiritual journey. Seemingly, from the beginning of time, humans have held metaphysical beliefs about death and dying.

In the United States, surveys conducted regularly since the 1940s show that about 70 percent of American citizens believe in some form of life after death, consistent with numbers across the developed world (Lawton, 2019). More recently, a survey conducted by Pew Research Center (2021) revealed that 61 percent of Americans believe in both heaven and hell, and, of the 26 percent who believe in neither heaven nor hell, 7 percent believe in some alternative afterlife. These respondents describe their ideas of an afterlife in various terms, including spirit/energy continuing to live on in another dimension, spirit/energy transformed, reincarnation, enlightenment, cyclical existence/rebirth, reunion with God or loved ones, and peace without suffering. Note that many of these visions of an afterlife aren't at all religious in nature.

If nearly everyone believes in some form of an afterlife—even those with no religious affiliation or spiritual orientation—there must be more to it than a cultural construct. Jesse Bering (2002), experimental psychologist and leading scholar in the cognitive science of religion, set out to understand the evolutionary mechanisms that underpin afterlife beliefs. In a study published in *The Journal of Cognition and Culture*, since widely replicated and expanded, participants read a one-page vignette describing a fictional character's emotions, physical sensations, and state of mind, ending with the character's sudden death. Each participant was then asked a series of questions about the dead character's current mental state, designed to assess five psychological domains: *psychobiological* (ability to register physical sensations), *perceptual* (operation of the senses), *epistemic* (ability to think, remember, believe), *emotional* (capacity to feel emotions), and *intentional* (existence of wants and desires). Based on responses to a questionnaire, participants were sorted into six categories according to their afterlife beliefs: *extinctivists* (complete cessation of consciousness after death), *agnostics, reincarnationists, immortalists* (consciousness survives after death and exists forever), *eclectics* (combination of reincarnationist and immortalist beliefs), and *other* (consciousness persists after death but in unknown form). Respondents across belief categories showed a remarkable similarity in how they perceived the mental states of the deceased. Regardless of their afterlife beliefs, they endowed the deceased character with thoughts, emotions, and desires. That is, though all acknowledged that psychobiological and perceptual functions cease after death, even individuals who claimed to believe that all consciousness ceases at death were inclined to say that certain psychological states persist. They were able to conceive of their bodies dying, but not their minds.

Bering (2008, 2011) attributes these findings to our natural biological proclivity to think of the minds of dead people in the same way we think of our own. Because we're unable to imagine the absence of certain psychological states in ourselves, we intuitively project psychological states and traits onto the dead. Our native, instinctive belief in an afterlife is underpinned by evolved cognitive mechanisms that enable us to form a "theory of mind"—the ability to think about the consciousness of others, even in their absence—and allow for complex social interactions. Within this framework, supernatural (including afterlife) beliefs are viewed as a default setting of cognition, rather than learned. Sociocultural factors determine what form this innate predisposition takes, whether religious or otherwise. With this theory, Bering offers a bio-social-evolutionary alternative to the notion that our afterlife beliefs result from religion, or from the need to shield ourselves from the terror of nonexistence. This construct would help explain why belief in an afterlife has held up even as religiosity has declined.

Regardless of our beliefs—religious, spiritual, atheist, or agnostic—we're all in the same boat: None of us know what happens after death. But, concerning death anxiety, it's not the actual postmortem reality that matters—it's what we believe while alive. And what we believe can provide either comfort or torment. What do you believe? Are you a "lights out" person who believes consciousness ends with the death of the body, or do you believe in some version of an afterlife, the immortality of the soul? If you're in the latter camp, is your belief informed by a particular religious tradition or an areligious spiritual orientation? Or, does your evolved human brain just naturally refuse to accept that death is the end, based on your innate biology? I invite you to reflect deeply on the impact of your beliefs—or absence thereof—on your fear of death. Religious and spiritual exploration is not about the adoption, rejection, or conversion of any belief system, but rather about better understanding how beliefs figure into your struggle with mortality. As I concluded in my questing youth, there are no right answers, only revelatory questions:

> It would be especially comforting to believe that I have the answer to the question, What happens when we die? Does the light just go out and that's that—the million-year nap? Or will some part of my personality, my me-ness, persist? What will that feel like? What will I do all day? Is there a place to plug in my laptop? [Roach, 2006]

Chapter 7

Death Rituals

> We humans have always needed rituals to draw like curtains over the chasms of the unknown. Without them we go mad, I think.—Patricia J. Williams, American legal scholar

Monty Python's 1975 comedy classic *Monty Python and the Holy Grail* is widely regarded as one of the funniest films of modern cinematography. And, arguably, the most quotable. Perhaps your annoying friends—or you—have repeated the frantic "Run away! Run away!" from scenes in which King Arthur and his not-so-courageous band of knights are beating a hasty retreat while being pelted with farm animals, attacked by the Killer Rabbit of Caerbannog, or the Black Beast of Arrrggghhh. It's funny because we can all identify with the impulse to flee when encountering danger. You've no doubt heard the term *fight or flight*, the instinctive human response to scary, threatening, or traumatic phenomena. It should be no surprise, then, that the earliest humans responded to the terrifying specter of death by, literally, running away.

In his book *Psyche and Death: Death-Demons in Folklore, Myths and Modern Dreams*, German psychotherapist Edgar Herzog (2001), describes preliterate cultures of Malaysia and North India who fled after the burial of one of their kinfolk, never to return to the burial ground. The practice of a particular Malaysian tribe was to abandon a dying person and return later to see if they had died. If so, they buried them with leaves and fled the resting place of their dead neighbor. Herzog views these primitive practices as marking the initiation of humans' confrontation with death. As humans evolved, so did their rites and rituals for integrating the concept of death into their existential understanding.

The deaths of members of a society were thus traumatic and potentially disintegrating experiences for the group. The development of practices surrounding disposal of the corpse served to reintegrate the community by allowing members to assert some manner of control over the society's relationship with death and the dead [Malinowski, 1948]. Cultural practices regarding disposal of the corpse thus became important in all human societies. These practices were subject to an infinite degree of variation, but in all cases they served a similar underlying purpose: bringing what was once an incomprehensible horror within the realm of an ordered understanding of the role of death in the human experience [Moore & Williamson, 2003].

Is denial and avoidance of death in our Western culture not a modern-day version of the flight of terror seen in primitive cultures? After all these millennia, are we not still screaming "Run away!," at least figuratively? As observed in Chapter 1, Western culture has lost its way with regard to honoring the sacredness of death through ritual observances—before, during, and after death. Regrettably, the consequences of abandoning these rites of passage are significant for the dying, the bereaved, and the death-phobic among us. Death rituals—whether religious, spiritual, or secular—serve important sociocultural functions, and play a significant role in relieving death anxiety.

A ritual, derived from the Latin *ritualis* (that which pertains to rite or *ritus*), has been defined as "a religious or solemn ceremony consisting of a series of actions performed according to a prescribed order" (Oxford University Press, 2024). Rituals are a feature of all known human societies and include liturgies of organized religions, as well as many secular observances such as weddings, showers, funerals, ceremonies, inaugurations, and various rites of passage (e.g., graduations, retirements). Arguably, there's no greater variety and scope of rituals than those surrounding death. Death rituals give form and structure to engaging with death. They provide prescribed practices for interactions with dying and dead bodies, disposition of the dead, funerary practices, mourning practices, and memorialization of the dead into the future.

Different countries, cultures, and religious traditions have unique—and sometimes extraordinary—ways of managing death. Regardless of the form they take, death rituals all serve a number of psychosocial functions for both the dying and the living. Most significantly, death rituals create a sense of meaning and comfort in coping with mortality. Established traditions and customs provide a familiar framework for navigating difficult transitions, as well as order and certainty in the face of disequilibrium and uncertainty. Rituals have tremendous power to mitigate fear of the unknown so central to death anxiety.

Death rituals serve to create a clear boundary between life and death while, at the same time, affording a sense of continuity to our existence—a connection among past, present, and future. In facilitating emotional expression in the form of shared stories, prayers, music, and vocal laments, death rituals provide an outlet for grief and an established forum for communal support. As rituals bring people together for a common purpose and shared experience, they connect us to a larger community and culture. They engender a sense of belonging and ease feelings of isolation. Finally, death rituals that are rooted in religious or spiritual traditions provide a framework for understanding death within a shared belief system. At their core, death rituals allow us to participate in a story we already know and, thereby, to become part of a larger, established narrative.

When you reflect on familiar death rituals in our Western culture, what comes to mind? Likely, you'll think of funerals, wakes, and memorial services. These are, undoubtedly, the most common ways we communally process death. Regrettably, most of us are unaware of the rich and diverse death rituals, ceremonies, and celebrations across time, cultures, and faith traditions. Exposure to radically different approaches to death, dying, and after-death can open our eyes and moderate our fear of death, particularly to the degree our fear is perpetuated by the limitations of our own culture's myopic perspective. To that end, let's take a brief cross-cultural, trans-faith world tour for a sampling of the vast range of practices used to engage with and come to terms with death. Content warning: Before proceeding, please note that the next two sections ("Funerary Rituals" and "Ancestral Veneration") include graphic descriptions of death rituals that you may find disturbing.

Funerary Rituals

Throughout history, civilizations have followed prescribed rituals for interacting with and parting with the bodies of their dead, each infused with meaning and symbolism reflecting regional, religious, and cultural belief systems. For most cultures, including Western cultures, disposition of the body after death involves some version of burial or fire cremation. But in some parts of the world, burial rituals involve uncommon means of disposal. For example, "sky burial" is a traditional Tibetan Buddhist practice in which the body of the deceased is disassembled and placed on a mountaintop or other elevated area to be exposed to the elements, as well as scavenging birds and other animals. This organic practice is believed to allow the soul to depart the empty vessel of the body while offering the remains back to nature to complete the circle of life. Believing that a dead body defiles everything it touches, followers of Zoroastrianism, an ancient Iranian religion, clean the body with bull's urine before cutting off clothing with special tools, later destroyed. The corpse is then placed on a stone structure called a *dakhma* or "tower of silence" where vultures consume it. Avoiding burial or cremation prevents polluting the elements of earth, fire, and water, or contaminating the living. In certain regions of China, Indonesia, and the Philippines, "hanging coffins" are suspended on cliffs or high rock formations, often with ropes or other supports. This practice is believed to bring the deceased closer to heaven and to protect the remains from animals and floods. The Maasai tribe of Africa returns their dead to the earth through "predator" burials. Believing that burial is harmful to the soil, the dead are smeared with fat or blood and left in the open for hyenas or lions to devour.

In a practice quite foreign to most modern cultures, certain Indigenous tribes of the Amazon dispose of their dead by consuming them. *Endocannibalism*, practiced for hundreds of thousands of years, is viewed as a profound act of respect, ensuring that the spirits of deceased kinfolk continue to live within the community. For example, the Wari tribe engages in a ritual process akin to wine-making. After being placed on racks to facilitate decomposition to a juicy state called *melarak*, the remains of the deceased are transferred to a large jar-like container to ferment. The liquid and solid remains are separated and the solids are buried. For the Wari, drinking the wine of a corpse holds great spiritual significance, both honoring the dead and transferring their wisdom to the living. The Yanomami peoples of the Amazon are known to consume a cremated tribe member's ashes, mixed with a soup made from fermented bananas. Everyone in the community is expected to drink the mixture, passed around in gourds. As explained by Tony Walter (2019), professor of death studies, "Across cultures, there is a common desire to hold onto and absorb, in a way, the energy of the deceased." As with sky burials and hanging coffins, endocannibalistic practices are also thought to help move the spirit of the deceased from their earthly body to their next destination (Lepinskie, 2022).

The death rituals of other cultures center around the skeletal remains of the deceased. For example, Naga tribes of India carefully collect the dried bones of their loved ones following the decomposition of the flesh. During *kotsuage,* a Japanese cremation ritual reserved for close family members, bone fragments are plucked from the cremains with special chopsticks and placed in a cremation urn. Picking out certain bones is viewed as gathering luck, strength, wisdom, or healing.

Some funerary rituals are notable for their degree of specificity. For example, Japanese death rituals, influenced by Buddhist and Shinto religious traditions, include performing a detailed, prescribed set of 20 steps to purify and prepare the spirit of the deceased for the spirit world. The first two steps involve washing the lips and the body of the corpse, and the last two steps include the aforementioned "picking of the bones" and, finally, *kika sai* (coming home), during which the remaining ashes of the deceased are placed on family shrines.

Fire and water figure prominently in the burial rituals of some cultures. In ancient Viking cultures, the deceased would be placed on a wooden ship with their belongings and the ship would be set ablaze and pushed out to sea in a fiery send-off to the afterlife, known as *Valhalla.* Today, pyre cremation, in which the body is burned on a pile of wood in the open air, is most commonly associated with Buddhist and Hindu religions. In these faith traditions, cremation is a way to free the spirit from the body, allowing the deceased to transition into the next phase of their existence. Scattering of cremains at sea, or another body of water, is a preferred means of disposition in many cultures. In a common Hindu ritual, cremains of loved ones are scattered in the Ganges River. Densely populated Hong Kong has designated areas where ashes can be scattered at sea, with a free ferry service for mourners.

In many cultures, funerary rituals mix sorrow with celebration, including festive parades and carnival-like revelry. In a Varanasi Indian tradition, the dead are paraded through the streets, their bodies clothed in colors that symbolically represent their particular virtues. During a "jazz funeral," practiced in Caribbean and Southern U.S. cultures (New Orleans, in particular), the funeral procession, led by a brass band, accompanies the body to the burial site playing somber music, followed by lively jazz music and dancing. Similarly, a jazzy Ghanaian funeral tradition involves hiring a group of professional mourners who sing, dance, and perform theatrical acts to entertain funeral attendees and honor the deceased. "Fantasy coffins," known as *abebuu adekai* or "proverb boxes," are the centerpiece of these funerary processions. These colorful, elaborate coffins are customized to represent the deceased's occupation, interests, or personality, celebrating their life creatively and symbolically. In Balinese Hindu cultures, the body of the deceased is placed in a decorated sarcophagus or *wadah,* representing the temporary vessel of the soul. The wadah is carried to the cremation site in a grand procession, accompanied by music and dance. Elaborate cremation ceremonies are joyous events, believed to release the soul from its physical form and allow it to continue its afterlife journey. Taiwanese funeral celebrations often include strippers (i.e., exotic dancers) to entertain mourners, appease wandering spirits, and celebrate the life of the deceased.

In Aboriginal Australian cultures, funeral rituals include smoking ceremonies, dances, songs, and storytelling designed to guide the dead back to the "Dreamtime"—a spiritual realm that connects the past, present, and future—where the deceased's spirit rejoins ancestors. The funerary rituals of Maori culture, Indigenous to New Zealand, similarly honor the deceased with wailing, singing, and dancing, including *haka*, a traditional war dance. As with other cultures that emphasize the connection between the living and the dead, it's believed that the spirit of the deceased remains near the family for some time before transitioning to the spiritual realm. Death is viewed as part of a larger spiritual and ancestral continuum. In blending mourning with celebration, these various party-like send-offs confront death with an affirmation of life.

Across cultures, funerary rituals include vocal expressions of mourning, including songs, hymns, chants, and death wailing. Among various Indigenous peoples of Africa, the Americas, Asia, and Australia, unrestrained expressions of grief are performed ceremonially in ritualized weeping, wailing, and shrieking. The traditional Irish and Scottish practice of *keening*, loudly wailing for the dead, is a notable example of vocalized grief. In some cultures, professional criers are hired to perform vocal laments at funerals.

These ritualized emotive displays are antithetical to modern Western culture's emphasis on emotional restraint and private grief. As a teen, I recall attending a funeral during which the widow of a 50-year marriage, overcome with grief, began wailing and flung herself on the floor. I watched in horror as the pallbearers forcibly removed her from the room as if to shield the other mourners from her unabashed grief. Though shocking at the time, in retrospect, I understand this as another manifestation of our culture's pervasive death aversion. The widow's uncensored response to death was intolerable in its evocation of internalized death terror among the living.

As you've read these accounts of cross-cultural funerary rituals, you may have noted that many of them involve intimate handling of dying and dead bodies, both in bathing and dressing them in preparation for burial and cremation and, in some cases, interacting with their remains and cremains. These customs are in direct contrast to Western practices in which medical and mortuary professionals handle these kinds of ministrations. No longer do we practice the deathbed and burial preparation rituals of bygone eras. Some of us haven't even seen a dead body, and many of us haven't touched one. Adults and children alike are protected from death, as if contagious. What consequences might this lack of normalized exposure have for our persistent unfamiliarity with dying and death and, consequently, our fear of it? Anthropologist Peter Metcalf (1987) suggests that how dead bodies are treated is key to understanding a culture's relationship with death. Likewise, how cultures engage with, remember, and honor their dead beyond their immediate disposition provides additional clues. Let's continue our world tour and investigate what this looks like in other cultures.

Ancestral Veneration

Veneration of the dead, a common practice in many countries, cultures, and religious traditions, honors deceased relatives and affords them a prominent place among the living. The dead are believed to exist beyond death and to have the power to intervene in the affairs of their descendants. Ancestral altars are set up in homes—typically with photographs of dead loved ones and urns of crematory ashes. Across cultures, death is celebrated with dedicated festivals and other ritualized memorials throughout the year. These joyous occasions typically include communal singing, dancing, and feasting.

During the annual *Qingming* Festival, also known as "Tomb-Sweeping Day," Chinese families visit the gravesites of their ancestors to clean the tombstones, burn incense, and make offerings. In *Sradh*, a Hindu ritual of remembrance performed annually on the death anniversary of loved ones, family members offer food and water to the departed soul during a ritualistic ceremony, thereby providing nourishment and support for the deceased in their journey beyond life. *Famadihana*, also known as "turning of the bones," is an ancestral ritual practiced by the Malagasy people of Madagascar during which they exhume the remains of ancestors from their tombs every few years, rewrap the bones in fresh shrouds, and dance with the ancestral remains before reinterring them. This practice is intended to speed up decomposition and facilitate the movement of their spirits toward the afterlife.

In Mexico and other Latin American countries, the dead are memorialized in a colorful and vibrant annual celebration called *Dia de los Muertos* (Day of the Dead). The spirits of the dead, believed to return to visit their loved ones at this time, are welcomed with special foods, music, dancing, parades, and storytelling. Families create altars, decorated with flowers, candles, photographs, and mementos meaningful to the departed. Celtic cultures, rich in folklore, maintain ongoing engagement with departed loved ones, consistent with their belief in a thin veil between the living and the dead. During *Samhain*, an ancient Celtic festival marking the end of the harvest season, ancestors are honored with bonfires and food offerings. Places are set at the table for the spirits of the departed. Among some Indigenous tribes of New Guinea, the skulls of deceased relatives are preserved and displayed in homes in a practice called "scull cult." Their spirits, believed to reside within the skulls, offer guidance and protection to living family members. In the North American Lakota tribe, a lock of hair is taken from the departed person and held over burning sweetgrass to purify it before being wrapped in a piece of sacred buckskin. This "soul bundle" is held by the "keeper of the soul," usually a relative, until it can be released.

In Japanese culture, many families maintain ancestral altars (*butsudan*) in their homes where they conduct daily rituals. The *Obon* Festival, an annual Japanese Buddhist holiday commemorating deceased ancestors, is a time when ancestral spirits are believed to temporarily return to this world to visit their relatives. Paper lanterns are hung in front of houses to guide them home and ritual dances (*bon odori*) are performed. *Jesa*, a Korean memorial ceremony held on death anniversaries to commemorate departed ancestors, involves ritual bowing, chanting, and prayers. The ceremony begins by invoking the spirit of the deceased and inviting them to join the feast. It ends with the burning of a ceremonial paper inscribed with the deceased's name, signaling that it's time for their spirit to depart. In Nepal, *Gai Jatra* (cow festival) is held to commemorate those who have died during the past year. Families of lost loved ones participate in a procession, often leading a cow through the streets. The cow is believed to help the soul of the departed transition to the afterlife. In many African cultures and religious traditions, specific days are set aside to honor ancestors with ceremonies and rituals designed to maintain a connection with them. Offerings of food, drink, and symbolic items are placed on ancestral altars or gravesites.

In the most literal example of communing with the dead, the Toraja people of Indonesia keep the mummified remains of their deceased relatives in their homes for years, until they have enough money to pay for a proper (i.e., elaborate) funeral. Meanwhile, their spirits are believed to hang around. Treated as sick rather than dead, their bodies are cleaned, dressed, and brought to family meals. For years after they're eventually buried in tombs, their remains are regularly exhumed in a ritual known as *ma'nene* (care of ancestors), during which they're cleaned, left in the sun to dry, and dressed in new clothes before being returned to the tomb. Family members take selfies with the corpses as yet another way to keep their memories alive.

Despite the diversity of these practices, there are several notable common elements of ancestral veneration rituals across regions, cultures, and religious traditions. First and foremost, they're designed to maintain a connection to dead relatives, honoring them with a continued presence in the lives of the living. As such, these rituals signify that death is seen as a transition and not the end. The boundary between the living and the dead is blurred and, in various ways, the dead are treated as if still present. Ancestors are seen as powerful spiritual beings who can influence the lives of their descendants and provide blessing, guidance, and protection.

An additional common element is the literal or symbolic interaction of the living with the physical remains of the dead, in whatever form they exist. Whether through sweeping and cleaning family gravesites, reciting prayers and chants, leaving offerings of food and drink, or caring for remains or cremains, the living-to-dead relationship is ongoing and honored. Ancestral veneration rituals share a social element—an opportunity for the living to connect with the dead and with each other. They reinforce familial bonds and provide a sense of continuity with past generations. Finally, through honoring dead ancestors, death is normalized and embraced as a natural part of life. With death ever-present in a loving, respectful, and celebratory cultural context, fear has no place.

This brief exploration of cross-cultural funerary and ancestral veneration rituals is a mere sampling of the vast array of practices across the globe. When viewed through the ethnocentric lens of our own culture, some of these practices may seem strange, shocking, or even repulsive. Perhaps you find them intriguing, as I do. But what are you to do with this information? And what do these global death rituals have to do with your fear of death? The diverse ways human beings, past and present, frame and interact with death have a lot to teach us about our own relationship with death and how we engage with it. As Western cultures have moved away from direct experience with the dying and the dead, away from explicit death rituals to provide meaning, guidance, and continuity, we've become ill-equipped to deal with death. Exposure to the rites and customs of other cultures can serve to shake up and disrupt the cultural aversion and denial that perpetuate our fear of death. We can all benefit from a bit of death desensitization.

As author and activist Anne Lamott opines, "Rituals are a good signal to your unconscious that it is time to kick in." Perhaps the most valuable lessons we can take from the death rituals of non–Western cultures are those conveyed to our subconscious psyches about life and death. We don't have to hang Aunt Myrtle's remains from a cliff, or dine with mummified Grandpa Joe. Cross-cultural awareness isn't about adopting these unfamiliar practices, or the religious and spiritual traditions that underpin them. Rather, we can use an understanding of the diversity of death rituals to normalize death as part of life. Through rituals, boundaries between life and death, material and spiritual, sacred and profane, become more permeable. When we lift the veil of secrecy, death becomes more natural and familiar, less mysterious.

The beauty of death rituals is that they don't have to be complicated or even culturally defined. They don't require a religious affiliation to afford a sense of transcendence and meaning in the face of mortality. A ritual can be as simple as lighting a candle or planting a tree. My favorite example of a DIY ritual is the wind phone. A man in Otsuchi, Japan, devastated by the loss of his cousin, placed a phone booth in his garden to talk to him, believing that the wind would carry his messages. Since then, he's opened his wind phone to the public, and wind phones have been installed worldwide (mywindphone.com). I invite you to reflect on the death rituals practiced by your own family, community, and faith traditions. In facing the death of loved ones, what rituals have proven meaningful and comforting to you? What rituals might you adopt to make death more sacred and less scary?

CHAPTER 8

Death Meditation

> Of all the footprints, that of the elephant is supreme. Similarly, of all mindfulness meditation, that on death is supreme.—Buddha

If I may ask an indelicate question, how do you feel about your body? Sure, there may be elements of it you're not crazy about—a fluffy tail, a prominent proboscis—but that's not what I'm getting at. I mean, how attached are you to your body? To what degree do you identify with it? Though you may be inclined to disavow your attachment or identification, consider your relationship with your body, a constant companion throughout your entire life. You've nourished, hydrated, cleaned, and clothed it. You've rested it, exercised it, and nursed it when ill. You've groomed it with countless haircuts, shaves, and products designed to enhance its appearance. You've consulted the mirror for feedback on the results of these ministrations. This body of yours is your home; it contains YOU and all your experiences—every pleasure and every pain. And yet, this cherished body of yours is ephemeral. It will decline, die, and decay. It embodies you, but it is not you. This profound experiential awareness is the essence of the ancient spiritual practice of death meditation.

Cultures throughout history have adopted spiritual meditative practices as a means of coming to terms with mortality. Death meditation, also known as contemplation of death or mindfulness of death, involves meditating on death and dying with intense focus. Though there are many different practices associated with various religious traditions, all are designed to promote awareness of mortality and invite death into daily life. The fundamental process of death meditation is to reflect deeply on the impermanence of the body and to practice detachment from it. Though counterintuitive, the benefits of death meditation are similar to those of many of the other approaches in this book: freedom from fear of death through exposure, familiarity, and rehearsal; enhanced vibrancy of life now; and peace when death comes. Death meditation is yet another means to live a good life and die a good death.

Though the scope of death meditation practices is vast, Stoicism and Buddhism are the most well-known and accessible philosophical and faith traditions, respectively, that teach mindful awareness of mortality. The secular Stoic practice of *memento mori* will be addressed in Chapter 11, but I'll focus on spiritual approaches here, as exemplified by Buddhist practices. There's a long, rich death meditation tradition in Tibetan Buddhism, known as *Maranasati*. In Pali, the language of the Buddha, *marana* means death, and *sati* means mindfulness. Maranasati, regarded as the ultimate meditative practice, includes an array of visualization and contemplative techniques, ranging from simple reflections on death to long and complex prescriptive practices. No matter their form, they all allow us to fully comprehend that we will die—not just intellectually or philosophically, but experientially. Through the "practice" of dying, we're better emotionally and spiritually prepared for a conscious and peaceful dying experience. This is wholly aligned with the Stoic exhortation to "rehearse death."

In the Buddhist tradition, death awareness practices are divided into four categories: meditations to help us contemplate that death is inevitable, that the time of our death is uncertain, and that our bodies and our lives are both impermanent and fragile; meditations to help us understand the physiologic process of our bodies shutting down in death; meditations to visualize the gradual decomposition of the physical body over time; and meditations concerned with the transition of consciousness into our next cycle of existence at the time of death (Roth, 2007).

The Buddhists of Tibet engage in a meditation called *Lojong* or "The Four Thoughts That Turn the Mind," one of which is the contemplation of death and impermanence. It consists of the following contemplations, designed to be practiced daily:

- All things made from other things are impermanent.
- The human body is a thing made from other things.
- Therefore, the death of the body is certain.
- The time of death is uncertain and beyond our control.

The "Five Contemplations" is another practice in the Buddhist death meditation tradition, outlined by the Buddha as follows:

- Just like everyone, I am of the nature to age. I have not gone beyond aging.
- Just like everyone, I am of the nature to sicken. I have not gone beyond sickness.
- Just like everyone, I am subjected to the results of my own actions. I am not free from these karmic effects.
- Just like everyone, I am of the nature to die. I have not gone beyond dying.
- Just like everyone, all that is mine, beloved and pleasing, will change, will become otherwise, will become separated from me.

The "Nine-Part Meditation on Death" is another traditional Maranasati practice, adapted from the teachings of Atisha, an 11th-century Indian Buddhist sage. It has three roots, with three contemplations for each:

- The inevitability of death
  1. Everyone has to die.
  2. Our personal life span is decreasing continuously day by day.
  3. Death will come, whether or not we are prepared for it.
- The uncertainty of the time of death
  4. Human life expectancy is uncertain.
  5. There are many causes of death.
  6. The human body is very fragile and vulnerable.
- Only spiritual practice can help us at the time of death
  7. At the time of death, our material resources are not of use to us.

8. Our loved ones cannot keep us from death.
9. Our own body cannot help us at the time of our death.

Though hardly cheery, these traditional Buddhist contemplations may seem tame compared to the "corpse meditation," a far more intense and visceral practice. Contemplation of the nine stages of decay, a practice dating back to early Buddhism and persisting in monastic settings to this day, involves imagining or observing the gradual decomposition of a dead body—from "bloated and festering" to "bones turning into dust." Each of the nine stages is similarly graphic and evocative. Traditionally, a practice known as *Chod* or "cutting through" was performed on charnel grounds where, before modern (14th century) burial practices, corpses were left exposed to decay above ground in the open air, similar to the tradition of the Tibetan sky burial. The nine stages of decay became a popular subject of Buddhist art and literature, both for their meditative function and aesthetic value. A widely respected practice in the Buddhist canon, modern Buddhist monks regularly perform corpse meditation, sometimes in the presence of an actual dead body, and sometimes with photographs depicting corpses in various stages of decomposition. It's common for monks to have corpse meditation photos with them at all times, even when dining or resting. Such photographs can even be purchased at religious shops throughout Asia.

The Buddha himself recommended corpse meditation and specifically discussed death visualization in the *Satipatthana Sutta*, the foundational text for contemporary *vipassana* (insight) meditation practice. At the end of his incredibly graphic outline of the stages of decay, he says, "Verily, exactly so is also my own body! It is of the very same nature. So fragile and feeble is it, it will inevitably turn into dust and it cannot ever escape this fate. Then he lives fearless, detached, and clings to nothing in this world!"

Meditating on real, pictorial, or imagined human remains is one way to contemplate death; another way is to imagine that you're a corpse. To practice this meditation, you simply lie down and pretend that you're dead, that your body is decaying and returning to the earth as nourishment, the source of new life. It's no coincidence that the final resting pose in yoga is called *shavasana*, literally "corpse pose," a not-so-subtle reminder of our ultimate fate. In a modern take on death meditation, billed as a wellness trend, people wrap themselves up in a white sheet like mummies and visualize their dead bodies. Death meditation practices and classes have infiltrated social media. One such class was advertised on Instagram as "a breath-guided meditation intended to contemplate death in many forms" (Joshu, 2023). Death-positive artist A.J. Hawkins addressed her death phobia by examining death through a creative lens. After compulsively studying the decomposition of the human body, she created "The Reclamation" (ajhawkinsart.com/the-reclamation), a stunning art series on the stages of decay, from death to dust, and how nature reclaims our bodies to perpetuate life.

From a Buddhist perspective, all suffering (including death anxiety) comes from attachment. Hence, regardless of the form death meditation takes, non-attachment to one's own body is the lesson. As practitioners, we're asked to come face to face, intimately, with the law of impermanence. Through the deep, lived understanding that we'll have to let go of our attachments in death, we attain an intuitive knowledge that forms the basis of wisdom. By dying to our attachments now, we reduce suffering in life and render death of the body less threatening.

In death meditation practice, we invite our fear of death to come closer rather than pushing it away. When death eventually comes, it will occur in an ordinary moment like this one. By simulating such a moment through meditation—approximating the experience of our actual death as vividly as possible—we allow the fear to arise so that we can learn to transcend its power. Larry Rosenberg (1994), American Buddhist teacher and founder of the Cambridge Insight Meditation Center, describes how death meditation directly addresses our fear of death:

> In learning more about death awareness meditation, we learn how to shine the light of death on life. It's not meant to be an exercise in morbidity or self-pity, or in terrorizing ourselves. In fact, one often feels light, happy, and unburdened after directly acknowledging the truth of our inevitable death. One way in which it is extremely invaluable is that it flushes out fear. It gives us an opportunity to work very carefully

with fear. Now remember, what we're afraid of is not really death but our idea of death. And this is one of the things to learn, that it's a very powerful idea.

If you're inclined to highlight important passages in fluorescent yellow, don't miss this one: *What we're afraid of is not really death but our idea of death.* This uncannily Stoic-sounding insight is a recurring theme across all approaches surveyed in this book.

Death meditation is designed to systematically evoke a sense of "spiritual urgency," or *samvega* in Pali, by centering the scarcity of time in our consciousness and calling us to live more in alignment with our most authentic values. When we "shine the light of death on life," many aspects of our lives collapse, while others become even more precious. Confronting death engenders perspective and puts our priorities in sharper focus. It is, quite literally, illuminating. Deep awareness of the transience of life also awakens us to its vibrancy. As expressed by Zen Buddhist priest and teacher Roshi Joan Halifax, "Whether or not enlightenment is possible at the moment of death, the practices that prepare one for this possibility also bring one closer to the bone of life." American novelist and playwright Zona Gale offers a similar, albeit secular, take: "When you look at a corpse you can always sense your own breath better."

At the heart of the Buddhist Maranasati tradition is the notion of death as transition, rather than end of life. It's believed that *bardo*—the intermediate or liminal state between death and rebirth—can persist for hours or days after the body dies, consistent with the practice of delaying cremation. Those who fear the finality of death often take comfort in the idea that death is not an end, but rather a transformation, a continuation of the cycle of existence. Thich Nhat Hanh (2002), beloved Buddhist monk, author, and teacher, explores this core idea in his book *No Death, No Fear: Comforting Wisdom for Life*:

> Our greatest fear is that when we die we will become nothing. We believe that we are born from nothing and that when we die we become nothing. And so we are filled with fear of annihilation. The Buddha has a very different understanding, that birth and death are notions. They are not real. When we understand that we cannot be destroyed, we are liberated from fear.

Chapter 8. Death Meditation

I saw and touched my first dead body—my father's—when I was 27. I remember being struck with the realization that, though his body looked like him, it wasn't him. He was no longer in or of his body. This was my first, albeit elementary, understanding of the body as shell, not self. Death meditation reminds us that we are not our bodies, that our consciousness didn't begin with our bodies and won't end with our bodies. As Rainn Wilson (2023) (aka Dwight Schrute of *The Office*), author of *Soul Boom: Why We Need a Spiritual Revolution*, so aptly describes it, "We are spiritual beings having a human experience, riding around in these flesh tuxedos." For those who adopt this perspective, death of the body is nothing to fear.

Unfortunately, because we tend to be attached to and identified with our bodies—fluffy tails and prominent probosces notwithstanding—it's hard to imagine existing without them. Those who suffer from death anxiety often express concerns about how they'll breathe without lungs, how they'll think without a brain, how they'll experience the world without their senses. Of course, such concerns are born of their current material existence. Death meditation erodes these fears by allowing us to access the vibrant core of our being—our immutable spirit—which is completely independent of the body, breath, and mind (Tigunait, n.d.).

In our death-averse Western culture, the idea of purposefully contemplating death is completely foreign. It might seem that increasing our awareness of mortality would cause us to be more fearful of dying, or even despairing. Yet, the opposite is true. The Buddha taught that mindfulness of our impermanence wakes us up from the delusion that causes so much suffering in this life (Roth, 2007). Consonant with the Stoic notion that "death is happening now," Buddhism reminds us that our bodies are in a constant state of decay. Death isn't something waiting for us at the end of the road; it's walking with us all along the way. Death meditation is about turning toward rather than away from this uncomfortable reality, about facing the truth of the matter. Paradoxically, meditating on death in a structured, intentional way can quiet distressing intrusive thoughts and worries about death over time. When we invite death in and make it welcome, it stops popping up uninvited.

Though death meditation can be a deeply transformative

practice, it's not for everyone. Some of these practices may be beyond your tolerance and are not recommended for those suffering from trauma, severe depression, or emotional instability. Others are best executed with the guidance of an experienced practitioner. Regardless, as with the seemingly macabre death rituals examined previously, there's benefit to simply being aware of the range of practices other peoples and cultures have used to make peace with mortality.

If you wish to explore death meditation further, there are abundant resources and sources of instruction available to you. Online, you can find scripts in both audio and text format, including simple guided meditations for beginners. Community meditation centers offer specialized classes and retreats. Though many death meditative practices derive from religious or spiritual traditions, you're welcome to appropriate them, regardless of your spiritual persuasion. In exploring these practices, it's important to find a balance between nurturing your psychological well-being and nudging yourself beyond your comfort zone for the sake of personal growth.

If you're not quite ready to observe (or pretend to be) a rotting corpse, there are many gentle, low-key ways of easing into death meditation that don't even involve sitting (or lying) still. Simply notice how change is a part of everyday life, that everything comes and goes. The next time you walk in nature, reflect on the transience of the plants you encounter. Consider that they will all eventually die and become nourishment for the soil and future plants. When you see a dead bird or squirrel, pause and reflect on the impermanence of all beings. Watch an old, classic movie and consider that each actor is now dead. Visualize the billions of people populating this Earth and ponder the reality that every one of them will die. If you're more of an auditory person, contemplate the lyrics of a death-themed song or, if classically inclined, listen deeply to one of the great Requiem Masses.

Death meditation, no matter how you engage with it, is yet another way of "rehearsing death." Across all approaches to making peace with mortality, there's reverberant consensus: Deepening our understanding of death and our acceptance of it—through meditation or other means—can radically affect how we live. Whether you approach it philosophically or spiritually, to learn how to die is to learn how to live. Grab your marker; that, too, is worth highlighting.

Part IV
Psychological Approaches

In contrast (and complement) to the philosophical and spiritual approaches previously covered, psychological answers to death anxiety are empirically based. That is, they're derived from—and verifiable by—observation, direct sensory experience, and experimentation, rather than theory, logic, faith, or tradition. The approaches in this section address thoughts, feelings, and behaviors associated with fear of death from different theoretical frameworks and methodologies traditionally used in clinical settings. Fortunately, they translate well to self-help books such as this one. Included are evidence-based psychotherapeutic modalities (Cognitive Behavioral Therapy and Acceptance and Commitment Therapy), as well as existential and consciousness-altering approaches.

Chapter 9

Cognitive Behavioral Therapy

> Don't believe everything you think.—Robert Fulghum, *All I Really Need to Know I Learned in Kindergarten*

Close your eyes for a moment and listen inside your head. What do you hear? Silence? Unlikely. Every waking moment of every day, we talk to ourselves. If you tune in, you'll hear constant chatter, a running monologue—or, perhaps, a dialogue, if you disagree with yourself. If you've ever tried meditation, you know how busy and noisy your mind can be. We can attempt to "quiet the mind," but the brain is a thinking machine. That's what it does. And most thoughts are sub-vocal speech—that is, language-based. For better or worse, we hear our self-talk and are powerfully influenced by it. When thoughts become repetitive or negative, they can devolve into obsessive worries or doubts, sometimes referred to as rumination, brooding, or overthinking. Whether merely chatty or abjectly tormenting, all our thoughts—also known as cognitions—are the (gray) matter of Cognitive Behavioral Therapy.

Cognitive Behavioral Therapy (CBT) is a structured, evidence-based approach to psychotherapy that combines basic principles from behavioral and cognitive psychology. Its core premise is that psychological problems arise from faulty or unhelpful ways of thinking. Goal-oriented and practical, CBT focuses on changing thought patterns that result in distressing feelings and maladaptive or limiting behaviors. CBT is a skills-based approach. Its overarching goal is to develop coping strategies that enable us to become more skillful at managing life's challenges, as well as our thoughts, feelings, and behaviors in response to life's challenges. CBT has proven effective in treating a wide array of psychological problems—especially depression and anxiety—and boasts an impressive body of supporting research evidence. It's considered the gold standard of psychotherapeutic interventions for managing death anxiety (Menzies et al., 2018).

CBT addresses death anxiety in two ways: by challenging distorted, unhelpful ways of thinking about death ("cognitive restructuring") and by systematic "exposure" (in real life or imagination) to death-related stimuli, previously avoided. As we consider these elements of CBT, listen for echoes of the Stoic constructs of dichotomy of control and premeditatio malorem. Hopefully, these reverberations are louder than the voices in your head.

Cognitive Restructuring

> There is nothing either good or bad, but thinking makes it so.—Shakespeare, *Hamlet*, Act II, Scene 2

CBT is the love child of psychology and Stoic philosophy. Consistent with the core Stoic premise that influenced its early development, CBT posits that people aren't disturbed by things that happen to them, but rather by their view of these things. This is contrary to the popular cause-and-effect, stimulus-response (S-R) notion that events (S) cause feelings and behaviors (R). But as you saw in the traffic jam thought experiment in Chapter 4, there's an intervening variable between stimulus and response: our thoughts (cognitions) about the stimulus. This is how we explain that no two people have exactly the same emotional or behavioral response to the same stimulus. If events were the direct cause of our responses, then everyone would be affected in the same way by an event. We see this with death anxiety. Death (S) happens to everyone, but not everyone fears it (emotional R) or avoids it (behavioral R), or at least not to the same degree. CBT concerns itself with the meaning we make of death, as reflected in our thoughts and beliefs about it.

The application of CBT to anxiety and other disorders starts by identifying the particular set of cognitions (i.e., thoughts, beliefs, attitudes, perceptions, judgments, assumptions, attributions, appraisals, interpretations, etc.) that are causing and maintaining emotional distress and behavioral dysfunction. CBT practitioners have identified categories of irrational or unhelpful thought patterns (*cognitive distortions*), with clever names such as *catastrophizing*, *fortune-telling*, *should-ing*, and *all-or-nothing thinking*, some of which you may recognize. Perhaps one of your smug, CBT-savvy friends or family has even accused you of engaging in these. Once the cognitive culprits are identified, CBT involves questioning and challenging the problematic thought patterns to expose faults in logic, functionality, and disparities with reality. Long-held beliefs and assumptions—often the product of parental or cultural indoctrination—are investigated, interrogated, re-examined, and put to evidentiary testing.

If, as CBT theory suggests, many of our problems result from misinterpretations and misattributions, it's fair to ask why we make these errors. The short answer is that our brains are lazy. But let's get "meta" and think about our thinking for a moment. It's not always slow, deliberate, or accurate, is it? We all have quick, automatic thoughts in response to things happening around us. We even have automatic thoughts in response to our automatic thoughts. (Rabbit hole, anyone?) These automatic thoughts or *cognitive biases* are based on cognitive "models" or assumptions we make about the world derived from our unique lived experiences, including cultural programming.

These mental shortcuts (aka *heuristics*) are quite efficient, as Daniel Kahneman (2011) points out in his bestselling book *Thinking, Fast and Slow*. They enable us to process information quickly without needing to think through every detail of everything we encounter. Jumping to conclusions takes much less time and energy than thoughtful analysis. The disadvantages of these cognitive models are that they're not always accurate, and, once formed, resistant to change. This is because of *confirmation bias*: We pay more attention to information that fits our models and less attention to information that contradicts them. We also develop blind spots and distort incoming information to fit our existing models. It's easy to see how this applies to death anxiety. If we think of our models as lenses through which we see the world and that color our perceptions, CBT suggests that we might be looking at death and dying through shit-tinted lenses. We have a cognitive bias against death.

Our brains also have a "better safe than sorry" attentional bias—a surveillance mechanism designed to run disaster scenarios and protect us from harm. The anxiety-prone brain can become hypervigilant, constantly scanning for threats and making it difficult to relax or concentrate on normal activities. The cognitive error here is that we assume worst-case scenarios, often magnifying a threat, or becoming more aware of it than necessary. Our worries directly influence what we notice. For example, the anxious person might be more attuned to the weather, traffic, or news reports of natural disasters than the non-anxious person. The death-phobic person tends to see threats to life and limb everywhere. Because attention is a limited resource, this attentional bias can take up more than its share of available bandwidth.

So, if changing faulty or maladaptive thought patterns is the solution to a host of thought-driven maladies, how do we do that? First, we tune in to our self-talk. We identify our cognitive biases or distortions and notice them when they arise. Next, we consciously and deliberately override these mental defaults by challenging them. CBT offers a series of challenge questions to test the validity of a thought or belief:

- Is the thought true or verifiable? What objective evidence do I have for it?
- Is the thought useful? Does it help me achieve my goals?
- How does the thought make me feel? Does it help me feel the way I want to feel?
- Does the thought involve an outcome I can control?
- What would the most sane and rational person I know say about the thought?
- Who would I be without the thought? How would my life be different?

Finally, we develop "counters" or alternatives to the existing thoughts that have proven untrue, invalid, irrational, or unhelpful. Cognitive restructuring isn't about ignoring or avoiding maladaptive thought patterns. Neither is it about lying to ourselves just to feel better. Rather, it's about revising, reframing, or reconfiguring our current thoughts and replacing them with more realistic and helpful ways to think about the things that disturb us. It's essentially counter-programming, designed to ensure that our thoughts work for us instead of against us.

Now that you see how CBT's cognitive restructuring works—at least in theory—let's apply it to your death anxiety. In general, death anxiety is associated with a tendency to overestimate threats and underestimate our ability to cope. Numerous identifiable thought patterns serve to foment or exacerbate fear of death. Here are some common culprits which illustrate the most "popular" death-related cognitive distortions:

- My death is going to be painful and I won't be able to stand it. (catastrophizing, fortune-telling)
- If I avoid danger and pay close attention to my health, I can avoid death. (magical thinking, illusion of control)
- I wouldn't be able to survive the death of my loved one. (catastrophizing, fortune-telling)
- Death is unfair and I shouldn't have to die. (should-ing)
- My death is going to ruin the lives of my loved ones, especially my kids. They'll never get over it. (fortune-telling, all-or-nothing thinking)
- I'll never be able to come to terms with my mortality because I don't cope well with uncertainty. (overgeneralization, all-or-nothing thinking, fortune-telling)
- Death feels terrifying, so it must be horrible. (emotional reasoning)
- The doctor is going to tell me I have cancer. (catastrophizing, fortune-telling)
- I must worry about death because if I don't, it might creep up on me. (magical thinking)
- This strange mole must be a sign of skin cancer. (catastrophizing)
- I know someone who became confused at the end of life. All people who are dying lose their mental faculties. (overgeneralization, all-or-nothing thinking)

- I'll be remembered as a failure. (mind-reading, fortune-telling)
- I'll be forgotten after I'm gone. (fortune-telling)
- If I think or talk about death, it might happen. (magical thinking)
- I should be able to control my thoughts about death. (should-ing, illusion of control)
- Death is always a tragedy. (overgeneralization, all-or-nothing thinking)
- I must accomplish all my goals in life before I die. (should-ing)

These are just a few examples of common faulty or unrealistic beliefs around death and dying. Note that the distortion categories aren't always discrete, and there's often overlap. Can you see how believing these thoughts fuels death anxiety? How many do you identify with? If not exactly your thoughts, perhaps some are adjacent?

To personalize your experience, I invite you to try an exercise. First, list the specific elements or bases of your fears about death. If you get stuck, you can refer back to the list at the end of Chapter 2, or the self-assessment in the Appendix, where you identified the components of death anxiety most troublesome to you. Translate each fear into a thought or belief in the form of a sentence, as in the examples above. Next, choose one particularly upsetting thought and subject it to the six challenge questions. Examine the evidence for your fear-producing thought. How does it hold up to scrutiny? If it proves untrue, invalid, or unhelpful, generate alternative ways of thinking about your fear—counter-arguments to the unrealistic belief. Once you've established this new set of responses to your belief, practice self-correcting the negative thought when it arises. Talk back to yourself, in other words. I promise it will get easier with practice. The trick is to catch your self-talk—automatic and stealthy—and address it before it takes on a life of its own and spawns more scary negative self-talk. Remember, you hear everything you think. But you don't have to believe it.

To illustrate this process, let's take one common cognitive distortion about death and dying from the above list and "CBT it." If we were sitting together, we'd pick one of yours, but here we are. So I'll choose one that I hear a lot.

Thought:

- My death is going to be painful and I won't be able to stand it.

Challenge questions:

- Is the thought true or verifiable? No. I don't have any evidence that my death will be painful. I don't know how I'm going to die or what the experience will be like.
- Is the thought useful? Does it help me achieve my goals? No. My goal is to live without fear and having this belief about pain at the end of life is getting in the way of that. With this belief on board, I'm living way too cautiously trying to avoid a painful death. Unhelpful.
- How does the thought make me feel? Does it help me feel the way I want to feel? The thought terrifies me and I don't want to feel that way.
- Does the thought involve an outcome I can control? No. I can't control that I will die or how I will die.
- What would the most sane and rational person I know say about the thought? In a word, "Nonsense!" Followed by, "I'll make sure that you're drugged into oblivion."
- Who would I be without the thought? How would my life be different? I would be free to live life without dreading the end of it so much. The thought isn't serving any function except to perpetuate my fear of death.

Counters or alternative thoughts:

- Death isn't necessarily painful. Pain can be a symptom of some terminal diseases, but dying itself isn't inherently painful.
- Even if I do experience pain, modern medicine has effective medications to relieve my suffering. There's no reason I'll have to die in pain.
- My idea that death is painful came from a story I heard about a death that occurred a long time ago, before the medical advances we have today.

- I can think of two people I know who died peacefully and with their pain well-controlled.
- There's no evidence that I wouldn't be able to stand pain or discomfort at the end of life. I've experienced pain before and, though not pleasant, I "stood" it.
- Death is a fact of life and I can't control when or how I die. But I can control the way I live and use the time that's been given to me. I also have control over my level of knowledge and understanding about death. Perhaps I can consult with my doctor or a hospice professional about end-of-life pain management options so I know better what to expect. I can also read Chapter 13.

Note that all of these counters are TRUE. Cognitive restructuring is not about selling yourself a bill of goods, rationalizing, or "thinking positively." Your alternative thoughts must be believable and convincing, or your mind isn't buying them. So, for example, "I'm not going to die" is NOT a valid alternative to "I'm afraid I'm going to die a painful death." With cognitive restructuring, we challenge invalid or unrealistic assumptions about death and dying and replace them with thoughts that are both true and helpful. Fear of death results from notions that death is something inherently horrific, and cause for constant worry. Reframing how we think about death—seeing it in a new, more balanced and accurate way—can make it much less frightening. But CBT isn't just about thoughts. Let's move on to the "B" in CBT—the behaviors associated with death anxiety.

Exposure and Response Prevention

The best way out is always through.—Robert Frost

Imagine attending your own funeral. In a novel program sponsored by a funeral service company in Seoul, South Korea, the Hyowon Healing Center enables you to do just that (Sang-Hun, 2016). After an instructional lecture and video, you're led into a dimly lit hall where you sit beside your casket and write your last testaments. You then put on a burial shroud and lie down in your coffin. A grim-looking man in a black robe—"the Envoy from the Other World"—hammers the lid closed. You're left encased in darkness for 10 minutes. At the end of the two-and-a-half-hour session, you're told, "Now, you have shed your old self. You are reborn to have a fresh start!" Would you sign up for this experience? If you're struggling with death anxiety, perhaps not. And yet, according to CBT's exposure and response prevention (ERP), it might be just the ticket to overcoming your fear.

As we've established, most people deal with death anxiety by avoiding anything and everything related to death, similar to how we often deal with other things that scare or worry us. However, the things we avoid tend to have the most power over us. How does this work? It's important to understand that the two primary motivations behind avoidance behaviors are to keep us safe and to prevent us from feeling uncomfortable. Sounds good, right? Hooray for safety and comfort! But when there's no actual threat (as is the case with anxiety), avoidance has problematic unintended consequences. Each time we avoid or escape a death-related stimulus (i.e., an internal or external reminder of death), we experience immediate relief from anxiety. And though this affords us a momentary "Phew!," the relief strengthens the avoidance behavior. Because relief from anxiety reinforces the behavior that precedes it, we're more likely to avoid the things we fear next time because avoidance works (i.e., it serves the intended function of minimizing or preventing discomfort).

Okay, so what's the problem with that? Why not just keep avoiding the things we fear? Though avoidance reduces anxiety in the short term, it serves to maintain our anxiety and worsens it in the long term. By avoiding a feared stimulus, we miss an opportunity to test our experience in two ways: We don't learn that the thing we fear isn't as awful as we think, and we don't learn that we can actually tolerate the anxiety associated with it. Hence, avoidance perpetuates fear. Another downside of avoidance is that it severely restricts and constricts our lives. Life becomes a minefield of potential triggers. We're constantly dodging bullets and stepping around experiences likely to produce anxiety. So, it's not just how we *think* about death that fuels our fear of it; it's also how we *act* in relation to it.

Consider an example. Let's say that your death anxiety manifests in avoidance of places that remind you of death, such as cemeteries. Unfortunately, you drive by a cemetery on your way to work every day, and doing so invariably spikes your anxiety. You begin to dread your commute. At first, you cope by simply turning away from the cemetery as you pass, and this reduces your anxiety somewhat. So you keep doing it, nearly crashing into a pedestrian at one point. You decide to avoid the cemetery altogether, driving a much longer route to work. Though inconvenient, it works. No more anxiety. So you continue to avoid the cemetery. But one day you're running late for work and forced to drive by it. You discover that your anxiety is worse than ever. What's more, you're now unable to drive by funeral homes or hospitals without anxiety. Whenever you travel out of town, you have to ensure there are no cemeteries, funeral homes, or hospitals in the vicinity. As long as you avoid these triggers, you're able to keep your death anxiety at bay. But the more you do so, the worse your death anxiety becomes. Because you have no experience to the contrary, you now believe that you'd be unable to cope if you ever inadvertently encountered one of these reminders of death. You're in a box of your own making. An avoidance behavior that once worked like a charm has ultimately backfired. Your fears loom ever larger. And your world is getting increasingly smaller.

Other behaviors serve to perpetuate death anxiety as well. *Safety-seeking behaviors* (aka *superstitious behaviors*) are commonly employed when we're unable to avoid feared situations. These are actions we take because we believe they'll keep us safe or prevent us from experiencing anxiety. Typically linked to the cognitive distortion of magical thinking introduced in the previous section, safety-seeking behaviors can easily become compulsions. Examples are holding your breath when walking past a graveyard, carrying a lucky coin when crossing a bridge, avoiding stepping on a crack, or (to get embarrassingly personal) watching a tiny virtual plane cross the screen on a flight tracker app whenever my son flies. (N.B.: I don't actually believe that my vigilance is keeping the plane aloft.) The problem is that when the feared outcome doesn't happen and we experience relief, our silly brains give credit to the safety-seeking behavior, rather than concluding that perhaps we've overestimated the likelihood of the threat. This misattribution reinforces the idea that our action prevented the feared catastrophe and precludes the discovery that it's actually unlikely to happen if we don't engage in the behavior. Safety-seeking behaviors, like avoidance, give us a false sense of security and perpetuate the idea that we aren't safe in the first place.

Reassurance-seeking is another behavior that affords temporary relief from death anxiety but maintains it in the long term. This typically takes the form of asking medical professionals or loved ones for assurance that we're safe, not suffering from a serious illness, and not going to die. It might also take the form of seeking reassurance that our loved ones are safe, or repeatedly replaying conversations that we found reassuring. Compulsive *checking behaviors*, such as scanning the body for signs of illness, or mentally reviewing whether or not we've touched a contaminated surface, are other behaviors that maintain death anxiety. Checking is self-perpetuating (i.e., you're more likely to repeat it because it decreases anxiety), and invariably leads to more checking, which leads to less confidence, which leads to more anxiety. Likewise, other compulsions such as repeating a particular phrase or counting in ritualistic ways—"just to be on the safe side"—only serve to perpetuate death anxiety in the long run.

Avoidance of death-related stimuli can also occur in the mind. Because certain thoughts and images evoke anxiety, we understandably try to suppress or control them. Maybe we use drinking, drugging, or comfort eating to temporarily numb ourselves and aid in banishing uncomfortable thoughts, images, or memories. Maybe we try to distract ourselves with mindless scrolling on our devices. If thinking about our death or that of a loved one is upsetting, just don't think about it, right? But, as I'm sure you've discovered, trying not to think about something doesn't usually work. Scary thoughts can be sticky. And, like other avoidance mechanisms, any relief we might experience in the short term comes at the cost of greater anxiety and less confidence in our ability to manage the distressing thoughts or the anxiety they produce.

When you think about your death anxiety, what are the "solutions" you've developed to manage it? If you recognize avoidance, safety-seeking, reassurance-seeking, checking, compulsions, or controlling your thoughts, can you see how these strategies, designed to keep you safe and free from anxiety, are actually contributing to your problem instead of solving it? I'll even go a step further to say that they've *become* the problem.

So what's the alternative to avoidance and other behaviors used to manage death anxiety? Exposure! Though not the indecent kind. (I confess that my errant brain invariably produces a mental image of a naked man in a raincoat. Just me?) Exposure is based on the simple idea that the more you face or confront a feared stimulus, the less afraid you'll become. Exposure therapy—technically, *exposure and response prevention (ERP)*—is a standard CBT treatment for phobias that entails putting yourself in situations where you're exposed to the source of your fear in a controlled, deliberate fashion.

The ERP protocol involves identifying *exposure tasks*—thoughts, objects, places, or situations that evoke anxiety—and then gradually moving from the least anxiety-provoking scenario to the most until each of them feels less overwhelming and more tolerable. So, for example, a spider phobia might be treated by viewing a picture of a spider in a magazine and working up to sitting next to a spider. New research suggests that proceeding through a graduated hierarchy (*graded exposure*) is unnecessary and that even more potent results can be achieved by jumping around the hierarchy in varied situations (Menzies & Veale, 2022). Though exposure therapy sometimes involves imagining scenarios you fear (*imaginal exposures*), confronting feared stimuli in real life (*in vivo*) is far more powerful. Regardless, the point is to "face the fear" by engaging with it in gradual and prolonged ways in order to normalize and adapt to it. You're intentionally triggering your thoughts, images, and bodily sensations to develop a different relationship with them and how you react to them. The idea is to get increasingly comfortable with being uncomfortable. Through exposure, you learn to tolerate feelings of anxiety and test out your predictions and expectations regarding the actual threat of a feared stimulus and your ability to manage it, also known as a *behavioral experiment*. In essence, exposure = learning.

It turns out that facing our fears not only reduces our anxiety over time but actually changes our brains. In a fascinating research study on the neurobiology of courage, scientists at the Weizmann

Institute of Science used functional magnetic resonance imaging (fMRI) to scan volunteers' brains as they decided whether to slide a live snake toward their heads on a conveyor belt. Subjects fearful of snakes who pushed themselves to advance the snakes closer were found to have activation in the subgenual anterior cingulate cortex (sgACC) and reduction in skin conductance (GSR)—an indication of bodily arousal—even though they reported a subjective experience of fear (Nili et al., 2010). This example of adaptive neuroplasticity suggests that voluntarily performing an action opposite to that promoted by ongoing fear has the potential to impact neural mechanisms associated with fear and courage.

Beyond the *exposure* element (the "E" of ERP), the *response prevention* part (the "RP" of ERP) is equally important. Response prevention involves resisting any avoidance, compulsion, or other behaviors that serve to afford temporary relief but maintain anxiety. So, for example, one would perform an exposure task (e.g., walking through a cemetery) without relying on escape (i.e., leaving the cemetery) or engaging in safety-seeking, reassurance-seeking, or compulsive behaviors designed to manage the anxiety that inevitably arises. The key to overcoming death anxiety within the ERP framework is to identify the factors that are maintaining it and eliminate them. In this way, CBT is a bit like firefighting. While the fire is burning, we're not interested in what caused it. Rather, we're focused on what's keeping it going and what we need to do to put it out.

ERP is extremely effective in addressing death anxiety. The process involves exposure to various feared aspects of death and dying without reliance on avoidance or safety behaviors. Thankfully, exposure to death-related stimuli needn't involve actually dying, or even a near-death experience. The exposure tasks you might undertake are limited only by your imagination. They can be any activities, situations, locations, objects, words, sounds, or ideas related to death that you tend to avoid—in imagination or real life—because they activate your anxiety. If you're game to build your own *fear hierarchy*, list your anxiety-provoking exposure tasks from least to most aversive. I encourage you to get creative in designing exposure tasks, tailored specifically to your particular fears about death and dying and your unique patterns of avoidance. The following ideas, in no particular order—some imaginal and some in vivo—are designed to spark your imagination:

- Read obituaries of people you don't know.
- Write your own obituary, eulogy, or tombstone inscription.
- Visualize or attend a funeral.
- Read books about death and dying, or fictional accounts of characters who die.
- Read hospice materials that discuss the dying process in detail.
- Read books about people who have cared for the dying and experienced loss.
- Read about or listen to inspirational first-person accounts of people who have faced their imminent deaths with equanimity.
- Watch movies or television shows depicting death scenes.
- Write a "death plan" in which you detail all of your end-of-life wishes.
- Write out your funeral wishes.
- Write your Will.
- Engage in conversations about death and dying, or what you believe happens after death.
- Write an imaginal story about your loved ones' lives after you die. Audio record it and replay it multiple times.
- Write an imaginal story about your journey from receiving a terminal diagnosis, to being on your deathbed, to your funeral and its aftermath. Audio record it and replay it multiple times.
- Walk through a cemetery and read tombstone engravings, especially those of people who died around your age.
- Visit a hospital, nursing home, hospice, or funeral home.
- Talk to someone with a terminal illness.
- Visualize your own death or the death of a loved one.
- Imagine what will happen to your dead body.
- Listen to the music of a famous person who died or to music with lyrics about death.

- Have a (simulated) out-of-body experience through a virtual reality program.
- Imagine in detail what you most fear about death or dying.

Though extreme, a notable example of an exposure task—actually designed as a stress-management tool—comes from Radboud University in the Netherlands. A chaplain there dug a "Purification Grave" for stressed-out students to lie in to "reflect on their lives." Students can book a time slot from 30 minutes to three hours. It's surprisingly popular (O'Leary, 2023).

As you proceed through subsequent chapters, you'll discover that some of these suggested exposure tasks have multiple benefits and are recommended for different purposes within other frameworks. So be on the lookout for additional opportunities—and reasons—to engage in death-facing exercises. Death meditation, covered in the previous chapter, is a form of exposure you've already encountered. Writing your end-of-life wishes (Chapter 14) also serves double duty as an exposure task and a practical means of preparing for death. Knowing that you're compounding your benefit can enhance motivation to do hard things.

If you decide to pursue ERP to address your death anxiety, here are some general considerations and guidelines to keep in mind:

- Plan your exposure tasks intentionally, rather than encountering them accidentally and being triggered.
- Exposure tasks can be done alone, with the support of family or friends, or with a therapist.
- Ensure that any imaginal exposure tasks are as detailed and vivid as possible.
- Choose targets that are challenging but not overwhelming. Conduct exposures at a high enough level of anxiety—and for long enough—to learn to tolerate the anxiety. Remember, the discomfort *is* the exposure. Stick with the anxiety; otherwise, you run the risk of reinforcing the idea that anxiety is harmful and to be avoided. Allow sufficient time to test out your expectations.
- Remember that anxiety, though uncomfortable, will not

cause you harm. The sensations of anxiety are just your body trying to prepare you for some threat that your brain (mis)perceives.
- Avoid using anxiety-reducing strategies such as substances, compulsions, or safety-seeking behaviors. Though tempting, this will defeat the purpose.
- Don't wait for your anxiety to subside during an exposure session. Anxiety may not reduce during an exposure but will diminish each time you repeat the exposure.
- Willingness to face your fear and sit with anxiety is crucial. Remember that you can't grow courage without feeling anxious. You're learning to get better at feeling anxious.
- Remember that exposures are behavioral experiments designed to test expectations and predictions. After each exposure, ask yourself what you've learned.
- Shift your focus from the problem of preventing harm or discomfort to the problem of tolerating anxiety. Keep your eye on the prize.
- Repeat exposures frequently enough to gain traction, as often as possible and in different situations. Daily exposure is a recommended minimum, but you can't do too much. Don't allow long gaps between exposure episodes. Try to incorporate exposure into your daily life and generalize your exposures across different contexts.
- Monitor your exposure tasks so that you can track your progress. Consider keeping a log of tasks completed, level of discomfort, how you coped, and what you learned about the expectations or predictions you tested.
- Read the self-help book devoted entirely to CBT for death anxiety: *Free Yourself from Death Anxiety* (Menzies & Veale, 2022).

Because CBT for death anxiety involves addressing both your thinking about death and the behaviors that maintain your anxiety, its application involves a combination of cognitive restructuring and exposure. Both are essential because the way you've thought about death and the solutions you've employed to manage your fear of it has become the problem. Remember that you're dealing with a worry problem, not a death problem.

In his book *The Conquest of Happiness*, 20th-century iconoclastic philosopher Bertrand Russell (2015) masterfully integrates the essence of Stoic premeditatio malorum with modern CBT's core tenets:

> When some misfortune threatens, consider seriously and deliberately what is the very worst that could possibly happen. Having looked this possible misfortune in the face, give yourself sound reasons for thinking that after all it would be no such very terrible disaster. Such reasons always exist, since at the worst nothing that happens to oneself has any cosmic importance.
>
> Now every kind of fear grows worse by not being looked at. The effort of turning away one's thoughts is a tribute to the horribleness of the specter from which one is averting one's gaze; the proper course with every kind of fear is to think about it rationally and calmly, but with great concentration, until it has been completely familiar. In the end familiarity will blunt its terrors; the whole subject will become boring, and our thoughts will turn away from it, not, as formerly, by an effort of will, but through mere lack of interest in the topic.

Again and again, we see that the answer to death anxiety is not to look away, but to look directly at—and move toward—that which we fear. CBT gives us a structured, proven way to do just that, informed by the wisdom of the ages.

Chapter 10

Acceptance and Commitment Therapy

> Get out of your mind and into your life.—Steven C. Hayes, originator of ACT

Imagine you're steering a ship far out at sea. You're the captain; there's no crew. Your destination is a particular shore of your choosing. Below the deck, out of sight, lies a vast horde of demons, all with enormous claws and razor-sharp teeth. These demons have many different forms. Some of them are emotions, such as fear about your inevitable death, or regrets about how you've lived your life. Some are memories of loved ones who have died and left you alone to grieve. Others are thoughts like "Death is terrifying" or "I'm going to die a painful death." Some of them are scary mental images, such as floating corpses or being buried alive. Others are unpleasant sensations, such as tightness in your chest, or a knot in your stomach. Still others are strong urges to drink too much, work too much, or endlessly scroll through social media, all designed to distract or numb yourself.

Now, as long as you keep that ship drifting out at sea, the demons stay below deck. But as soon as you start steering toward shore, they swarm onto the deck, flapping their membranous wings, baring their fangs, and threatening to tear you into little pieces. Naturally, you don't like that much, so you make a deal: "If you demons stay down below deck, out of sight, I'll keep the ship drifting out at sea." The demons agree, and everything seems okay—for a while. The problem is, eventually you get fed up drifting aimlessly and directionless. You feel lost, bored, and stuck. You see plenty of other ships heading into shore, but not yours.

But here's the interesting thing: Although these demons are very good at threatening you, they can't actually cause you any physical harm. All they can do is growl and wave their claws and look terrifying. Their only power is the ability to intimidate. And once you realize this, you're free. You can take your ship wherever you want, as long as you're willing to accept the demons' presence. The demons may howl and protest, but they're powerless because their power relies entirely on your belief in their threats. But if you've got to keep them below deck at all costs, then your only option is to stay adrift at sea. Of course, you can try to throw the demons overboard, but while you're busy doing that no one is piloting the ship, so you risk crashing into the rocks or capsizing. Besides, it's a struggle you could never win because infinite demons are in the hold.

"But that's horrible!" you may well protest. "I don't want to live surrounded by demons!" Well, I regret to inform you that you already are. They're your thoughts, feelings, memories, images, sensations, and urges. And those demons will keep showing up, again and again, as soon as you start to take your life in a valued direction. But here's the good news: If you keep steering your boat toward shore, despite the demons, many of them will give up and leave you alone—maybe even dive over the side and swim off. As for the ones that remain, you'll get used to them after a while. And if you look closely, you'll realize they're nowhere near as scary as they first appeared. You'll see that they've been using special effects to make themselves look a lot bigger than they really are. Sure, they'll still look ugly, but you'll find them less frightening and intimidating. You'll find that you can let them hang around without being so bothered by them. And as you do that, you'll realize there's much more in your life than just those demons. There's all that sea and sky out there; there's sun on your face and a breeze in your hair. In addition to demons, you'll also encounter flying fish, mermaids, and dolphins. It doesn't matter how far away from the shore you are. The instant you start heading toward it, you're living life, having an adventure, and moving in a valued direction. You sail onward, confident in your ability to right-size your demon companions.

Chapter 10. Acceptance and Commitment Therapy

The above metaphor was adapted from Russ Harris's 2022 book *The Happiness Trap*, based on *Acceptance and Commitment Therapy (ACT)* principles. ACT was developed in the 1980s by psychologist Steven C. Hayes in response to his own struggles with anxiety. It's an empirically-based, skills-oriented approach to psychotherapy that derives from traditional Behavior Therapy and Cognitive Behavioral Therapy, with a broader focus on mindfulness, presence in the moment, and living in accordance with one's values. The theory behind ACT is that trying to control unwanted thoughts, emotions, or sensations is counterproductive. Instead of blocking, fighting, repressing, or changing our difficult internal experiences, we can focus on changing how we *relate* to them. In the words of mindfulness guru Jon Kabat-Zinn, "You cannot stop the waves, but you can learn to surf."

A common myth in popular psychology is that we should be able to control our minds and "think positively" at all times. Negative or destructive thoughts are often met with self-criticism or, perhaps, the criticism of others. We worry that something's wrong with us and try to banish or change thoughts we deem unacceptable. But try, for a moment, not to think of a purple rhinoceros with yellow polka dots. Just don't think about it. Certainly don't picture it. How's that going? Sometimes thoughts just pop up (or are implanted!) for no apparent reason, and sometimes they're negative or unpleasant. But ACT doesn't see this as a problem. According to Hayes (2009),

> We as a culture seem to be dedicated to the idea that "negative" human emotions need to be fixed, managed, or changed—not experienced as part of a whole life. We are treating our own lives as problems to be solved as if we can sort through our experiences for the ones we like and throw out the rest. Instead of a discrepancy-based mode of mind, we need to develop a modern integrated style of consciousness that can take us out of our minds and into our lives. Acceptance, mindfulness, and values are key psychological tools needed for that transformative shift.

ACT is quite different from traditional Cognitive Behavioral Therapy (CBT)—and its Stoic predecessors—in that it teaches people how to accept and be present with unpleasant thoughts, feelings, and sensations rather than trying to change, reframe, or reason our way out of them. In contrast with CBT, ACT holds that there are valid alternatives to restructuring our thinking. Within the ACT framework, the content of our thoughts isn't the problem; it's how we engage with them. True change happens when we learn to sit with discomfort and uncertainty and to make choices based on our values rather than our fears. The "Demons on the Boat" metaphor illustrates the tremendous quality-of-life cost of avoiding or fighting unpleasant thoughts and feelings to keep them "below deck."

A central concept of ACT with direct applicability to death anxiety is *cognitive defusion*, also known as *deliteralization*. Cognitive defusion is an empirically-supported strategy to change our relationship with problematic thoughts by observing them from a distance, without automatically identifying with, attaching to, or buying into them. It's about looking *at* thoughts rather than *from* them. Becoming a witness to our thoughts creates space between us and them, affording us the flexibility and freedom to be fully present and focus on our broader experience.

In this context, the concept of "thoughts" encompasses all internal cognitive (mind) experiences, such as images, memories, beliefs, attitudes, and assumptions. Boiled down, they're merely a passing stream of sounds, pictures, words, stories, and snippets of language. Nonetheless, we can so easily get caught up in our thoughts. Especially when they're distressing, thoughts can be all-consuming, making it difficult to focus on anything else. When we fixate on a thought, this is referred to as being *fused* or *hooked* in ACT parlance. With cognitive fusion, our thoughts become reality. We over-identify with our thoughts, elevate their importance, take them seriously, and amplify them to the status of "facts" and "truth." We believe what we think. And we hold on to these beliefs so tightly, we forget they're beliefs. When we become attached (fused) to thoughts in this way, it's easy to see how they can feel so compelling. This is especially true with anxiety-producing thoughts and images about death. Like the demons on the boat, it seems we're at their mercy.

Cognitive defusion is a tool to break free of this trap by shifting attention from the *content* of thoughts to the *process* of thinking, thereby loosening the hold thoughts have over us and enabling us to view them more objectively. Derived from mindfulness meditation practices, defusion is about observing the thoughts themselves, rather than watching the world *through* the thoughts. We learn to regard thoughts as just thoughts and let go of struggling with them or trying to suppress them. We're not compelled to engage them, believe them, or get caught up in them—we simply notice them as neutral observers. We allow them to hang out with us above deck.

Defusion isn't some clever mental trick to control thoughts or emotions—rather, it's the skill of becoming untangled from them. When we change our relationship with the steady stream of thoughts that flow through our heads, thoughts can come and go and we choose how much attention to pay them. Our thoughts are only as powerful as we allow them to be. I'm reminded of the folktale of a grandfather telling his grandson about a fight between two wolves. One of the wolves represents light and hope; the other represents darkness and despair. The grandson asks, "Which wolf wins?" and the grandfather replies, "Whichever one you feed."

To better understand how cognitive fusion and defusion work, I invite you to try this exercise. Imagine that your hands are your thoughts. Slowly bring your hands up to your face and hold them about two inches in front of your eyes. Notice how hard it is to see beyond your hands (thoughts). Very little information can get in because the environment is obstructed from your view. Being disconnected from the world around you makes it difficult to act effectively. This perceptual challenge illustrates fusion. Now, slowly move your hands away from your face. Notice what happens between you and the room when the space between you and your hands increases. You've widened your view to incorporate more information. You can still see your hands, but now you can also see everything else in the room. This is what's meant by defusion. When we get some distance from our thoughts, they don't disappear, but we can see past them.

What does all this have to do with your death anxiety? When you're afraid of death, your mind can get very busy generating scary thoughts (words, images, memories, worries, etc.) related to death and dying. Sometimes these thoughts are *intrusive*, meaning they come uninvited and it's hard to get rid of them. You get caught up in them or fused with them. If you have recurring intrusive thoughts about death and dying, you know how disruptive these can be to your concentration, your mood, and your overall well-being. Your instinct is to resist or suppress the thoughts, which usually requires trying to think about something else. However, this strategy invariably backfires and produces a rebound effect, making the unwanted thoughts even more tenacious. You may have heard the expression "What you resist persists." This is that.

Has your death anxiety ever taken you down a rabbit hole in a disturbing chain of thoughts? As an example, let's imagine that your particular fear is dying of cancer. You've seen friends struggle with this disease and you're haunted by memories and images aplenty. So one day you have a headache out of the blue. The thought pops into your head that you might have a brain tumor. From there, you compulsively consult "Dr. Google" for confirmation—or reassurance. You imagine undergoing tests and being told you have cancer. A cascade of worried thoughts about your decline and ultimate death follow. You try to distract yourself—or think about something else—but the cancer thoughts are persistent and keep coming back with a vengeance. In psycho-babble, this is called *obsessive rumination*.

The good news is that ACT, cognitive defusion in particular, is extremely effective in managing intrusive thoughts about death. An Iranian study investigated the effectiveness of ACT for the treatment of death anxiety and obsessive-compulsive disorder (OCD) with eight adult women. ACT resulted in a 60–80 percent decrease in death anxiety, and a 51–60 percent decrease in obsessive-compulsive symptoms, demonstrating ACT's promise for the treatment of OCD and death anxiety (Davazdahemami et al., 2020). Other researchers have provided an evidence-based account of how ACT can help people confront and grow from existential concerns—including loss, illness, and death—and lead a more vital life (Ciarrochi et al., 2022).

Now that you understand the rationale behind this approach and how it works, let's apply it to your fear of death. Below is a list of techniques, adapted from widely available ACT resources, including the Association for Contextual Behavioral Science (n.d.) and *The Big Book of ACT Metaphors* (Stoddard & Afari, 2014), for defusing disturbing thoughts that fuel death anxiety. I invite you to try the ones that you find most appealing, practice them for 30 seconds each, and see which ones work best for you. You may feel silly initially, but, like my cringey elevator experience, we can all survive a little embarrassment.

The first step in experimenting with cognitive defusion of anxious thoughts about death is to identify specific thoughts that reflect your particular fears. You can reference the list you developed in the previous chapter and choose one thought to practice with. To illustrate how defusion techniques work—and how they differ from CBT techniques—let's use the same fear we practiced with previously: the fear of experiencing pain while dying. The thought associated with this fear is "My death is going to be painful and I won't be able to stand it." Because you haven't yet actually died a painful death, the culprit in creating your anxiety is the thought, not the reality. So we'll work with that thought as we move through the exercises. Once you get the hang of it, you can apply the techniques to your own distressing death thoughts.

Observing Thoughts. Instead of saying/thinking, "I'm going to die a painful death," say, "I'm having the thought that I'm going to die a painful death." This creates distance between you and the thought, thereby loosening its grip on you. Then go a step further and say, "I'm noticing that I'm having the thought that I'm going to die a painful death." When you notice a thought as a thought, you're freed from believing it as truth. The effect of this strategy can be likened to moving from the front row to the back row of an IMAX movie theater and taking off your 3D glasses: The action sequences aren't nearly as heart-pounding or compelling.

Leaves on a Stream. Imagine that you're sitting on the bank of a slow-moving stream in early autumn. Colorful leaves are floating down the stream. When the distressing "I'm going to die a painful death" thought or image pops up (as it inevitably will), imagine placing it on a leaf and watching it gently float by. Put the next thought that arises on the next leaf and watch it sail away until it disappears out of sight. Continue to notice the leaves carrying your death-fear thoughts as they float past you. This image serves as a reminder that all thoughts are impermanent and ever-changing.

Zoom Out. Think of your death, including the painful death that you fear. Then zoom out and picture yourself floating high above the Earth, where everything below looks tiny and insignificant. See your house and the street you live on. Then zoom out further and see your city, your country, and planet Earth. Behold the solar system and the limitless expanse of the universe, glittering with light and energy. Do your fear-based thoughts feel as significant from this distance?

Repeat the Thought. Write down your distressing thought—"I'm going to die a painful death"—and read it out loud. Now try manipulating the sound of the thought in each of these ways. Repeat the thought over and over until only sound remains. The thought is just words and sounds, not reality. Now repeat the thought over and over in a silly voice. Try impersonating your favorite cartoon character or a favorite actor. The more ridiculous the better. When the thought inevitably comes up again, always hear it in the same ridiculous voices. See how seriously you take your mind when it's jabbering on like Elmer Fudd or Homer Simpson. Try singing the thought to the tune of "Happy Birthday" or any other familiar song—again, the goofier the better. You'll find it harder to think the thought when repeated in these ways. As with the other techniques, manipulating the thought doesn't get rid of it, but helps you not take it so seriously.

Thank Your Mind. Whenever "I'm going to die a painful death" or other fear-based thought pops into your head, rather than getting hooked by it or trying to suppress it, thank your mind for having the thought. After all, your brain thinks it's helping. Try saying, "Thanks for the feedback, mind," or "Thank you for this interesting thought." Responding in a sarcastic tone, as you would to a rebellious teen trying to provoke you, can help you avoid getting into a power struggle with your challenging thoughts.

Label Your Thoughts. Notice your specific death-fear thoughts when they arise and label them. You might say, "There's that painful death thought again." Or, "There's that cancer thought again." You might also use labels to describe your inner experience, such as "Worry, there is worry." Or, "I see you, mind—catastrophizing again." Avoid judging thoughts as good or bad. Instead, use descriptive words and be as specific as possible. Labeling your thoughts with detachment and objectivity softens your attachment to them.

Mindful Thought-Watching. Mindfulness involves observing your thoughts with openness, acceptance, and curiosity. When you have the "I'm going to die a painful death" or other fear-based thought, practice noticing your thought instead of struggling with it, interpreting it, analyzing it, elaborating on it, or trying to process it. But a thought can be seductive, no? It may seem that if you just chew on it a little longer, you'll have some clarity and then be able to let it go. This rarely happens. So when you notice that the pesky thought is back again, thank yourself for noticing and return to the observer position. By practicing this "coming back" maneuver over and over, it will become easier to allow thoughts to float in and out of awareness without getting caught up in them or engaging with them.

You've Got Mail. Visualize your "I'm going to die a painful death" thought appearing in your email inbox on your computer. Notice the subject line, read the message once, but don't reply to it or delete it. Just let it remain in your inbox as a "read" message. By resisting the impulse to delete it, you're deliberately agreeing not to suppress the thought and to tolerate it just being there. Alternatively, imagine your "I'm going to die a painful death" thought appearing as a new voicemail message on your cell phone. Listen to the message once but don't delete it. Allow it to remain in your imaginary voicemail. Each time you notice it, say "I see it's still there." You can also try this approach with an imagined text message.

Suggestion Box. Think of your mind as a suggestion box. Though it intends to be helpful, it doesn't always come up with ideas that serve your best interest. Your mind is always entertaining new thoughts, so you never have to take any particular thought or impulse too seriously. If you wait a moment, it will come up with another idea. The "I'm going to die a painful death" idea is just a suggestion, and you have the prerogative to reject it or any other unhelpful thought that arises.

Brain Drain. Imagine that your brain is clogged up with distressing, unhelpful thoughts about dying a painful death. To break up the clog, try a stream-of-consciousness writing session. Take a few minutes to write down whatever comes to mind, unedited and unfiltered. This purge-fest will clear your head and allow your thoughts to flow more freely. Draining your brain is particularly beneficial when performed first thing in the morning or before going to sleep at night.

ACT's cognitive defusion is a powerful tool for managing difficult thoughts and feelings related to death and dying. Facing your demons—in this case, your death fears—doesn't mean throttling them, only to have them return another day to plague you. Neither does it mean avoiding, suppressing, keeping them below deck—or even reasoning with them, as Stoicism and CBT would suggest. It means making room for them and willingly entertaining them. (Recommended reading to internalize this more deeply: "The Guest House" by Rumi, 13th-century Persian poet and mystic.) If your death anxiety manifests in distressing thoughts, images, or sensations, practice being a neutral observer of them when they arise. By noticing them come and go, you won't banish them, you won't change them, but you'll change your relationship with them. And, like the demons on the boat, you'll learn to co-exist and sail on.

Chapter 11

Existential Approaches

> Some refuse the loan of life to avoid the debt of death.—
> Otto Rank

Though quite different in both theory and practice, existential approaches to mortality are complementary to Cognitive Behavioral approaches. Existential psychology (and psychotherapy) focuses on the "givens" of human existence: freedom, responsibility, isolation, meaning, and mortality. Influenced by thinkers like Viktor Frankl, Rollo May, Otto Rank, and Irvin Yalom, existential psychology, like existential philosophy, views death anxiety as a fundamental aspect of the human condition. Such approaches to fear of death posit that humans are born with an innate need for meaning, that meaning derives from the finite nature of existence, and that fear of death is a problem of meaning in life. From this perspective, the answer to death anxiety lies in cultivating meaning by engaging in pursuits that provide a sense of purpose and transcendence. Per existential theorists, meaning-making is achieved through examining and clarifying personal values and beliefs, cultivating gratitude, considering legacy and impact, and fostering awareness of mortality. Let's explore the application of these meaning-making pursuits to your fear of death.

Memento Mori

> If we kept in mind that we will soon inevitably die, our lives would be completely different. If a person knows that he will die in a half hour, he certainly will not bother doing trivial, stupid, or, especially, bad things during this

half hour. Perhaps you have half a century before you die—what makes this any different from a half hour?—Leo Tolstoy

In ancient Rome, generals were honored with magnificent parades for their victories on the battlefield. The proud victor at the center of the procession wore a laurel crown and purple toga adorned with gold, otherwise reserved for kings. His luxurious four-horse chariot parted the streets lined with adoring fans chanting his praises. This was the greatest honor a Roman general could receive, the ultimate tribute. In this moment, he was at the center of the universe. But there was a problem. The Senate and other political bodies were concerned that a highly celebrated general might become "too big for his britches," and attempt to take over the state and declare himself king. (You may recall Julius Caesar's assassination resulted from several senators fearing his aspirations to crown himself.) So, the Romans devised a plan to keep the ego-driven ambitions of triumphant generals in check. While a horse-drawn chariot carried the honoree of the day through the streets of Rome amidst a cheering crowd, a slave sitting right behind him whispered in his ear *memento mori*, meaning "remember you will die" (Holiday, n.d.). This buzzkill was designed to serve as a reminder that all his fame and glory were temporary and that death was inevitable, even at the height of his power. In his greatest moment of triumph, he was still a human, still mortal.

The philosophers of this time and place likewise adopted this memento mori practice, a cornerstone of Stoic philosophy. The Stoics believed that reminders of death's inevitability could inform their approach to life, a notion that infused all of their thinking about how to live a good life and die a good death. Consequently, "memento mori" was always on their lips and in their thoughts.

Centuries later in Elizabethan England, a similar memo was on Shakespeare's mind as he penned his last play—*The Tempest*. In the final scene of his final play, the character Prospero (notably, a middle-aged man) says, "And thence retire me to my Milan, where *every third thought* shall be my grave." Every third thought. One might wonder what Shakespeare, speaking through Prospero, thought about his own mortality. He died five years later, at age 52.

A world away in premodern Japan, samurai soldiers used daily contemplation of death to conquer fear and become better warriors. The samurai bible, known as *The Hagakure: The Way of the Samurai*, exhorted samurai warriors to contemplate their death—by every possible means—*morning and evening*. Per the *Bushido* (code of conduct), "Every day, without fail, one should engage in the practice of death ... considering whether it will be here or be there, imagining the most sightly way of dying, and putting one's mind firmly in death. This is the substance of the Way of the Samurai." Warriors of another time and place—Native Americans—were said to enter into battle accompanied by the death song, "Today is a good day to fight. Today is a good day to die," intoned by Sioux Chief Crazy Horse. These words were also used in the daily lives of many Native American tribes as a reminder to embrace mortality and live fully.

High in the Himalayas, the Bhutanese people of every generation have adopted the discipline of contemplating death *five times a day* to promote happiness and a sense of gratitude. As you've learned, Buddhist monks practice *Maranasati*, a death meditation that involves visualizing the nine stages of a corpse decomposing, as a reminder of the transitory nature of their bodies. Historically, Sufi (Muslim) mystics, referred to as "people of the graves," hung out in graveyards to keep their mortality top of mind.

And so we see that memento mori is an idea that has spanned generations and geography. Its imprint is evident in all disciplines of life, from philosophical discourse, to spiritual practice, to warfare. From Stoics to Buddhists, practitioners have attempted to keep death in the forefront of consciousness in myriad ways—thoughts, whispers, visual reminders, ritual practices—to engender a greater appreciation for life in its finitude and imbue existence with vibrancy.

Might we all benefit from such reminders? Five times a day? Every third thought? Morning and evening? As we're riding our metaphorical chariots of success? Research studies on the numerous benefits of mortality awareness suggest that we would. For example, in a clever study designed to test the effects of mortality salience (reminders of death) on emotional response, several dozen students were divided into two groups: one was told to think about a painful visit to the dentist and the other was instructed to contemplate their own death. Both groups were then asked to complete stem words like "jo_," which can either be completed to become a positive word like "joy" or a neutral word like "jog." Students asked to contemplate their own death were far more likely to form positive words than the students asked to contemplate a painful visit to the dentist. Orienting to positive emotional information in response to mortality salience was immediate and unconscious, leading the researchers to conclude that "death is a psychologically threatening fact, but when people contemplate it, apparently the automatic system begins to search for happy thoughts" (DeWall & Baumeister, 2007). In numerous publications and lectures, Arthur C. Brooks (2023), Harvard professor and the world's foremost authority on the science of happiness, boldly proclaims that contemplating mortality isn't morbid but, rather, "the key to happiness!" Ancient global traditions and modern science concur: Mindfulness of death promotes happiness and psychological resilience.

Beyond mere happiness, existential psychologists remind us that mortality awareness is an essential element of meaning-making in life. Counterintuitively, keeping death top of mind is particularly potent medicine for those who fear death. But no matter how life is going, it's all too easy—and convenient—to forget that we're going to die one day. Remembering to remember our mortality doesn't come naturally, especially if thoughts of death evoke anxiety. So how can we adopt a memento mori practice and make a habit of eating our existential vegetables? Unlike cultivating more neutral daily habits such as drinking more water or applying sunscreen, we're naturally disinclined to think about death. So we need robust strategies to override our defaults of denial and avoidance. Fortunately, there's an app for that. And some other tools, too.

WeCroak App

Five times a day, my phone reminds me that I'm going to die and invites me to open and read one of thousands of quotes from literature, philosophy, popular culture, religion, and medicine about life, death, and the essence of existence. The free *WeCroak* app (wecroak.com), with a winsome poison dart frog as its logo, is inspired by the aforementioned Bhutanese practice of contemplating death five times daily. Each day, the subscriber receives five invitations to stop and think about death. The blunt message is always the same: "Don't forget you're going to die." According to the app's website, these notifications "come at random times and at any moment, just like death," and are meant to encourage "contemplation, conscious breathing, or meditation." The app has many favorable reviews, the most glowing of which rates it "second only to the Holy Quran."

Unlike many apps whose sole purpose is distraction (I see you *TikTok*), *WeCroak* keeps us laser-focused. No escapism here. The app serves as a reminder that death is a fate from which there's no escape. What might seem like a downer instead offers a dose of perspective. Whatever minutia you're fretting about at the moment are, in the grand scheme, not such a big deal. You're reminded that however you're spending your time, it's finite and not to be wasted. But aren't these incessant interruptions intrusive? Why, yes. That's the point. Whatever you're doing, the "death pings" don't knock you off track—rather, they put you back on. We have apps for everything else, so why not one to keep mortality top of mind? Unless you have the luxury of sitting on a rock in the bucolic Himalayas with plenty of time and opportunity to contemplate death like it's your job.

Life Calendars

Though there are many versions of this interactive tool, life calendars (aka memento mori calendars) are all designed to allow you to visualize the entire span of your life in weeks, usually in poster format "suitable for framing," as they say. Some versions are customized to start with your actual date of birth, while others simply display a certain number of weeks based on a hypothetical lifespan (e.g., 4,680 weeks for a 90-year life or, less optimistically, 4,160 weeks for an 80-year life). Generally, each week is represented by a square that you can darken to illustrate, in stark relief, how long you've lived so far, where you are in your finite lifespan, and how much time you have left. Of course, none of these yet-to-be-filled squares are guaranteed. But the ritual of filling in a square each week serves as an accountability check to help you focus on what really matters and make the most of your time. While 80 or 90 years of life may be difficult to grasp, a week is quite knowable and within the realm of your lived experience. A week can slip by very quickly. When you consider your life as a whole, it may seem like it's made up of countless weeks. But with a life calendar, there they are, fully countable, staring you in the face. If you're lucky, you have a few thousand—a number small enough to fit neatly into a single image.

To fully appreciate the use of this tool, remember that each square—each week—only represents a week that you'll be alive. But there's an important distinction between *lifespan* (the number of years someone lives from birth until death) and *healthspan* (the number of years someone is healthy without chronic or debilitating disease). How many of these weeks will be spent living well—doing the things you love, or that give your life meaning? Remember, it's not just the weeks in your life; it's the life in your weeks. Cheesy, but true.

Purveyors of life calendars—you can Google "life calendars" for a dizzying array of options—tout all sorts of benefits to filling a new square with each passing week, including improved focus, a heightened perspective on life, and motivation to take consistent action, accomplish more, live better. One ad boldly proclaims: "Visualize your life in weeks and unlock your true potential!" Another includes the warning: "You may experience some existential crisis followed by a rush of motivation to get the most out of every week." Your mileage may vary.

Visual Cues

For much of history, memento mori was more than a thought exercise; it was a lifestyle. Across civilizations and cultures, people intentionally surrounded themselves with visual reminders of their mortality and the fragility of human life. Enter the tchotchkes!

Human skulls are a perennial favorite for keeping death top of mind. As early as 7200 BCE, skulls of dead ancestors were displayed on shelves and benches in Middle Eastern homes. In 13th-century Latin America, the Aztecs displayed the heads of warriors defeated in battle on skull racks (Weingarten, 2011). Skull imagery became the hallmark of *Dia de los Muertos* (Day of the Dead), an annual skeleton-centric celebration of Mexican culture. Stoic philosophers of ancient Greece and the Roman Empire used visual prompts to aid their daily memento mori practice, including human skulls strategically placed on their desks.

Skull iconography featured prominently in European decorative art in the mid–1300s, after the bubonic plague killed a quarter of the population (Weingarten, 2011). The skull was commonly depicted on drinking goblets, reminding people that life is short and to be enjoyed. Medieval monks kept human skulls in their monastic cells to aid in their daily contemplation of mortality. During the second wave of the "Black Death," European churches ran out of burial space as dead bodies began to pile up. Out of necessity, they started the practice of displaying skeletal remains as decoration. Churches throughout Europe are adorned with centuries-old skulls and bones to this day. A notable example is the "Bone Church" (Sedlec Ossuary) in the modern Czech Republic. An ossuary beneath the church of Santa Maria in Rome, built in 1630, is decorated with the remains of 4,000 friars, including an entire "crypt of pelvises." Therein hangs a plaque with the inscription: "What you are now, we once were; what we are now, you shall be." Memento mori, in other words.

Sixteenth-century essayist Michel de Montaigne, introduced in Chapter 5, wrote of an ancient Egyptian custom wherein a dried skeleton would be brought out during their feasts, and it would be said, "Drink and be merry for when you're dead you will look like this." Montaigne famously suggested writing in a room with a window overlooking a cemetery to sharpen one's focus.

During the late Middle Ages and early Renaissance, memento mori jewelry became popular, especially among European social elites. These coveted collectibles featured motifs of skulls, bones, and names of the departed, inscribed in precious metals. Ivory carvings with a human face on one side and a skull on the other were prized status symbols. Memento mori prayer beads likewise kept death top of mind. In 16th-century England, Mary, Queen of Scots, famously owned a large silver watch in the shape of a skull, inscribed with the words "Pale death knocks with the same tempo upon the huts of the poor and the towers of kings." (Ironically, she was beheaded for treason at the age of 44.)

Seventeenth-century Europe saw the emergence of *Vanitas* (Latin for "vanity"), an allegorical art form that used symbolism to highlight the transience of life, the futility of pleasure, and the certainty of death. The paintings of this period typically depicted still-life images of transitory objects. The most famous example of this genre—"Still Life with a Skull"—was painted by Philippe de Champaigne in 1646. It features the three iconic memento mori symbols: the tulip (life), the skull (death), and the hourglass (time). *Danse Macabre* (Dance of Death) and the *Grim Reaper*, personifications of death, were other symbolic commentaries on death's inevitability that emerged during this period.

In the Victorian era, death-themed objects were commonly scattered throughout homes. Desks and tables held skulls, and walls were adorned with paintings featuring symbols of death, including skeletons, hourglasses, soap bubbles, wilting flowers, clocks, and extinguished candles. Memento mori medallions could be found in pockets and purses, along with spare change. Visual reminders of death were everywhere.

In stark contrast, in modern Western society, symbols of death are relegated to cemeteries, tombstones, and "Goth" subculture, all easily avoided. Sweeping such reminders under the rug serves to perpetuate the death taboo so prevalent in our culture. As many ancient societies and non–Western modern cultures have taught us, visual prompts can normalize the presence of death in life. You don't need to display an urn of Uncle Ralph's ashes on the mantle or entertain guests with skull-themed shot glasses. But visual cues in your environment, obvious or more subtle, can serve to keep mortality top of mind. I keep an hourglass on my desk, and skull art as wallpaper on my mobile phone. A death educator colleague of mine wears skeleton earrings. Be creative! You're going to die! Why not get that "memento mori" tattoo you've always wanted?

Habit Formation Through Stacking

When I turned 60, I began to fret about the (unlikely) possibility of falling and breaking a hip, thereby concluding my life as I know it. In defense of my neurosis, this fear was not entirely unfounded as, statistically, falls are the leading cause of injury, disability, and injury-related death in older adults. Following my own sage advice to "do instead of stew," I decided to preempt catastrophe by improving my balance. The plan was to adopt a daily practice of standing on each foot for 30 seconds at a time. But how would I remember to do such a thing, despite my good intentions? I thought about setting an alarm on my phone, but knew that those reminders would invariably come at inopportune times when I couldn't perform my balancing act.

As a behavioral scientist, I knew that new habits are best formed by pairing them with existing ones. This hack, called *habit stacking* is based on the neurological phenomenon of *synaptic pruning* (i.e., neural connections). So, I decided that each time I brushed my teeth, I'd balance on one foot, then the other, for the two-minute duration. My fancy electric toothbrush would alert me to shift feet with each 30-second interval per mouth quadrant, for a total of 60 seconds on each foot. After doing this twice daily for about a month, I was ready to walk a tightrope across Niagara Falls—or at least avoid tipping over on my way to the bathroom in the wee hours. The point of this intimate glimpse into my dental hygiene practices is that if you wish to make a habit of thinking about your mortality, one efficient way to do it is to pair it with something you already do regularly every day, such as feeding a pet, walking to the mailbox, or brewing your morning coffee. If you're curious, I'm happy to report that my tooth-brushing regimen is now accompanied by balancing on one foot *and* contemplating my mortality—hopefully not correlated.

Mindful Living

Another, more organic, strategy for maximizing the benefits of mortality awareness is to accompany your daily activities with reflections that are relevant to those activities. Essentially, you perform the simple acts of living—things you do each day—more mindfully. Examples of such mortality-mindful reflections are as follows:

- As I wake up in the morning, I remember that one morning I will not wake up.

- As I eat a meal, I remember that this might be my last meal.
- As I'm going to sleep at night, I remember that I may not wake up tomorrow.
- As I'm walking, I remember that I'm closer to my final destination with each step.
- As I'm aware of my breathing, I remember that one day I will take in my last breath.
- As I'm getting a haircut or clipping my nails, I remember that one day I will discard this body as easily as I'm able to let go of these hairs and nails.
- As I notice the flowers in the vase wilting, I remember that all forms of life eventually decay and die.

Lest you recoil at these suggestions, it's important to note that memento mori is not intended to foster a morbid preoccupation with mortality. As you endeavor to change your relationship with death, the goal is to neither fear it nor fetishize it. Instead, the intent is to normalize it by making it more common, a part of daily life. By whatever means, you can use reminders of your mortality to live life to the fullest and to remain in the present moment. Death illuminates the preciousness of life. Remaining mindful of the inevitability of death—the impermanence of all things—focuses us on living with intentionality and purpose. Instead of letting death loom in the distant future, we bring it closer. Instead of anxiously avoiding all thoughts of death, we lean in. Rather than morbid or depressing, as you might imagine, mortality awareness is invigorating and life-affirming. As encapsulated by British novelist E.M. Forster, "Death destroys a man, but the idea of death saves him."

Gratitude, the Antidote to Regret

> No amount of regret changes the past, no amount of anxiety changes the future, any amount of gratitude changes the present.—Ann Voskamp, Canadian author

When you review your life, what regrets do you have? List them now, if you're willing. If you're having trouble identifying regrets, try completing the sentence "If only ..." as many times as proves generative. What feelings come up for you? Perhaps you feel sadness, heaviness, guilt, bitterness, or longing. Now, consider all the things in your life for which you're grateful. List them now, if you're willing. If you get stuck, try completing the sentence "I appreciate ..." As you continue this gratitude exercise, what happens to your feelings of regret? Likely, they've dissipated or were replaced by your subsequent feelings of gratitude. The point here, hopefully experienced firsthand, is that regret and gratitude are incompatible at any given moment. Of course, they co-exist as entities in our minds, available for access at any time, but they can't be experienced simultaneously. As you'll soon discover, gratitude is a potent counter to regret, a neuropsychological reality with significant implications for death anxiety.

Regret is a central concern for many who suffer from death anxiety. Indeed, studies have confirmed that an unfulfilled life, or poorly lived life, is highly correlated with fear of death. It makes intuitive sense that one's assessment of how well they've lived—things they've done and failed to do—would directly impact their perspective on mortality and their ability to face death without fear. In her book *Top Five Regrets of the Dying*, Australian hospice nurse Bronnie Ware (2019) identifies the following regrets of those facing imminent death:

- I wish I'd had the courage to live a life true to myself, not the life others expected of me.
- I wish I hadn't worked so hard.
- I wish I'd had the courage to express my feelings.
- I wish I had stayed in touch with my friends.
- I wish that I had let myself be happier.

Do you identify with any of these regrets? If so, how might they impact your fear of death?

When we examine the experience of regret, we realize that it exists in the past. It regards past actions or inactions. It's that nagging feeling that we could or should have made different choices. Whether a missed opportunity, a bad decision, wasted time or money, or words spoken or left unspoken, regret is a heavy burden to carry. It casts a shadow over our experience of the present and, in the case of death anxiety, the future. Essentially, we're afraid to die with regret. We understand regret to be a reflection of the life we've lived. Of course, regret has an upside. We can use it to course-correct in the time we have remaining, akin to Nietzsche's eternal recurrence thought experiment. Used constructively, regret can serve as a learning opportunity—a tool to avoid its further accumulation.

All well and good, but what to do about the futile practice of revisiting past actions or omissions without discernment or correction, especially as it impacts our ability to face our mortality? We invoke the arch nemesis of regret—gratitude! In the last two decades, the phenomenon of gratitude has received a great deal of attention within the "positive psychology" movement. And for good reason. Gratitude has a myriad of positive effects on our mental and physical health and well-being (Emmons & McCullough, 2003; Wood et al., 2010). It's been shown to lower stress, reduce pain, promote faster recovery from trauma and injury, and even improve our immune systems, blood pressure, heart function, and sleep quality. Psychologically, gratitude has been linked to decreased anxiety, depression, and loneliness, and increased happiness, self-confidence, life satisfaction, and resilience (Bouchrika, 2024). Most importantly for our purpose, gratitude figures prominently in constructing a life of meaning, a powerful buffer against death anxiety.

So what is it, actually? To get etymological, gratitude derives from the Latin word *gratis*, meaning gratefulness or thankfulness. Psychologists have defined gratitude as the feeling of appreciation for benefits received that are unexpected or felt to be undeserved. According to gratitude researchers Emmons and McCullough (2004), the feeling of gratitude involves two core components: acknowledgment of goodness in our lives, and recognition that sources of this goodness lie outside of ourselves. Gratitude can be felt toward a person, an animal, or an abstract or non-human entity (e.g., nature, God). Stoic philosopher Cicero named gratitude the greatest of the virtues, the "parent" of them all.

Research studies consistently demonstrate a negative correlation between death anxiety and gratitude. That is, individuals who exhibit greater gratitude fear death less. In a study of Lebanese adults following the 2023 earthquake, gratitude, mediated by optimism, was associated with reduced fear of death (Al Boukhary et al., 2024). Likewise, a brief gratitude induction procedure was found to be highly effective in reducing death anxiety in older Chinese adults (Lau & Cheng, 2011). Breast cancer survivors experienced significantly lower death-related fear of recurrence after undergoing a gratitude intervention, mediated by the pursuit of meaningful personal goals (Otto et al., 2016).

By what mechanism(s) does this work? It has been suggested that gratitude diverts our attention and memory away from negative aspects of the past and grounds us in the present. Viewed through the lens of a treatment approach called *habit reversal training*, gratitude is framed as a competing response, an action that's incompatible with regret or other negative mental habits. As you may have experienced at the start of this section, you simply can't experience regret and gratitude simultaneously. According to neuroscientist Alex Korb (2012),

> Gratitude can have such a powerful impact on your life because it engages your brain in a virtuous cycle. Your brain only has so much power to focus its attention. It cannot easily focus on both positive and negative stimuli. So once you start seeing things to be grateful for, your brain starts looking for more things to be grateful for. That's how the virtuous cycle gets created.

In his book *The Upward Spiral*, Korb (2015) suggests that during experiences or expressions of gratitude, our brain is automatically redirected to pay attention to what we have, producing enhanced awareness of the present. Consciously practicing gratitude trains the brain to attend selectively to positive thoughts and emotions, as opposed to those associated with regret—an attentional bias that works to our benefit.

It has also been posited that the influence of gratitude on death anxiety is mediated by an enhanced sense of meaning in one's life and engagement in goal-directed behavior. This theory is consistent with both TMT (death anxiety decreases with the pursuit of culturally derived goals) and MMT (creation of meaning in life promotes death acceptance and neutralizes death anxiety). By reexamining life events with a thankful attitude, we become less fearful of death due to a sense that life has been well-lived.

The link between gratitude and mortality acceptance is also explained neurobiologically. Like so many things that are good (and bad) for us, gratitude changes the brain. Studies have demonstrated that feelings of gratefulness are evoked in the right anterior temporal cortex (Zahn et al., 2007) and that people who express and feel gratitude have a higher volume of gray matter in the right inferior temporal gyrus (Zahn et al., 2014). Neurochemically, gratitude catalyzes neurotransmitters such as serotonin, dopamine, and norepinephrine—the brain chemicals that mediate emotions and stress responses. Feelings of gratitude have also been associated with a marked reduction in levels of cortisol, the stress hormone (McCraty & Childre, 2004). Remarkably, the effect of gratitude on the brain is long-lasting (Zahn et al., 2007).

Neuroscientist and gratitude researcher Glenn Fox explains that gratitude conditions the brain: "I think that gratitude can be much more like a muscle, like a trained response or a skill that we can develop over time as we've learned to recognize abundance and gifts and things that we didn't previously notice as being important." This notion was extremely personal for Fox as his mother, diagnosed with stage 4 ovarian cancer, practiced gratitude journaling as she was dying. It profoundly affected her ability to stay in the moment and appreciate the time she had left. Fox himself benefited tremendously from the practice as he processed his grief after her death (Tung, 2019).

In the quest to overcome death anxiety, your brain on gratitude is a powerful alternative to your brain on regret. So how do you replace regret with gratitude? Remember, the wolf you feed is the one who wins. Here are some scientifically proven practices to cultivate gratitude in your daily life:

- Daily expressions. Make a habit of saying "thank you" to others for even the smallest gestures or acts of kindness throughout the day.
- Gratitude journaling. Jot down a few of the things you're thankful for each day.

- Gratitude letter. Communicate your appreciation to someone in writing.
- Gratitude visit. Take the gratitude letter a step further by visiting the person you're grateful to and reading your letter aloud to them.
- Gratitude meditation. Sit quietly and give focused attention to the things and people in life that you're grateful for.
- Bookend your day. Begin and end each day by taking a few moments to acknowledge three things you're grateful for.
- Gratitude jar. Decorate a glass jar and fill it with daily gratitude entries. When the jar is full, read the entries and savor what was appreciated.
- Mental subtraction. Imagine what your life would be like if certain positive events hadn't occurred, or if certain negative events had. Sometimes the greatest gifts in life are the troubles you don't have. Be thankful for the hardships you've escaped or overcome, the bullets you've dodged.
- Gratitude walks. Take a walk—in nature or in a city—and think about the people, places, and things you appreciate along the way.
- Make it social. Enhance the benefits of any of these practices by sharing them with a friend or family member.

Whatever practices you might adopt, remember that you're training and rewiring your brain away from regret and toward gratitude. If you think of gratitude practices as mental exercise, you're strengthening your gratitude muscle. Not only will you derive benefit in the moment, but you'll be addressing your fear of death by diminishing regret and consciously infusing your life with meaning. The kind of meaning that, according to existential psychologists, makes your life one worth dying from. And, per gratitude neuroscience, you might even sleep better in the meantime.

Rippling

> Just as ripples spread out when a single pebble is dropped into water, the actions of individuals can have far-reaching effects. —Dalai Lama

My presentation had gone well, but I was tired and anxious to get back to my hotel. I had returned to the city of my graduate school, 30 years later, to speak at a psychology conference. As the crowd began to thin, a young woman lingered and, with some hesitation, approached me. She introduced herself as a local psychologist and the daughter of a woman I had treated three decades ago during my clinical training. Though I didn't recognize her mother's name, her story came back to me instantly. I had treated her for a severe case of postpartum depression following the birth of the woman now standing before me. As I was reeling from the serendipity of this chance encounter, the young psychologist thanked me for saving her mother's life and, in turn, hers. Her mother had struggled with both suicidal and homicidal ideation, including the impulse to kill her infant daughter. Thankfully, she recovered and came to embrace her role as a new mother—to the great benefit of her daughter who, 30 years later, was inspired to become a psychologist. Apparently, when she was old enough to understand, her mother/my patient told her the story of her descent into madness and the therapeutic relationship that pulled her out. The mother had referenced me by name over the years, enabling her daughter to connect the dots when attending my presentation—quite randomly, she confessed. I had no idea—and couldn't have imagined—that my impact on a single patient as a young, inexperienced psychologist-in-training would extend to her offspring and beyond, to the many patients she would help as a psychologist. I was compelled to reconsider the long-held, oft-bemoaned notion that my impact as a psychologist was limited to the patient sitting in front of me.

This spine-tingling vignette illustrates the phenomenon of *rippling*, introduced by existential psychiatrist Irvin D. Yalom (2008) in his book *Staring at the Sun: Overcoming the Terror of Death*. According to Yalom,

Rippling refers to the fact that each of us creates—often without our conscious intent or knowledge—concentric circles of influence that may affect others for years, even generations. The effect we have on other people is in turn passed on to others, much as the ripples in a pond go on and on until they're no longer visible but continuing at a nano level.

Parenting is, perhaps, one of the most obvious examples of rippling—even beyond projecting ourselves biologically onto our offspring by transmitting our genes. Contrary to the "Don't do as I do, do as I say do" model of parenting (not recommended), our children watch and absorb everything we do. Our imprint is indelible as we model behaviors we desire them to emulate. Our potential to shape and inspire them is infinite. The goal of parenting—to raise our child to become a good person—is all about rippling, because our impact on them as parents will, in turn, impact every person they encounter in profound ways. And what parent doesn't dream for their child to make the world a better place by virtue of their existence? (Sadly, rippling also has a dark side in this familial context, as malignant patterns of abuse and dysfunction can be passed down in the form of intergenerational trauma.) One needn't be a parent to practice rippling via *generativity*, a concern for the next generation and a desire to nurture and guide them. Even if you don't have children or grandchildren, you can ripple by tutoring a neighborhood kid or mentoring a junior colleague at work.

Yalom draws an important distinction between the (futile) hope to preserve your personal identity after you're gone and "leaving behind something from your life experience; some trait; some piece of wisdom, guidance, virtue, comfort, that passes onto others, known or unknown." It's the former—this core sense of "self" or "ego"—to which we're so attached, the anticipated annihilation of which is the source of much suffering, including death anxiety. But what if we conceived of "self" beyond this subjective, internal identity to include the wisdom we've accumulated, our deeply held beliefs, values, and worldview, as reflected in our behavior? Are these not so much more durable? Impervious to annihilation, even? We are, after all, defined by what we do. It's our behavior, regardless of our intent, which makes an impression on others. The good news is that the intangibles of our existence are independent of—and therefore outlive—our existence on this Earth. Death need not be the annihilation of self that we fear. Our names and identities will pass out of memory, but our rippled influence continues.

Now, you might be thinking, I'm no big deal. What kind of influence or impact could I have beyond my earthly existence? In fact, the most anonymous of us can lay claim to rippling. It isn't limited to the "big" things like groundbreaking scientific discoveries or leadership of a social movement. Neither is rippling about monuments or hospital wings with our names on them. Rather, it applies to each of us every day, in every action we take. Everyone has the potential to affect others for years, decades, and even centuries after departing this Earth. We are, in essence, inter-generational conduits.

Okay, so my impact doesn't have to be big, but what's the currency of rippling? What can I do or say that counts for something? Perhaps the most concrete and literal way to "leave something of yourself behind" is organ donation. Imagine the rippled impact of giving the gift of sight by donating your corneas to a blind person, for example. But what acts count, day-to-day, while I'm still alive? Rippling includes simple acts of care, comfort, generosity, and kindness. On a micro level, it can be as simple as offering a kind word or gesture to a stranger you'll never see again. Holding a door open or letting someone ahead of you in the grocery line can ripple. Simply acknowledging someone's existence with a smile, nod, or wave can improve their mood and impact the people they encounter the rest of the day. Imagine this scenario: The clerk at the checkout is having a bad day. You smile at them and compliment their glasses (which are, in fact, totally cool). Their mood improves, if ever so slightly, and when they go home, they're more patient with their kids. Their kids respond positively and, when they go to play at a friend's house, they positively impact their playmates who, in turn, make life a bit easier for their parents who, when they go to work, are more pleasant with their co-workers who go home to their families in a better mood, and on and on. Rippling is why I smile at strangers. And why, during the COVID-19 pandemic, I learned to smile with my eyes above my masked face. Maya Angelou spoke truth when she said, "I've learned that people will forget what you've said, people will forget what you did, but people will never forget how you made them feel."

The point of rippling, though, is that our impact isn't limited to those we encounter directly. Our influence never ends with the person in front of us. Because every encounter we have with someone changes both them and us, we will ripple outward to impact everyone we—and they—come in contact with. The effect may not seem large or even noticeable, but it's always there. And while our name or image may not remain attached to the ripples of our actions, that's beside the point. What matters is that in ways we may not realize, we leave something of ourselves as we inevitably influence the world around us. How we affect others endures even when we are no more. In my own life, for example, the lessons I've imparted to my son, my students, and my patients will continue to ripple long after I'm gone. I take great comfort in this. Remember that your sphere of influence is greater than you think, or will ever know. Indeed, "Your legacy is every life you've ever touched."—another Maya Angelou pearl.

Skeptical? It's science! Harvard scientists Fowler and Christakis (2008) looked at the emotional well-being of 5,000 people who were followed over 20 years in the renowned Framingham Heart Study. They found that happiness spreads through social circles due to the phenomenon known as *emotional contagion*. Happy emotions felt by those at the center of the social circle spread out to the rest of the social network in a classic rippling effect. One person's happiness triggers a chain reaction that benefits not only his friends, but his friends' friends, and his friends' friends' friends. Remarkably, the effect lasts for up to one year.

With the emotional contagion of rippling, timing matters, too. The messages we send with our behavior may land in a particularly meaningful way to someone who needs to hear them—or is particularly receptive to being influenced—at that moment, for whatever reason(s). I'm reminded of the Buddhist saying "When the student is ready, the teacher will appear." In this sense, we're all teachers, with every word and deed.

Does all of this sound too far-fetched or idealistic to have any meaningful impact on your death anxiety? Well, admittedly, there are three catches to this whole rippling thing. First, our influence on others is impossible to measure, so we may never know the extent of our impact, or how far and wide our ripples have extended. Second, because we rarely get feedback from others about how meaningfully we've influenced their lives, we may never know that we had an impact at all. Even profound impacts we've had may remain unknown to us. Finally, the impact of our existence is often not immediate. By their very nature, ripples can ripple across time and space, across generations. Though we're planting seeds every moment of every day, they may not yield fruit immediately, or even in our lifetime. Regardless, we're cosmically rewarded for "paying it forward" to future generations, as this Indian proverb reminds us: "Blessed is he who plants trees under whose shade he will never sit."

So how do we know that rippling works, especially if we're not around to enjoy the shade of the trees we planted? On the rare occasion we're gifted with feedback about the difference we've made—often years later—we know it to be true. Failing that, we must rely on the evidence of rippling all around us—including how we ourselves have been beneficiaries of rippling—and accept that we may never fully know our impact.

Of all the strategies Yalom employed in working with patients afflicted with death anxiety, he found the concept of rippling to be the most powerful of all. According to him, "Rippling offers a potent antidote to those who claim that meaninglessness inevitably flows from one's finiteness and the transience of all things." In some sense, knowing that our impact can and will outlast our bodies is a path to immortality. Though we are finite, our rippled influence is perpetual and everlasting. The notion that we continue to exist through our impact on others—that we can leave meaningful parts of ourselves behind after death—can be a tremendous consolation. Rather than chasing permanence through prestige, recognition, or fame, we can ask ourselves: What matters to me? What ripples do I hope to make in my time here? What kind of legacy do I wish to leave to the world? Rippling is certainly a preferred alternative to stacking up regrets about what we've done or failed to do. But alongside the comfort afforded by rippling comes immense responsibility. In ways large and small, we all have the power and potential to shape the world for the better. As expressed by philosopher William James, "The greatest use of life is to spend it for something that will outlast it."

Chapter 12

Altered States of Consciousness

> There are pockets of time, she thinks, where every sense rings like a bell, where the world brims with fleeting grace.—Dominic Smith, *The Last Painting of Sara de Vos*

While traditional psychological approaches to death anxiety involve working directly with distressing thoughts, feelings, and behaviors, approaches outside of the mainstream target those "hard to reach" areas of human experience—namely, spiritual or existential distress and despair. The disciplines of psychology and psychiatry have long explored the use of "non-ordinary" states of consciousness to facilitate deep psychological work (Tarrant, 2022). These alternative approaches—including mindfulness meditation, hypnosis, psychedelic trips, lucid dreaming, and other numinous experiences—all involve alterations or expansions of consciousness designed to transcend mental and emotional constrictions associated with death anxiety.

Better Dying Through Psychedelics

> Psychedelics are to the study of the mind, what the microscope is to biology and the telescope is to astronomy.—David E. Nichols, American medicinal chemist

When you think of "tripping out," you no doubt recall the hippie drug culture of the '60s or, perhaps, the aforementioned philosophy major/barista living in a van. And yet, psychedelics have been used to alter consciousness, promote healing, and accompany religious ceremonies dating back thousands of years, particularly well documented in Indigenous cultures. Psilocybin, the naturally occurring psychoactive, hallucinogenic compound found in "magic" (psychedelic) mushrooms, is one of the most commonly used and heavily researched psychedelic substances.

Early research into the therapeutic use of psychedelics for a host of mental health conditions, including existential angst, yielded promising findings. Psychiatrist Humphry Osmond, who coined the term *psychedelic* (which means "mind-manifesting"), pioneered experimentation with LSD-assisted psychotherapy in the 1950s. But, alas, the countercultural free-for-all of the '60s—promoted by legendary Harvard psychology professor Timothy Leary—eventually led to moral outrage and political backlash in the United States. In 1970, President Nixon signed the Controlled Substances Act, which classified psychedelic substances as highly restricted Schedule 1 drugs, deemed as having "no medical use" and a "high potential for abuse." The party was over, and research into the therapeutic benefits of these promising drugs came to a screeching halt.

The decades-long ban on psychedelic research ended in 1999 when Roland Griffiths of Johns Hopkins University pioneered a series of studies on the effect of psilocybin on psycho-spiritual distress, the angst that stems from facing the inevitability of death. In 2006, he and his team published a landmark study that sparked a renewal of psychedelic research worldwide. The study, published in the *Journal of Psychopharmacology*, demonstrated the clear benefit of psilocybin for anxiety and depression in cancer patients. It also jump-started a "psychedelic renaissance," the second wave of psychedelic research in the U.S. The study found that after two or three psilocybin sessions, a majority of participants reported significant positive changes in their mood and well-being, and one-third rated the experience as the most spiritually significant experience of their life, comparable to the birth of a first child or the death of a parent (Griffiths et al., 2006). A 48-year-old survivor of adult-onset leukemia who participated in one of Griffith's studies reported, "I now have the distinct sense that there's so much more ... that death is not the end but just part of a process, a way of moving into a different sphere, a different way of being" (Slater, 2012).

Subsequent and ongoing research has yielded similar results. In two of the largest and most rigorous double-blind, placebo-controlled clinical investigations of a psychedelic drug to date, researchers at Johns Hopkins University (Griffiths et al., 2016) and New York University (Ross et al., 2016) studied the effect of psilocybin on end-stage cancer patients with clinically significant anxiety or depressive symptoms, referred to in the literature as *end-of-life distress*. Both studies, published in the *Journal of Psychopharmacology*, found that a single high dose of psilocybin administered in a psychotherapeutic context produced rapid, significant, and sustained decreases in anxiety and depression, increases in quality of life and life meaning, increases in ratings of death acceptance, and decreases in anxiety about death among patients with advanced cancer. Both studies found that effects were dose-dependent (i.e., higher doses yielded more robust effects) and that patients who had a stronger mystical experience also showed a better outcome, whether or not they reported being religious. Remarkably, improvements persisted at 6-month follow-up and, in the case of the NYU study, even at 4.5-year follow-up. Participants overwhelmingly attributed positive life changes to the psilocybin-assisted therapy experience (Agin-Liebes et al., 2020).

Out-of-body, near-death, and other non-ordinary experiences have likewise been shown to significantly reduce fear of death through altered states of consciousness. Though undoubtedly profound and transformative, such experiences are rare and tend to occur accidentally, usually under extreme circumstances. The Johns Hopkins research team became interested in whether these naturally occurring experiences could be mimicked with psychedelic drugs such as psilocybin, lysergic acid diethylamide (LSD), or N,N-dimethyltryptamine (DMT). A recent retrospective survey study of more than 3,000 participants compared psychedelic near-death experiences with near-death experiences that weren't drug-related and found "remarkable" similarities in attitudes toward death and dying between the two groups. Nearly 90 percent of survey participants in both groups reported having less fear of death and dying after their experience, whether naturally occurring or via psychedelic drugs. Seventy-five percent of the psychedelic group and 85 percent of the non-drug group rated their experiences as among the top five most personally meaningful and spiritually significant events of their lives. Participants in both groups reported enduring changes in personal well-being and life purpose and meaning (Sweeney et al., 2022).

Though clinical and survey results certainly contribute to our understanding of the impact of psychedelics on fear of death, my interest in the subjective experiences of those undergoing therapeutic trips led me to investigate first-person accounts. Common recurring themes include alterations in perceptions of time and space, visceral experience of the present, childlike wonderment and awe, ego dissolution, oneness with everything, interconnectedness with all beings, unparalleled clarity, transcendence, reverence, access to deeper resources, access to the unconscious mind, big picture perspective, expansiveness, boundlessness, authoritative truth, simulated death and re-birth, fearlessness, pure love, and a deeper sense of joy and gratitude in life. However described, it's clear that psilocybin-assisted psychotherapy consistently facilitates improvements in psychiatric and existential distress, quality of life, and spiritual well-being—not just during psychedelic sessions but for months afterward.

Significantly, participants near life's end who had been palpably terrified of death replaced their fear with profound acceptance. They acquired an unprecedented ability to live in the present, an increased appreciation for the time they had left, and motivation to invest their days with meaning. The ratio of banality to wonder was flipped. The limitations of the body—and identification with it—were transcended. In letting go of ego and body, participants essentially "rehearsed death," as the Stoics would say. By dying before dying, many became convinced that consciousness survives the death of the physical body. As I've read these accounts, I'm reminded of ineffable conversion experiences, such as Montaigne's accident or Paul's encounter on the road to Damascus.

Without nerding out too much on the neuroscience of psychedelics, it appears that these substances have a direct impact on the neural circuits of the brain involving the neurotransmitter serotonin. This occurs primarily in the prefrontal cortex, the command center of executive functioning—the overthinking part of the brain that can get us into trouble. Psychedelic-induced states of "unrestrained consciousness" are associated with a deactivation of regions of the brain that integrate our senses and our perception of self (Slater, 2012). Specifically, post-psilocybin brain scans have shown decreased activation in the *default-mode network (DMN)*—the brain's ego center—consistent with participants' reports of a diminished sense of self and of being connected to everything. "It appears that, with the ego temporarily out of commission, the boundaries between self and world, subject and object, all dissolve. These are hallmarks of the mystical experience" (Pollan, 2015).

Further evidence suggests that psychedelics promote neuroplasticity, essentially allowing us to reboot the brain. Deep grooves that lock us into maladaptive psycho-neurological patterns of thought and behavior are dissolved—or at least temporarily suspended—providing an opportunity for novel neuronal connections. De-automatization or disruption of these stereotypic patterns can "relax the grip of an overbearing ego and the rigid, habitual thinking it enforces" (Pollan, 2015). By whatever mechanisms of action, it's clear that psychedelics such as psilocybin seem to untether the senses and shake something loose in consciousness, opening a door to a different way of experiencing life. According to Michael Pollan (2015), psychedelic explorer-advocate and author of the *New York Times* bestseller *How to Change Your Mind: What the New Science of Psychedelics Teaches Us About Consciousness, Dying, Addiction, Depression, and Transcendence*:

> Existential distress at the end of life bears many of the psychological hallmarks of a hyperactive default-mode network, including excessive self-reflection and an inability to jump the deepening grooves of negative thought. The ego, faced with the prospect of its own dissolution, becomes hypervigilant, withdrawing its investment in the world and other people. It is striking that a single psychedelic experience—an intervention that Carhart-Harris calls "shaking the snow globe"—should have the power to alter these patterns in a lasting way.

If the notion of disrupting negative habitual thought patterns sounds familiar, you may be hearing reverberations of CBT and ACT. As you've discovered with each and every approach to death anxiety so far, viewing life—and death—from a new perspective is fundamental to making peace with mortality. Whether through philosophical thought experiments, cognitive restructuring, cognitive defusion, or drugs, we recalibrate our relationship with death.

Despite voluminous literature regarding the neuropsychiatric utility of psilocybin and other psychedelics, they remain Schedule 1 substances with "no currently accepted medical use in treatment in the United States," according to the federal government. Aside from clinical trials, psychedelic treatments are available only under state and federal "Right-To-Try" laws which afford gravely ill patients access to experimental drugs without having to wait for FDA approval. However, the qualification criteria are quite stringent, usually requiring a terminal diagnosis. But why limit this "existential medicine" to end-of-life applications? Hopefully, psychedelics will one day be available to help anyone struggling with ordinary angst about death and the meaning of life, not just those with a life-limiting illness.

In the meantime... Don't try this at home! In contrast with recreational or even self-medicating use of psychedelics, psychedelic-assisted therapy occurs in a highly controlled and structured therapeutic setting, facilitated by experts. In the typical clinical protocol, you'd undergo pre-treatment assessment, screening, and preparation. Your journey of several hours would take place in a cozy, den-like room. You'd lie on a couch with eyeshades and headphones with a carefully curated playlist, inviting attention to your internal experience. You'd have two guides (trained therapists) with you at all times, and you'd return the next day for a period of "integration" to help you process and interpret your experience. Pollan (2015) asserts that the only commonality between recreational and therapeutic use of psychedelics is the molecules being ingested.

Though you might not plan (or happen) to have a near-death, out-of-body, or psychedelic-induced experience in your quest to make peace with mortality, I hope to reassure you, once again, that changing your fearful perspective on death—with or without the aid of substances—is possible. Let's explore another, more accessible (and legal) consciousness-altering approach. One that you *can* try at home—or waiting in line at the grocery store.

Mindfulness Meditation

> Whenever you step out of the noise of thinking, that is meditation, and a different state of consciousness arises.—Eckhart Tolle

At a recent dinner party, the conversation turned to meditation. The host looked at me and asked, "Do you meditate?" This query felt a bit personal, as if he had asked if I sing in the shower, or put both socks on before shoes (yes to both), but it was clear that meditation status had become a thing: All the cool kids are doing it. A similar party in the '60s might have discussed tripping in the same way. In my self-referential take on the zeitgeist, meditation is the new LSD, the new path to enlightenment. Though it's been around for thousands of years, meditation is experiencing a renaissance, moving from the hippy-dippy "alt" fringes to more mainstream parts of the lifestyle and wellness movement. Despite all the hype, it's no lightweight fad. It's free, it's safe, it's legal. And, clearing the bar for inclusion in this book, it happens to be a powerful, consciousness-altering means of addressing death anxiety.

Broadly defined, meditation is an ancient—now evidence-based—practice that involves focused attention on the present moment and non-judgmental awareness of thoughts, feelings, and bodily sensations. It's a complex mind-body process that involves changes in cognition, sensory perception, brain chemistry and circuitry, hormones, and autonomic nervous system activity. The past 15 to 20 years have yielded an explosion of scientific research demonstrating that a short daily dose of meditation can confer a host of compelling benefits for mental, emotional, and physical well-being. Mental health benefits include stress reduction, increased self-awareness, enhanced focus and concentration, improved emotional regulation, increased resiliency and coping abilities, and relief from depression, anxiety, and PTSD. Among many physical benefits are improved sleep, reduced blood pressure, boosted immune function, decreased inflammation, better management of chronic pain, and even enhanced sports performance (Carlson, 2012; Carlson & Garland, 2005; Kabat-Zinn, 2013). The science is impressive; if meditation were a pill, everyone would be taking it.

There are many forms of meditation from different cultures and traditions, some spiritually based and some secular. Common variants include Mindfulness Meditation, Transcendental Meditation, Loving-Kindness (*Metta*) Meditation, Guided Visualization, and Mantra Meditation. *Vipassana* (Insight) Meditation and Zen Meditation (*Zazen*) are practices that originate from the Buddhist tradition. These varied approaches share several features, including heightened awareness, a deep state of relaxation, and, in some cases, insight or spiritual growth. Meditative techniques can involve focusing on the breath, bodily sensations, a word or phrase (mantra), or a question or riddle (koan). *Mindfulness-Based Stress Reduction*, developed by Jon Kabat-Zinn, is a particularly effective, evidence-based form of meditation. Combining various mindfulness meditation techniques with body awareness exercises, its primary goal is to cultivate openness, receptivity, and attention to whatever is unfolding in the present moment—internally and in the external environment—without judgment, attachment, or suppression.

Meditation can produce an altered state of consciousness, signaled by a shift in perception of time and space and changes in brain activity, including electrical activity as measured by electroencephalography (EEG). A meditative state is typically associated with increased alpha and theta wave patterns (8–12 Hz and 4–8 Hz, respectively)—sometimes referred to as the *relaxation response* (Benson, 2000)—slower in frequency than the beta waves of normal waking consciousness and active thinking. Delta waves (0.5–4 Hz), the slowest brain waves, may be experienced during deep meditation or hypnosis, profound relaxation, or certain shamanic practices. Such states can allow access to the unconscious mind. As a result, meditators may experience detachment from their surroundings and an increased connection to their inner thoughts and emotions, creating a unique state of consciousness different from their normal waking states. Like a psychedelic trip without the baggage.

Though meditative states may appear placid on the surface, a lot is going on under the hood. Neuroscience has demonstrated the beneficial impact of meditation on at least a dozen neurotransmitters and neurohormones, including GABA, dopamine, serotonin, and cortisol, the stress hormone (Newberg & Iverson, 2003).

Like psychedelics, meditation alters the brain in ways that show up in brain scans of practitioners. For example, fMRI scans of experienced meditators show less activity in their default-mode networks relative to novice meditators, consistent with findings of psychedelic research (Brewer et al., 2011).

Tuning into the raw data of the senses naturally attenuates the brain's default-mode network, acting as a circuit-breaker on habitual rumination. This is particularly relevant to anxiety, including death anxiety, in that most mental health concerns are associated with diminished levels of psychological and cognitive flexibility. Essentially, the mind becomes stuck in certain patterns that are no longer useful (Tarrant, 2022). Altered states of consciousness induced by meditation, hypnosis, progressive muscle relaxation, autogenic training, breathwork, vibroacoustics, and neurofeedback—all means of slowing brain wave frequencies and impacting neurochemicals—are thought to operate similarly to psychedelic-induced states by calming the constant self-referential chatter in the brain and facilitating mental flexibility, insight, and acceptance (Carhart-Harris & Friston, 2019). The mind becomes "unstuck" and less rigid, affording greater "spaciousness"—a particularly resonant construct in mindfulness meditation.

Abundant empirical evidence suggests that mindfulness meditation reduces anxiety in general, and death anxiety in particular. It works on death anxiety by shifting focus from worries about the future, including death, to being more engaged with and grounded in the "here and now." By cultivating present-moment awareness, mindfulness meditation promotes a greater sense of acceptance and peace with the inevitability of death. Developing a non-reactive, non-judgmental posture toward thoughts and emotions about death enables one to observe them objectively without getting caught up in them. Meditation researchers have coined the term *decentering*, described as "a process through which one is able to step outside of one's immediate experience, thereby changing the very nature of that experience" (Safran & Segal, 1990). It's the difference between experiencing an experience and identifying with it—the difference between "I notice anxiety" and "I am anxious," for example. If this sounds familiar, decentering is akin to ACT's cognitive defusion.

Meditation helps facilitate this mental maneuver by creating space in which we can develop new ways of responding to life's challenges, including the prospect of death. Death-related thoughts and feelings are viewed as transient and, therefore, less threatening. By strengthening our ability to tolerate unpleasant internal experiences, we build resilience and become better equipped to face existential concerns with clarity and perspective.

A core feature of meditation, linking it to other altered states, is the sense of transcending one's primary identification with the physical body. This is commonly associated with feelings of connection to something larger than oneself and a sense of awe, similar to the *overview effect*—the vastness experienced by astronauts when viewing Earth from space. Whether induced by a psychedelic trip, a trip to outer space, or a meditation session, this perceptual shift enables us to reframe our reality and our place within it. The experience of self as separate from the body can change our core identification from a limited, finite vessel to a more expansive sense of self, thereby rendering the prospect of death of the physical body less terrifying.

It's important to note that mindfulness meditation isn't designed to "clear your mind" or banish unpleasant thoughts about death. As you've learned, resisting something or trying to make it go away only gives it more power and keeps you stuck in it. Rather, mindfulness meditation is a tool to practice being with unpleasant thoughts, feelings, and sensations without pushing them away or trying to think your way out of them. It's a refreshing alternative to getting caught up in all of the pesky thoughts, beliefs, and judgments that fuel death anxiety. You don't stop the chatter; you give it a compassionate nod of recognition and return to the breath or other point of focus. The goal is acceptance of what is, *as it is*. You're not trying to resist, avoid, suppress, or change anything. The affinity between mindfulness meditation and ACT is notable here.

The beauty of meditation is its accessibility and everydayness. It's potent, but not precious. In the absence of extraordinary or rarefied altered states such as those occasioned by out-of-body, near-death, or psychedelic experiences, one can tap into mindful awareness at any time and any place. You don't have to sit on a cushion—or a rock (the philosophers' perch)—or even be still. There's no set method or time requirement. The practice can be incorporated throughout your day in "mini mindfulness moments," such as stopping to take a slow, deep breath, tuning into the hum of your refrigerator, or feeling your feet on the ground as you walk.

Mindfulness pioneer Jon Kabat-Zinn (2017) explains that meditation isn't a technique, but a way of being. He describes mindfulness, the psychological state brought on by meditation, as "paying attention, on purpose, in the present moment, non-judgmentally." It doesn't matter what you pay attention to—it could be anything—it's the attending that matters. When your mind wanders, as it inevitably will, the idea is to gently bring your attention back to whatever you've chosen as your attentional "anchor." Getting distracted, noticing, and starting again—and again—is a crucial part of the practice. Dan Harris, meditation evangelist and author of *10% Happier*, calls it "bicep curls for the brain."

If you don't already have a meditation practice and are interested in giving it a try, there are abundant apps, audio recordings, and videos that offer guided meditations with step-by-step instructions. They needn't be specific to death anxiety to be beneficial for this concern. Mindfulness meditation is a skill that requires disciplined practice. Consistency and regularity are key to experiencing the full benefits. Start with short sessions—even a few minutes each day—and gradually increase the duration as you become more comfortable. Think of it as exercising your acceptance and resiliency muscles. With sustained practice, they'll power on automatically.

Along with other consciousness-altering, brain-altering approaches, mindfulness meditation is a powerful tool to befriend all aspects of your life and experience, including mortality. In an interview with UMNCSH (2015), Kabat-Zinn describes mindfulness as a "love affair with life," echoing Nietzsche's amor fati, and giving legs to his exhortation to "consummate your life." Whether through medi*ca*tion or medi*ta*tion, altered states of consciousness are another means of changing your relationship with death. Neurologically and psychologically, you can learn (i.e., rewire your brain) to embrace your impermanence with greater peace and equanimity and awaken to your aliveness.

Part V
Functional Approaches

Functional approaches to death anxiety serve a practical or utilitarian role, distinct from the previous structural approaches that provide formalized and established frameworks, perspectives, practices, and interventions, informed by their respective disciplines. Let's round out this sprawling survey of philosophical, spiritual, and psychological approaches by exploring death education and literacy, practical considerations for end-of-life preparation and planning, and comforting alternative perspectives on death—courtesy of the theater, the natural world, the animal kingdom, cosmology, and comedy.

Chapter 13

Death Education and Literacy

Knowledge is the antidote to fear.—Ralph Waldo Emerson

Imagine that you're pregnant with your first child. Congratulations! The only problem is that you don't know the first thing about birthing a baby and you're terrified. You have so many worries about the labor and delivery process: Will it be painful? What are my birthing options? What could go wrong? Being a resourceful person, you'd likely manage your anxiety by educating yourself. You'd read books and articles on the subject, consult Google, watch YouTube videos on childbirth, and interrogate everyone you know who's been through it. You might even hire a birth doula to help you navigate the process and, ultimately, you'd make a detailed birth plan.

Now, imagine that you're going to die—a less hypothetical proposition. Being a resourceful person, you'd likely educate yourself and make a detailed end-of-life plan, right? Because we fear what we don't know, becoming more fluent in death is a powerful remedy for death anxiety. Knowledge neutralizes fear; familiarity breeds comfort. Death education illuminates the dark places where fears, born of imagination, reside. The more you understand about dying and what to expect when your time comes to die, the more at ease you'll become with it. Maybe not thrilled—as with an impending birth—but certainly less terrified. Though I can't offer you "everything you've always wanted to know about death and dying" in this short psycho-educational chapter—perhaps *Death for Dummies* will be my next book—I can coach you on resources for becoming more death literate and conversant, and launch you on your autodidactic journey. But first, some reassuring intel to dispel fear-perpetuating rumors.

Demystifying Death

> Just as when we come into the world, when we die we are afraid of the unknown. But the fear is something from within us that has nothing to do with reality. Dying is like being born: just a change.—Isabel Allende, *The House of the Spirits*

There are, essentially, only two ways to die: fast and slow. Examples of the former include suicide, homicide, accidents, or sudden medical events, such as a heart attack or stroke. I'll focus here on the process of a gradual, expected death, such as that from old age or disease. You're aware that you're dying. You have time to be scared—or prepared.

Undoubtedly, no matter the particular bases of your death anxiety, you fretfully ponder the question of what it's like to die. Though the dead are keeping this secret from us, we have many clues about the dying experience from people who are dying, people who have nearly died and come back, and medical professionals—particularly palliative care and hospice workers—who have witnessed thousands of deaths. From diverse vantage points, these "participant observers" all convey precisely the same resounding message: Dying isn't nearly as scary as you imagine. A natural, expected death is a chapter of life, not a moment in time. Hence, it needn't be a mystery or a surprise.

Death isn't the opposite of life; it's the opposite of birth. One an entrance and the other an exit, these gateways are strikingly similar biological imperatives. No one teaches us how to die, and no one teaches us how to be born, either. Both are natural, innate physiologic processes with an "automatic" factory setting. Our bodies are pre-programmed to die, and when the time comes, they'll know exactly what to do and how to do it. Mercifully, our bodies are designed to take care of us throughout the dying process.

Barbara Karnes, American hospice pioneer, end-of-life educator, and renowned authority on the dying process, is at the forefront of normalizing and de-awfuling death. Having witnessed hundreds of deaths, she observed that each death follows a nearly identical sequence and script, the inspiration for her "dying manual" *Gone from My Sight: The Dying Experience*—the "Little Blue Book" that transformed the hospice industry. Karnes (2014) describes the "labor of dying" as a process akin to birth. But unlike the labor to enter this world, the labor to leave it is harder on the observers than on the one doing the work. She identifies three factors that can affect the labor of dying and make it more difficult to exit our bodies: physical pain, fear, and unfinished business. Hospice professionals are experts at managing the first, and you're addressing the other two by reading this book and preparing yourself for a peaceful death, free of fear and loose ends. As strange as it may sound, Karnes tells us that the key to dying is to relax. In a relaxed state, we can simply ease out of our bodies.

When it comes to wrapping our heads around what it's like to die, metaphors abound. Karnes likens the labor of dying to a little chick trying to free itself from its shell. Elisabeth Kübler-Ross (2014), author of the groundbreaking book *On Death and Dying*, compares dying to shedding the physical body, like a butterfly shedding its cocoon, or a hermit crab discarding its old shell. Dying has also been likened to removing a tight shoe or taking off an old coat. Ernest Hemingway, knocked out by an exploding shell in Italy in World War I, describes slipping out of his body like a handkerchief being pulled out of a shirt pocket. (He came back into it after a few minutes, to drop this metaphor.) Leo Tolstoy characterizes death as the destruction of the "scaffolding" of the body after the building is up and finished. The Dalai Lama likens death to a change of clothes. To John Lennon, death is as simple as getting out of one car and into another.

Sandra Kerr (2023), founder of the Centre for Sacred Deathcare, compares the last minutes of dying to the experience of falling asleep in class. No matter how interesting the subject or how hard you struggle to stay awake, you just can't force your eyelids open or resist surrender to the magnetic pull of drowsiness. Another comforting description, attributed to an unnamed Twitter account years ago and oft-repeated is, "I hope death is like being carried to your bedroom when you were a child and fell asleep on the couch during a family party. I hope you can hear the laughter from the next room." Notably, none of these illustrative attempts to capture the essence of dying are painful, dramatic, or frightening. In truth, death is Nature's final mercy—the most kind, gentle, and generous of her forces.

Whether from an aging body, illness, or the progression of a disease, an ordinary, expected death unfolds in a recognizable, predictable chain of events over months, weeks, days, and hours. All the bodily systems that normally and automatically hum along in perfect balance begin to unwind and dysregulate. The body is gradually shutting down; it knows that it's dying. Over time, this winding down process is signaled by changes in breathing patterns, skin color, and temperature. Awareness of and interest in surroundings gradually fade as the dying person detaches and withdraws from the outer world. Activity and communication decrease. As the dying body no longer requires nutrition or hydration to maintain itself, hunger and thirst diminish and eventually disappear. The digestive system is shutting down and metabolism is slowing.

Typically, in the last few weeks of life, the dying person will grow increasingly drowsy, weary, and weak. As energy diminishes, naps will become more frequent and last longer, interspersed with ever-briefer periods of wakefulness. As death approaches, sleeping will give way to periods of unconsciousness. This distinction can be quite subtle, marked only by unresponsiveness or inability to arouse the dying person for medications or visitors. Slipping in and out of consciousness isn't unpleasant or scary for them, as unconscious people don't know they're unconscious.

This pattern of waking and sleeping, in and out of consciousness, continues until, eventually, the dying person is unconscious all of the time. Next, changes in breathing occur. In unconsciousness, the brain drives automatic, reflexive breathing patterns which can alternate from deep to shallow, regular to irregular, fast to slow, and sometimes panting or gasping. Deeply relaxed, the dying person stops clearing the saliva that builds up in their throat (*terminal secretions*) and produces a gurgling noise as their breath passes over it. Regrettably called the *death rattle*, this phenomenon is not unpleasant or uncomfortable for them, but it can be alarming for loved ones who don't know to expect it. At the very end of life, breathing becomes increasingly shallow and irregular, often with long pauses (*apnea*)—known as *agonal* or *Cheyne-Stokes breathing*—until one final out-breath isn't followed by an in-breath. This cessation of breathing is often so subtle and gentle that loved ones don't even notice it. There's nothing special about that last breath, no grand Hollywood finale. To borrow the poetic rhetoric of T.S. Eliot, we go out "not with a bang but a whimper." People commonly express the desire to die in their sleep. This wish is invariably granted.

Many fear a painful death but, in reality, dying doesn't hurt. Pain, when it does occur, is typically associated with underlying disease processes and/or side effects of treatments, not the dying process itself. And there's no reason to believe that this pain will be any worse or different than that of illnesses already experienced. Though natural death is commonly devoid of suffering, end-of-life professionals are adept at managing any distressing symptoms that arise (e.g., pain, shortness of breath, agitation) when necessary. Mercifully, as the body shuts down, a number of natural, built-in physiological mechanisms kick in to conserve energy, protect from discomfort, and ease the transition out of the body. For example, sodium levels decrease and calcium levels increase, causing increased sleep. Reduced blood circulation and hypoxia (low oxygen levels) likewise minimize conscious awareness. The dying body naturally releases endorphins and other endogenous opioids which serve to dull pain and minimize discomfort. In particular, the neuroprotective activity of the brain's serotonergic system eases dying through the mood-enhancing function of the neurotransmitter serotonin (Wutzler et al., 2011).

At the end of life, the "actively dying" person gradually loses senses and sensations, one by one. Symptoms that observers might interpret as signs of pain or discomfort, such as agonal breathing or the death rattle, are not distressing to the dying person at all. Decades of hospice and palliative care data assure us that the dying are much more comfortable and peaceful than we might imagine. Often the disturbing things we see in dying individuals are merely reflexive, unconscious operations of the shutting down body. Due to prevailing cultural mythology and cinematic misrepresentation, what actually happens at the end of life is often not what we expect.

When I've explained the dying process to terminally ill patients and their families, their typical reaction is, "That's all there is to it?" Yes. As Barbara Karnes is fond of saying, "Death is sad, but it doesn't have to be bad."

The notion that our dreadful perceptions of death may not reflect reality has empirical, as well as clinical, basis. Two studies compared the affective experience of people facing imminent death with that of people imagining imminent death, using language as a window into their emotional lives (Goranson et al., 2017). In the first study, researchers analyzed the writings of regular bloggers with either terminal cancer or ALS, all of whom died during the study. They compared them to blog posts written by a group of participants who were told to imagine they had been diagnosed with terminal cancer with only a few months to live. The second study compared the last words and poetry of death row inmates with a group of participants asked to imagine that they were about to face execution. In both studies, blog posts of those facing imminent death were found to have considerably more positive words and fewer negative ones than those imagining they were dying. What's more, their use of positive language increased as they got closer to death. The participants who imagined what it would be like to die were more fearful and negative than those who, due to terminal illness or execution, were actually approaching death. Overall, those facing imminent death focused more on what makes life meaningful. The researchers concluded: "Evidence that dying is more pleasant than expected may suggest a reassessment of one of humanity's great fears." Reassessment? Yes, please.

Many of our worst fears about death are unrealistic and unfounded, based on our mythology-fueled imagination. Though we may have adopted our cultural narrative of death as terrible and tragic, there's abundant evidence—clinically, empirically, anecdotally—that this is a false narrative. Unfortunately, deeply-rooted, long-standing ideas that death is dreadful die hard. But if we're wrong, which I suggest that we are, we die more than once. In the prescient—and ironic—words of Abraham Lincoln: "If I am killed, I can die but once; but to live in constant dread of it, is to die over and over again."

It's important to bear in mind that when we imagine our death, we imagine it happening in our current state of ability—physically and cognitively—and not from the perspective of being old, ill, infirm, or in decline. This is crucial because the vantage point from which we view death colors our judgment of it. Our perspective determines whether death is experienced as a tremendous loss and deprivation or a blessed relief and release from suffering, or even tedium. Those who are dying of old age may have lost many of their loved ones, their mobility, their senses, and their ability to enjoy life. Those dying of disease are often experiencing pain and disability, or side effects of treatments designed to prolong their lives. For many, death brings an end to suffering. From a Buddhist perspective, life itself is suffering (because we wish things to be different than they are). Christians refer to the sorrows and tribulations of life on Earth as a "vale of tears." And yet, when we think of loss of life, we think only of losing the pleasures and delights of life. If we're honest, much of life is routine and mundane, is it not? Alain de Botton, contemporary philosopher and king of the aphorism, astutely observes, "How we feel about 'the nature of existence' is largely determined by what we have to do in the next few hours."

Perhaps, upon reflection, there are many aspects of life that you won't mind giving up: alarm clocks, taxes, traffic, deadlines, dental visits, mosquitoes, etc. When Shakespeare's Hamlet spoke of "shuffling off this mortal coil," he was referring to shedding the tangle (i.e., messiness) of daily life. For a fun perceptual shift, try generating your own list of the *benefits* of death—the toils, troubles, and turmoil you might not mind "shuffling off." This exercise in no way diminishes your investment in the grand adventure of life; rather, it enlarges your perspective on it. As German philosopher and historian Hannah Arendt observes, "Death not merely ends life, it also bestows upon it a silent completeness, snatched from the hazardous flux to which all things human are subject."

Our perspective on death—whether dreaded or welcome—is informed by our perspective on life. Whatever your vantage point, I invite you to consider alternatives to the "death is horrible and scary" narrative. Because—while I'm on a de Botton aphorism roll—"unhappiness can stem from having only one perspective to play with."

As you've likely noticed, this entire morality-facing journey is about trying on different frames of reference for fit—and acuity.

Strange, Wonderful Things

> Science has explained nothing; the more we know, the more fantastic the world becomes and the profounder the surrounding darkness.—Aldous Huxley

Having examined physical aspects of the natural dying process, several fascinating, inexplicable phenomena that often occur at the end of life provide an additional window into what it's like to die—and how very not-terrible it is. The most common of these—though no less extraordinary—include terminal lucidity, deathbed visioning, and near-death experiences.

Terminal Lucidity

Ask any hospice nurse and they'll tell you tales of patients at death's door, many of whom have been immobile and unresponsive, who suddenly become awake, alert, and nimble in the last hours of life. It's not uncommon for dying people with severe cognitive impairment—perhaps from dementia or a stroke—to suddenly regain memory and other mental abilities and to communicate clearly and cogently. In "the rally," as it's commonly called, the dying person will often pop out of bed and move about their home or request a specific meal after not having moved or eaten for days or weeks. They typically die shortly thereafter. Though terminal lucidity has been recognized and studied since the 19th century, we still don't have an explanation for it. Perhaps it's one of Mother Nature's final blessings at the end of life.

Deathbed Visioning

In a phenomenon so common that hospice professionals often tell loved ones to expect it—or, at least, to not be alarmed if it happens—people who are dying report visitation by deceased loved ones or pets in the final hours of life. The dying are often observed staring at, pointing to, talking to, and reaching for beings that others in the room can't see. They begin to use "journeying" language, suggesting that they sense they're getting ready to go somewhere. They invariably describe these experiences as deeply comforting and reassuring, never frightening, as familiar faces assemble to greet and escort them on their journey. In my personal witness, I can only describe these "reunions" as blissful, with dying faces lit up and beaming.

Near-Death Experiences

Perhaps the closest one can come to experiencing death without actually dying is through a *near-death experience* (*NDE*). This profound psychological event typically occurs when an individual is close to death or experiences a life-threatening medical emergency from which they're revived. These widespread and widely-reported phenomena share a set of uncannily common elements, including out-of-body experiences, moving through a dark void into bright light, encounters with deceased loved ones or otherworldly beings, life review, intense emotions, and returning to the body after encountering some sort of barrier. Though clinically "dead," near-death experiencers universally report a heightening of their senses and intense, overwhelming feelings of well-being, serenity, warmth, light, floating, joy, love, calmness, compassion, wholeness, and interconnectedness with all beings.

People who have died and come back describe death as a place of profound peace. They often report reluctance to return to their bodies and disappointment when they regain consciousness. These vivid, surreal experiences appear to mimic altered states of consciousness associated with psychedelics. They also comport with end-of-life experiences reported by the dying on the way out of their bodies. According to Peter Fenwick (2017), eminent neuropsychiatrist and NDE researcher, "There are so many common features between near-death experiences and end-of-life experiences that one can only conclude that the former are giving us a glimpse of another, different reality, one which we can hope to experience when we do actually die."

Invariably, these close encounters with death have a profound, lasting impact on those who have experienced them. In his book

Extraordinary Awakenings, Steve Taylor (2021) documents such stories of transformation, including new perspectives on life and death, and significant changes in attitudes, beliefs, values, and even identities. Following NDEs, people often become more spiritual, compassionate, altruistic, appreciative, sensitive to beauty and nature, and generally happier and more positive. Nearly dying is commonly associated with an increased sense of purpose and a renewed zest for life, along with a marked decrease in death anxiety. It makes sense that someone who has "been there, done that" would no longer experience fear of the unknown, especially if their glimpse beyond the veil was so compelling that they were reluctant to come back to life. If fear of the unknown figures prominently in your death anxiety, you might find it useful to read accounts of those who've "gone" before us.

First investigated by Raymond A. Moody, Jr., and chronicled in his 1975 bestseller *Life After Life*, researchers have widely documented and studied NDEs. There are numerous published accounts of people who have nearly died and come back to life to report on the experience. The most confounding element of these experiences is that they occur in the absence of physiological or neurological activity, leading to questions about the persistence of some form of consciousness even after the heart has stopped beating. A recent groundbreaking study, published in the *Proceedings of the National Academy of Science*, found evidence of increased gamma activation—associated with consciousness—in the brains of comatose patients removed from life support, suggesting the existence of covert consciousness in dying humans (Ralls, 2023).

These "phenomenal" near-death experiences cast doubt on the reductionist, materialistic worldview that equates human consciousness with brain activity. They raise questions of whether consciousness may be independent of the brain, and thus able to survive brain death. Though more research is needed to solve the mysteries of how someone with severe structural brain damage can regain consciousness (terminal lucidity), or how consciousness appears to persist in the absence of brain activity (NDEs), these phenomena may not be fully explicable in conventional neurophysiological terms. Nonetheless, compelling evidence that disembodied consciousness persists after death has implications for our understanding of death and its aftermath. Whether these inexplicable near-death and end-of-life experiences are mystical and metaphysical, or merely glitchy operations of the dying brain, we know that they're universally and unquestionably positive and transformative. I encourage you to let this well-documented finding inform your fearful perceptions of death.

Let's Talk About It

> When we avoid difficult conversations, we trade short-term discomfort for long-term dysfunction.—Peter Bromberg, American organizational consultant

How do you feel when someone brings up the topic of death? Do you cringe and change the subject to something more palatable? If so, you're not alone. A primary consequence of the death taboo in Western culture is a conspiracy of silence. We don't talk about death and, if we do, we sugarcoat the topic with euphemisms. Unfortunately, silence serves to perpetuate fear, and, in turn, fear perpetuates silence. I'm on a mission to break the silence. Like learning about death, talking about death can help alleviate fear. Fortunately, the death positive movement has given rise to a variety of tools, resources, and platforms designed to normalize and facilitate conversations about death.

Death Cafes provide an organized forum for informal conversations about death in a safe and supportive environment. A typical event is a pop-up gathering of strangers casually chatting about death over tea and cake (traditionally) or coffee and doughnuts. Participants have the opportunity to freely and openly voice their thoughts, fears, and questions about death in an accessible, respectful, and confidential space. Discussions of death are non-facilitated (i.e., group-directed) and have no agenda or theme, distinct from grief support groups or group counseling sessions. The stated objective of Death Cafes is "to increase awareness of death with a view to helping people make the most of their (finite) lives." The hope is that by allowing death to have a safe place in our conversations, the stigma and anxiety related to the topic of death can be lessened. Death Cafes are conducted on a not-for-profit basis, with no intention of leading people to any conclusion, product, or course of action. Having originated in Europe in 2004 and crossed the pond to the U.S. in 2012, Death Cafes are currently available in 89 countries across the globe. Both a movement and a public service, the Death Cafe model is a "social franchise," meaning anyone can organize and host an event, guided by the principles and methodology of the organization. You can locate (or organize) a meeting in your area through the official website (deathcafe.com).

For a more intimate experience, consider hosting a dinner party with death on the menu. *Death Over Dinner*, a concept similar to Death Cafes, is a platform for stimulating conversations about death—specifically, end-of-life wishes—over a meal. The movement originated in the U.S. in 2013 and gained awareness and momentum through a popular TED Talk. Per the official website, "We have gathered dozens of medical and wellness leaders to cast an unflinching eye at end of life, and we have created an uplifting interactive adventure that transforms this seemingly difficult conversation into one of deep engagement, insight, and empowerment." The website (deathoverdinner.org) offers unique tools and instructions on how to have end-of-life conversations with friends and family, and how to do a test run of the dinner. The site also provides selections for guests to read, listen to, and watch in preparation for an unforgettable dining experience.

According to the Conversation Project National Survey (2018), 92 percent of Americans say it's important to discuss their wishes for end-of-life care, but only 32 percent have had such a conversation. How we want to die is the most important and costly conversation America isn't having. *The Conversation Project* (theconversationproject.org) is a public engagement initiative of the Institute for Healthcare Improvement, which offers free tools, guidance, and resources designed to facilitate such conversations. A questionnaire on the website solicits feedback about what's important at the end of life and helps individuals determine where, when, and how to discuss these wishes with family members.

If death cafes with strangers or death dinners with intimates aren't your cup of tea, bring on the party games! Spurred by the death positive movement, several enterprising companies have devised games and fun conversation starters, including specialized playing cards, to facilitate non-threatening and low-key conversations about death. One of the most popular is *The Death Deck* (thedeathdeck.com), a set of 112 cards with a playful mix of multiple-choice and open-ended questions designed to spark lively discussion around "the topic we're all obsessed with but often afraid to discuss." By predicting other participants' responses, you'll be horrified to discover just how little you actually know about your friends and family. Your sister wants to be buried with her raggedy old stuffed iguana from childhood? Who knew?! The *Go Wish Game*, sponsored by Coda Alliance (codaalliance.org), is a similar card deck, focused on end-of-life wishes. *Hello* (commonpractice.com), another conversation game in both a "home edition" and an "event kit," is an "easy, non-threatening way to start a conversation with your family and friends about what matters most to you."

Life Support (life-support.uk), a clever interactive website designed by the London-based creative studio The Liminal Space and funded by the U.K. government, is a digital tool that proclaims, "Talking about dying won't make it happen." Born of COVID-19 and the dire need for end-of-life conversations, the site offers a curated curriculum to answer all your burning questions about death and dying. As you scroll through the interface, you're offered a selection of topics to explore. You swipe through for answers from palliative care and other experts, either in stylized blocks of text or recorded audio for you to play back. The tool empowers people to have difficult conversations by offering practical tips on how to discuss death, as well as sharing experts' personal experiences around varied end-of-life topics. Users can also download and share tips to aid in initiating conversations with loved ones.

Beyond these established conversational platforms and tools, death is increasingly creeping into our everyday conversations. Though this is an encouraging development, death is not yet a household word. So, here are some guidelines for initiating and engaging in dialogue about death and dying with anyone and everyone in your life:

- Look and listen for natural opportunities to talk about death. Organic openings are best, such as those presented by current events involving death, or mutual acquaintances who have experienced loss. If you pay attention, points of entry abound.
- Avoid initiating a death conversation with "We need to talk." That's never a good idea.
- Start by introducing the topic impersonally or abstractly—such as the death of a celebrity or a death-related topic such as green burial—before moving to more direct or personal conversations.
- Share books, articles, news stories, or movies about death that you've found interesting or thought-provoking.
- Avoid euphemisms in talking about death. Try to catch yourself in old habits and self-correct. But don't catch and call out others. You're not the euphemism police.
- Share stories about your personal experiences with death and dying. Self-disclosure begets self-disclosure.
- Read the room. Pay attention to and gauge the reactions of your audience as you move deeper into conversations about death. Notice body language, tone of voice, and eye contact. A little discomfort is okay, but don't scare the hell out of anyone.
- Model frankness, openness, and comfort with discussing death (fake it 'till you make it, if necessary) to convey the message that death is a natural part of life to be discussed accordingly. Maintain eye contact. Be present. Stay calm and grounded. Breathe.
- Don't be afraid of silence—or feel compelled to talk incessantly—during conversations about death.
- Don't be afraid to cry—or laugh. Death is a profound, emotionally charged topic.
- Initiate conversations about end-of-life planning with someone by asking about their experiences with the deaths of loved ones and which elements they'd wish to be different for themselves.
- Don't avoid friends or co-workers who have experienced

loss just because you don't know what to say. Don't miss this opportunity to engage authentically with someone for whom the experience of death is real and present.
- Be curious. Ask questions about others' experiences with death. People have stories and relish opportunities to tell them. Be an attentive listener.
- Be honest and authentic. If you're feeling uncomfortable, say so. If you're scared, say so. Share your personal journey to normalize death and overcome anxiety in your own life.
- Above all, "keep it real."

Though talking about death—a morbid topic in our death-averse society—may feel awkward or anxiety-provoking at first, you'll become more comfortable with practice. Consider these conversations "exposure tasks," as introduced in Chapter 9. By having conversations about death and dying, you can build up your tolerance for discomfort and, with time, your death anxiety will diminish. And, as a bonus, your brave forays into these difficult conversations will help destigmatize the subject of death for others. As a death-awareness evangelist myself, I can attest to this. I haven't alienated *too* many people. So break the silence, bust the taboo, and bring others along with you as you seek to increase your own comfort with death and dying.

Diving Deeper

Having completed this crash chapter on death education and literacy, you now know just enough to know what you don't know and what more you'd like to learn. Though I hope that this rudimentary introduction to the biological and psychosocial basics of death and dying has already begun to soften your fear, learning and talking about end-of-life issues is an ongoing process. To facilitate your further exploration, I've curated a list of resources not cited elsewhere in this book. Though certainly not exhaustive, these books, podcasts, documentaries, and websites are recommended next steps on your quest to become more fluent in death.

Books

Advice for Future Corpses (and Those Who Love Them): A Practical Perspective on Death by Sallie Tisdale

The Art of Dying by Peter Fenwick

The Art of Dying Well: A Practical Guide to a Good End of Life by Katy Butler

A Beginner's Guide to the End: Practical Advice for Living Life and Facing Death by B.J. Miller and Shoshana Berger

Being Mortal: Medicine and What Matters in the End by Atul Gawande

Can't We Talk About Something More Pleasant?: A Memoir by Roz Chast

Death's Summer Coat: What the History of Death and Dying Teaches Us About Life and Living by Brandy Schillace

The Dying Process: Your Essential Guide to Understanding Signs, Symptoms & Changes at the End of Life by Katie Duncan

Dying Well: Peace and Possibilities at the End of Life by Ira Byock

The Five Invitations: Discovering What Death Can Teach Us About Living Fully by Frank Ostaseski

From Here to Eternity: Traveling the World to Find the Good Death by Caitlin Doughty

The Good Death: An Exploration of Dying in America by Ann Neumann

How We Die: Reflections on Life's Final Chapter by Sherwin B. Nuland

Mortality by Christopher Hitchens

Nothing to Fear: Demystifying Death to Live More Fully by Julie McFadden

Smoke Gets in Your Eyes: And Other Lessons from the Crematory by Caitlin Doughty

The Tibetan Book of Living and Dying by Sogyal Rinpoche

Tuesdays with Morrie: An Old Man, a Young Man, and Life's Greatest Lesson by Mitch Albom

What Really Matters: 7 Lessons for Living from the Stories of the Dying by Karen Wyatt

When Breath Becomes Air by Paul Kalanithi

With the End in Mind: Dying, Death, and Wisdom in an Age of Denial by Kathryn Mannix

A Year to Live: How to Live This Year as if It Were Your Last by Stephen Levine

Podcasts

Best Life Best Death
Conversations on Death
Dead Talks
Death Happens—An Insider's Guide to Dying
Death in the Afternoon
End-of-Life University Podcast
Endwell
When You Die
You're Going to Die: The Podcast

Documentaries

Alternate Endings: Six New Ways to Die in America (2019)
End Game (2018)
End of Life (2017)
Extremis (2016)
The Good Death (2018)
How to Die in Oregon (2011)
The Last Ecstatic Days (2023)
My Last Days (docu-series) (2012)
Passing On (2016)
Prognosis: Notes on Living (2021)
Surviving Death (docu-series) (2021)
The When You Die Trilogy: In the Realm of Death and Dreaming; Saying Goodbye: Preparing for Death; Architecture of Death: The Inner World of Dying (2021–2024)

Websites

bestlifebestdeath.com
bkbooks.com
endwellproject.org
goingwithgrace.com
hospicenursejulie.com
livingdying.org
orderofthegooddeath.com
sacreddeathcare.com
talkdeath.com
whenyoudie.org

Chapter 13. Death Education and Literacy

> If thou expect death as a friend, prepare to entertain it;
> If thou expect death as an enemy, prepare to overcome it;
> Death has no advantage, except when it comes as a stranger.—Francis Quarles

Don't let death be a stranger.

Chapter 14

Ready to Go

Practical Considerations

> When the time comes to die, make sure that all you have to do is die.—Jim Elliot, *The Journals of Jim Elliot*

During my years as a health psychologist, I served as a consultant to the oncology service at a large medical center. My patients were living with various forms of cancer, navigating various phases of their cancer journeys. While making rounds with my favorite breast cancer specialist, we came to the room of a newly diagnosed patient who had been admitted for radical mastectomy. The surgery had not gone well, and the surgeon enlisted me to accompany him on his mission to deliver the bad news. At the end of a difficult conversation, he said, "I suggest you get your affairs in order." Now, I'd heard this directive so many times before, it was almost cliché. But for some reason, it landed differently this day. I began pondering what "getting your affairs in order" really meant. What it meant for this 36-year-old patient with two young children. What it might mean for me. What are these affairs? What constitutes getting them in order? Why do we wait until we've received bad news and the accompanying directive to do so, even though we know that we could go at any time?

Unpreparedness is a common basis of death anxiety. Lack of practical planning and preparation for death is both cause and consequence of denial, avoidance, and fear. That is, we put off planning and preparing because we fear death, and we fear death because we're unprepared to die. Our affairs are not in order. I contend that we invest more time and effort planning and preparing for a trip than we spend planning and preparing for our death. We research our destination, book flights and accommodations, devise an itinerary, consider the weather, purchase clothing and gear, pack, make arrangements for the pets, purchase travel insurance, take time off work, etc. If traveling abroad, we update our passport, study a language, and obtain vaccinations. We think about it, talk about it, plan for it. No detail escapes our consideration. And much of this planning and preparation is, by necessity, done well in advance. We're quite accustomed to making elaborate, carefully orchestrated plans for things we anticipate happening in the future—except our death.

Is it not also the case that we spend more time worrying about and preparing for things that may never happen than death which is sure to happen? Anyone who struggles with anxiety, obsessive worry, or compulsive behaviors designed to ward off anticipated catastrophes can attest to this. But when it comes to death, we don't want to think about something so unpleasant and terrifying. We'd rather worry about something about which we have, at least, an illusion of control. And if we're thinking about death at all, we assume we have plenty of time. Unlike the upcoming trip (which evokes temporal urgency) or the imagined catastrophe (which evokes psychological urgency), we believe we can postpone preparation for our final journey. But can we? As I see it, the only circumstance under which end-of-life planning can reasonably be postponed is if you're privy to your expiration date. If you know how much time you have left, you can plan accordingly. But procrastination only works with a clear deadline. Otherwise (as in 100 percent of cases), my best advice is to be ready to go at any time. Just in case. After all, "It's always too early until it's too late."

Though the inevitability of death is beyond our control, our ability to prepare for it—in all ways—is well within our control. In addition to philosophical, spiritual, and psychological means of coming to terms with death and overcoming fear of it, there are many practical considerations that, once addressed and resolved, can engender a greater sense of peace about mortality. But the task of "end-of-life planning" can seem daunting and overwhelming. Hundreds of books and websites offer guidance and innumerable checklists of "things to do before you die." No wonder we put off planning and preparation.

In the interest of helping you move past whatever avoidance you've been experiencing, I've distilled and consolidated this vast information into a concise, actionable format, along with curated resources. As Desmond Tutu once wisely observed, "There is only one way to eat an elephant: a bite at a time." I've broken down this "elephant" into six digestible bites: medical, legal/financial, material, practical, relational, and after-death. Let's do this!

Medical

In the event of a medical emergency at any age or state of health, it's important to have a fast and efficient way to convey crucial medical information to emergency responders. There are numerous options—from forms, to wallet cards, to refrigerator magnets—designed to provide first responders with your identifying information, emergency contacts, medical conditions, medications, allergies, blood type, donor status, support needs, etc. One such resource is the *File of Life*, offered by a nationally recognized non-profit organization (thefileoflife.org). Alternatively, if you're a smartphone user, most smartphones have a built-in medical ID feature that enables emergency responders to access important life-saving information and emergency contacts, even when your phone is locked. The minutes it takes to set this up is a wise investment.

Beyond medical emergencies, there may come a time when you can no longer communicate your wishes about your medical treatment, due to an accident, injury, old age, disease, or failing health. *Advance care planning* is the broad term that consists of considering, discussing, deciding, and communicating your healthcare preferences if you're unable to speak for yourself. Such planning isn't just about your end-of-life wishes, but all of your choices regarding how you'd like to be treated—or not—throughout your entire lifespan. Advance care planning is a process that's informed by an individual's values, preferences, and medical issues. An *Advance Directive* is the record of that process.

Though an Advance Directive is a legal document, valid as soon as you sign it in front of the required witnesses, you don't need a lawyer to complete one. Laws governing Advance Directives vary from state to state, and each state has its own guidelines and documents. An Advance Directive only goes into effect if you're unable to communicate your wishes due to incapacity (e.g., coma, stroke, dementia, under anesthesia). But, as the name suggests, it must be prepared in advance. An Advance Directive doesn't expire and remains in effect until you change it. If you complete a new one, it invalidates the previous one. It's important to review your Advance Directive periodically to ensure that it still reflects your wishes—especially when any major life events (e.g., divorce, move) or significant changes in your health occur.

Though Advance Directive is the broad, umbrella term for any legal document(s) concerning your wishes about your future medical care, it generally includes two components: a Healthcare Power of Attorney and a Living Will. A *Healthcare Power of Attorney* (also known as a *Durable Power of Attorney for Healthcare* or *Durable Medical Power of Attorney*) gives a trusted individual the authority to make medical decisions on your behalf should you be unable to do so for yourself. These decisions could be about treatment options, surgery, medications, and end-of-life care. The person you designate as your *healthcare proxy* (also known as *representative*, *surrogate*, or *agent*) should be familiar with your values and wishes and willing to serve as your representative. Unlike a General or Financial Power of Attorney, no financial authority is granted with this document. A Healthcare Power of Attorney only takes effect if you become incapacitated, either temporarily or permanently. Unlike a Living Will (discussed below), a Healthcare Power of Attorney is not limited to a terminal illness or permanently unconscious state. Even if you're temporarily unable to make your own medical decisions, a healthcare proxy can speak for you.

While the Healthcare Power of Attorney authorizes a representative to make medical decisions on your behalf, a *Living Will* (not to be confused with a Last Will and Testament) specifies your predetermined wishes regarding end-of-life care should you become incapacitated or otherwise unable to express your preferences yourself. You can indicate which common medical treatments you'd want, which ones you'd prefer to avoid, and under which conditions each choice applies. Issues addressed in a Living Will generally include life-support measures such as tube feeding, dialysis, and mechanical ventilation; comfort care and pain management; antibiotics and other medications; and resuscitation and other life-saving medical interventions. You may choose to receive every possible life-sustaining measure, some, or none.

A Living Will is especially important if you don't want aggressive intervention, as this is the default in our Western medical system. The decisions that your designated healthcare proxy makes on your behalf must align with the wishes you've expressed in your Living Will. Without this document, family members and healthcare providers are left to guess your preferences regarding treatment. This does not always go well. Though both a Living Will and a Healthcare Power of Attorney are legal documents that comprise an Advance Directive, it's important to understand that a Living Will applies specifically to end-of-life medical treatment, while the Healthcare Power of Attorney encompasses all types of medical treatment at any stage of life.

It should be noted that having an Advance Directive does not guarantee that medical personnel will follow it, or even know of its existence. In contrast, two medical order forms, signed by a licensed physician, relay instructions among healthcare professionals about a patient's care: DNR and POLST/MOLST. Because these forms convey specific instructions regarding life-sustaining treatments, they're intended for people who are seriously ill or at the end of life. Both forms must be completed in collaboration with your physician and will be recorded in your permanent medical record.

A *DNR* (*Do Not Resuscitate*) form—also referred to as *allow-natural-death* or *no-code*—conveys that you don't want to receive life-saving treatment (resuscitation) in the event of cardiac or respiratory arrest. You and your physician should sign a DNR order if you'd prefer that medical personnel not perform CPR or restart your heart and instead allow for a natural death. Without this document, emergency medical service providers are obligated to try to resuscitate someone whose heart or breathing has stopped. So, the DNR is an "opt-out" document.

Designed to improve the quality of care for seriously ill people, a

POLST (Physician Orders for Life-Sustaining Treatment) or *MOLST (Medical Orders for Life-Sustaining Treatment)* outlines your wishes for end-of-life care—treatments you want or don't want—especially regarding an existing diagnosis or life-limiting illness. POLST and MOLST are different names for the same thing, depending on the state. A POLST/MOLST is a medical order form, similar to a prescription, signed by a licensed physician. A primary benefit of the POLST/MOLST form is that it's "portable" and moves with the patient through the healthcare system (e.g., hospital, nursing care, home health care). It must be honored by all healthcare providers in all settings. Though less comprehensive and nuanced than an Advance Directive, it carries more weight.

A *HIPAA Release* is another opt-out form to consider. The Health Insurance Portability and Accountability Act (HIPAA) requires that medical records be kept confidential. While this is an important provision, it can have serious unintended consequences. If you were to become incapacitated, your family wouldn't be able to obtain information regarding your medical condition and treatment. A HIPAA release allows medical providers to discuss your medical situation with whomever you've specified in the document. Permitting your doctors to talk with your family or other caregivers differs from naming a healthcare proxy. A healthcare proxy can only make medical decisions on your behalf if you're unable to do so yourself.

Finally, organ and tissue donation is an opt-in decision to consider. You can register as an organ donor at your local Department of Motor Vehicles when you renew your driver's license or online at organdonor.gov. You may also choose to donate your brain to advance scientific research (braindonorproject.org), or even your whole body (anatomygifts.org) if you're feeling particularly generous.

Here ends the medical part of preparing to die. If all of this feels overwhelming and you'd benefit from step-by-step guidance with advance care planning, *Five Wishes* (fivewishes.org) is an advance care planning resource created by the non-profit organization Aging with Dignity in conjunction with the American Bar Association and leading medical experts. Described as "the living will with a heart and soul," it's now available in paper and digital formats, including fully digital signing and witnessing options. Wishes 1 and 2 are both legal documents (Healthcare Power of Attorney and Living Will) and meet most states' legal requirements for an Advance Directive. Wishes 3, 4, and 5 are unique to *Five Wishes*, in that they address matters of comfort care, spirituality, forgiveness, and final wishes.

Legal/Financial

Unlike advance care planning which can be done on your own or with the assistance of online tools, legal and financial planning for the end of life generally require the assistance of a legal professional. *Estate planning* is the process of establishing a framework to manage your assets upon death, disability, or incapacity. Even people with modest assets can benefit from such planning. A little forethought about how you'd like things to go once you're incapacitated or gone can give you great peace of mind now, as well as spare your loved ones heartache and hassle later. With the disclaimer that I'm not an attorney dispensing legal advice, just a prepared mortal helping you become a prepared mortal, the following legal documents are typically involved in "getting your affairs in order."

The fundamental purpose of a *Last Will and Testament* (aka *Will*) is to specify how your estate—property, money, and other assets—will be distributed and managed when you die. A Will can also specify guardianship (legal responsibility) for the care of your minor children, adult dependents, and pets after your death. For those whose death anxiety centers around concern regarding what will happen to their dependents after they're gone, making and documenting provisions for their care can be immensely helpful in allaying this particular fear of death.

When you create a Will, you name an estate *executor*, a person you trust to handle the distribution of your estate and carry out the terms of your Will. A Will becomes effective only after you die, so it doesn't confer any power to the executor or benefits to the beneficiaries during your lifetime. If you don't choose an executor, the probate court will name a representative to carry out the instructions contained in your Will. A Last Will and Testament should not be confused with a Living Will, discussed previously, which documents medical care preferences. A Will can be changed at any time, assuming you're mentally competent.

Everyone over 18 should have a Last Will and Testament. Without a Will, your estate will be distributed according to the laws of your state. You should not assume that the state will make the same choices you would. There are many ways you can make a Will, from enlisting the services of an attorney to writing your own Will with the aid of online services or software programs. A do-it-yourself online Will can be a viable, affordable option for those with simple estates and wishes.

A *Durable Power of Attorney* (also known as a *Financial Power of Attorney*) allows you to empower someone else (called an *agent* or *proxy*) to act on your behalf to make legal and financial decisions when you're unable to. This highly customizable document enables you to designate an agent to help with a specific task—such as selling property—or to take over all your financial affairs should you become incapacitated. The agent's powers begin at a time or circumstance specified in the document and end at your death or when you revoke the document. It's critically important that you trust the person to whom you assign this power, as they have complete legal authority to act on your behalf.

Although they have similar names, the Durable/Financial Power of Attorney and the Healthcare Power of Attorney are separate documents and serve completely different functions. Naming an agent in one does not make them the agent in the other. Therefore, you may wish to appoint two different people to fill these roles. If you choose to have the same agent for both healthcare and financial matters, you must create both documents. Likewise, the estate executor appointed in your Last Will and Testament and the agent appointed in Your Durable/Financial Power of Attorney are two different roles. If you choose to appoint the same person to both roles, you must create both a Will and a Durable Power of Attorney.

A *Living Trust* names and instructs a person, called the *trustee*, to hold and distribute property and funds on your behalf when you can no longer manage your affairs due to incapacitation or death. Setting up a Living Trust involves transferring ownership of your assets to the Trust, a legal entity. You, the grantor, retain control over any property within the Trust throughout your lifetime. When you die, your pre-chosen successor trustee gains control of the Trust and will distribute your assets per your instructions. It's a good idea to leave assets in trust if your beneficiaries are minors, legally incompetent, or not fiscally responsible.

Like a Last Will and Testament, a Living Trust is a tool to manage and distribute your property after you die. But, unlike a Will, a Living Trust is a legal entity, meaning it can "own" property. A primary advantage of a Living Trust, as distinct from a Will, is that the assets in trust can bypass probate (the costly and time-consuming court-driven process of validating your Will and distributing your assets), thereby streamlining the process of transferring your assets to your beneficiaries and settling your estate.

Even though they feel like family, pets are considered property by the law. Hence, it's important to have a plan for them in the event of your death. Otherwise, they may end up being placed in a shelter. To avoid this, you can designate a caregiver for your pets in your Will, and even set aside funds to pay for their care. If you want to be sure your pets are cared for in a particular way after you die, you may go one step further and establish a *Pet Trust*. Like a Living Trust you set up for human beneficiaries, you can establish a Trust for your pet(s) by naming a successor trustee to manage your Trust after you die and by funding the Trust with assets that will pay for your pet's care. A Pet Trust may be a good option if you have a pet with a long lifespan, have a pet that's expensive to care for or has special needs, and/or want to offset the cost of caring for your pets when you're gone. You can learn more about Pet Trusts from the ASPCA.

Certain assets, called non-probate assets, can skip probate and transfer directly to a beneficiary when you die—a designation called *transfer-on-death* (*TOD*). Examples include life insurance policies, pensions, and retirement accounts such as 401(k) and IRA accounts. To set up beneficiaries for these assets, you must fill out a specific beneficiary designation form from the institution where you have the asset. Other accounts, such as bank, CD, and money market accounts, can also be set up—or amended—to have a *payable-on-death* (*POD*) designation. Otherwise, these assets will likely be unnecessarily probated upon your death. Accounts and policies with designated beneficiaries will pass directly to them when you die. Therefore, your TOD and POD beneficiaries must be up-to-date and consistent with your wishes. Periodic review is recommended, especially following significant life changes.

If you have dependents and don't already have a life insurance policy, it may be worth considering one as part of your end-of-life planning. Life insurance helps protect the people who rely on you financially after you die. The payout from a life insurance policy can be used to cover your family's day-to-day and long-term expenses. It can also be used to pay for expenses associated with your death, such as funeral or probate costs. Consider consulting an insurance agent or financial planner to help determine your coverage needs and options.

Material

For some people, their material possessions are a barrier to the prospect of letting go and anticipating a peaceful, unencumbered death. As "stuff" can be a burden and source of anxiety during life, it can also cause tremendous anxiety when facing death. What's going to happen to all my stuff? How will I distribute it? Will my kids fight over it or be burdened by it? Please don't take offense, but it's quite likely that nobody wants your stuff. Behold this list of recent headlines from reputable news outlets:

- "Time to Face Reality: Your Kids Don't Want Your Stuff" (*Kiplinger*)
- "Aging Parents with Lots of Stuff, and Children Who Don't Want It" (*New York Times*)
- "Your Kids Don't Want Your Stuff" *(NerdWallet)*
- "Sorry, Parents, Millennials Don't Want Your Stuff" (*The Simplicity Habit*)
- "The Family Heirlooms That Our Children Don't Want" (*Wall Street Journal*)
- "Sorry, Nobody Wants Your Parents' Stuff" (*Forbes*)

Shocking, I know.

One way to deal with your stuff is to take inventory of the possessions you'll leave behind. Survey the inside and outside of your home with a video camera or old-school pen and paper and list items with monetary value (e.g., vehicles, electronic equipment, collectibles, art, antiques, jewelry). Then list all the items with sentimental value (e.g., family heirlooms, photographs, mementos). As you go, consider who you'd like to leave each item to. Though you don't need to designate beneficiaries for every one of your worldly possessions, doing so can avoid family squabbles—or, in many cases, the hassle of dealing with your stuff.

If you feel overwhelmed by the prospect of inventory-taking, distributing, and bequeathing—or want to avoid burdening your survivors with stuff that they (apparently) don't want—there's another way to approach end-of-life planning with regard to your possessions: Swedish death cleaning or *döstädning*. Introduced by Margareta Magnusson (2020) in her book entitled *The Gentle Art of Swedish Death Cleaning*, the idea is to declutter your home and life as if you're dying (which, of course, you are) so that others don't have to do it for you. By cleaning up after yourself before leaving this Earth, you're not only doing your survivors a favor. Unburdening yourself now can also make for a better life—and death—for you.

Practical

Beyond medical, legal, financial, and material considerations, there are several miscellaneous practical matters to consider in planning for your death.

Digital Assets. According to tech.co (Rowe, 2023), the average person in the United States has around 100 passwords. In addition to online banking, investment, and insurance accounts, you likely also have social, shopping, and other recreational accounts that will need managing upon your death. Most social media platforms have legacy options that allow you to select someone to take over your accounts, but you should also consider websites, blogs, and all of your other online activities. Consider using a digital vault or password manager to keep track of all your login credentials, and decide who should have access to them after you die. You can also name a digital executor in your Will who will manage or shut down your online accounts. Be mindful of security questions and two-factor authentication when empowering someone to manage your digital assets.

End-of-Life Housing Arrangements. Even if you're healthy and independent now, it's worth considering where you may want to live in your final days. For example, would you prefer to live in a nursing home or assisted living facility, or receive in-home care from a caregiver? Do you intend to move in with family members such as your adult children? If you'd like to receive hospice care, would you prefer that to happen in your own home or a hospice home or other institution? Think about the costs and tradeoffs associated with each living arrangement. Speak with your loved ones about your wishes to make sure you're all on the same page.

Important Documents and Contact Information. When getting your affairs in order, it's important to gather and organize your records and documents, including personal, financial, legal, and health information. Whether physical or digital, your executor or other trusted person will need to access the following records: income, assets, and debts; credit card, investment, and bank accounts; Social Security information; tax returns; education, employment, and military records; insurance policies (life, health, long-term care, auto, home); titles, deeds, and official certificates (birth, marriage, etc.); and, of course, all the medical, legal, and financial documents you've assiduously created. It's also important to compile contact information for your physician, attorney, insurance broker, financial advisor, relatives, and friends who would want to be notified of your death. Numerous tools are available to assist you in completing these tasks, including an "in case of death" binder or digital folder. It's recommended to review and update your documents regularly, keep them in one place, and ensure that at least one person can access them upon your death. If your documents are stored in a home safe or bank safe deposit box, be sure to consider keys and combinations.

Secrets. Though perhaps an indelicate topic, you might want to avoid leaving an accidental legacy. It's important to ask yourself if your survivors might be surprised, or even shocked, by anything you've unintentionally left behind. An "oops" from the grave could be as innocuous as a secret diary of indiscretions from your misspent youth, or as destructive as evidence of an extramarital affair, or even a secret double life. I once had a patient who discovered that her husband was gay only after his death. Another discovered a secret "love child" who turned out to be her half-sister. We all have secrets, of course, but it's important to be mindful of those you'd prefer to take to your grave or, perhaps, reveal before you die. Whether your goal is to protect your loved ones' feelings or your own reputation, it's best to be intentional about what your survivors will find after you're gone. Speaking of survivors ...

Relational

For most people, preparation for death involves consideration of their loved ones. In some cases, concern for the well-being of those left behind is a primary basis of death anxiety. Though getting your affairs in order is a tremendous posthumous gift to your family, honoring and tending to your significant relationships can also take other forms, both before and after your death. Ideally, preparing for death involves saying and doing everything that needs to be said and done while you're alive. This can include sharing verbal or written expressions of love, gratitude, regret, and seeking or extending forgiveness. The *Stanford Letter Project* (med.stanford.edu/letter), a website that offers free tools and templates for writing a last letter, is a helpful resource to facilitate the process of conveying personal parting messages.

Dying can be a time of letting go of regrets, resentments, and ill will. Taking care of any "unfinished business" is crucial to a peaceful death. Though it's not always possible or desirable to mend broken relationships before dying, finding closure in whatever ways make sense for you is an important part of unburdening your heart and mind in preparation for dying. End-of-life conversations—whether about practical, emotional, or relational matters—can be extremely meaningful and healing. Writing your obituary with loved ones is a particularly powerful exercise in conducting a life review and preparing both yourself and significant others to face your death. You might ask your family and friends to write your eulogies and read them aloud in your presence. Or, better yet, plan a *living funeral* to celebrate your life while you're still alive. It's such a pity that dead people don't typically get to hear all the kind words said about them at their funerals.

Legacy projects are a way to tend to the emotional well-being of loved ones after your death—to remain present in your absence. For example, you can gift them with mementos that persist beyond your physical presence, such as simple art pieces, poems or essays you've written, voice recordings of your life stories or stories read to your children, videos of you speaking, singing, or dancing (!), or favorite family recipes to pass down. One of my dying patients wrote birthday cards to be delivered to each of her grandkids every year through their 18th birthdays. Another pre-paid for flowers to be sent to his widow on their wedding anniversary for years into the future. If you would benefit from assistance with finding creative ways to help your loved ones survive your death, you might choose to be guided through this legacy work with a death doula or other end-of-life professional.

After-Death

A final component of end-of-life preparation and planning is the consideration of what will happen after your death, including what will happen to your body. Whether or not organ/tissue donation is right for you, there's a decision to be made regarding the disposition of your remains. Currently, legal options in the United States include conventional burial, flame cremation, water cremation (alkaline hydrolysis), green burial, burial at sea, and natural organic reduction (human composting). You can make arrangements in advance with a funeral home, crematory, or other service provider, and even pre-pay if that brings you peace of mind.

If you die at home, your survivors have the option to keep your body there with them for a limited amount of time, depending on the state. Death is not an emergency; you don't have to be hauled off immediately. Most states allow loved ones to prepare your body and make necessary arrangements themselves if you choose not to be embalmed or cremated. Though embalming has been the default option for many years in the West, it's actually optional, most typically elected for traditional burials with open casket and viewing. Some people choose alternative dispositions (e.g., green burials, human composting) to avoid the environmental impact of embalming chemicals and to avoid delaying natural decomposition. There's a recent movement advocating for home funerals. The National Home Funeral Alliance (homefuneralalliance.org) is a helpful resource if you're interested in this decidedly retro option.

Beyond your preferences regarding the disposition of your body, it's important to consider how you'd like to be memorialized and to plan for your final arrangements. Do you prefer a funeral soon after your death, a memorial service later, or both? Do you want a wake? What about visitation? If you've chosen a conventional burial, do you prefer your casket to be open or closed? How do you want to be clothed? Who will be the pall-bearers? Do you want to have anything buried with you? What type of service do you prefer? Religious or secular? Venue? Who will eulogize you or otherwise speak? Who will officiate your service? Do you have preferences regarding musical selections or readings? Do you wish to be memorialized with flowers or with a donation to your favorite charity? Where will you be buried? What should be engraved on your tombstone? If you choose to be cremated by water or flame, how would you prefer your cremains to be distributed and by whom? Any religious, spiritual, or cultural traditions you'd like to have honored should be specified in your instructions. These are just a few of the seemingly infinite variables to consider, ideally in conjunction with the loved ones who will be carrying out your wishes. The goal is to orchestrate your departure in accordance with your collective preferences.

Are you (more) ready to get ready to go? Though the process isn't simple or easy, one of the most strategic and impactful ways to address your fear of death is to prepare for it in these practical ways. So, have the conversations, create the documents, do the organizing, toss the stuff, record the videos, write the letters, make the arrangements. And, by all means, don't forget about that secret diary!

Chapter 15

More(tality)

Alternative Perspectives

Lagniappe is a French-Cajun word I acquired during my 18-year exile in Louisiana. It means "a little something extra." In context, it's the practice of a shopkeeper giving a customer a gratuitous bonus or unexpected benefit, by way of good measure, such as an extra donut with the purchase of a dozen. Having surveyed a literal dozen philosophical, spiritual, psychological, and practical approaches to death anxiety in Chapters 3 through 14, consider this final chapter your extra donut.

Dress Rehearsals

> In each thing there is an insinuation of death. Stillness, silence, serenity are all apprenticeships.—Federico Garcia Lorca, Spanish poet and playwright

In the theater world, a *dress rehearsal* provides an opportunity to run through a full show, complete with costumes, props, and all the technical elements, to simulate the real thing—the first actual audience performance—as closely as possible before the show opens. The purpose of this "dry run" is to avoid surprises on opening night and build confidence that the show will run smoothly. The Stoics, the Buddhists, and the Cognitive Behaviorists teach us to "rehearse death" for the very same reasons. Chances are, you've been doing this all along without even knowing it.

As we've established, death is feared as the greatest unknown and unknowable human experience. But is it entirely? If you've slept, sneezed, experienced illness, loss, or orgasm, you've already "died." Or at least previewed the main event. Though, indeed, life itself is not a dress rehearsal, life contains many dress rehearsals for death within it. None of us are complete strangers to death, really.

Every night when you fall asleep and slip into unconsciousness, you experience a foretaste of death. Likewise, if you've ever undergone surgery under anesthesia, you may recall counting down to oblivion. If you never awoke—from sleep or anesthesia—you would not have known it. Dying is thought to be like going into a dreamless sleep and never waking up. One relinquishes conscious awareness and never regains it.

The relationship between sleep and death has long been portrayed in poetry, literature, art, and iconography. In Greek mythology, exemplified by Homer's epic poem the *Iliad*, *Hypnos* (the personification of sleep) and *Thanatos* (the personification of death) are twin brothers, children of *Nyx* (the goddess of night). Shakespeare eloquently likens sleep to death in Hamlet's soliloquy: "To die, to sleep—To sleep, perchance to dream—ay, there's the rub—For in that sleep of death what dreams may come..." Likewise, Lord Byron references death in this line of his poem *Lara*: "That sleep the loveliest, since it dreams the least." John William Waterhouse's famous painting—*Sleep and His Half-Brother Death*—depicts Thanatos and Hypnos resting side by side. It was completed in 1874 after both of Waterhouse's younger brothers died of tuberculosis. To this day, funerary iconography—on tombstones and the like—bids the dead to "rest in peace."

In *Book of Laughter and Forgetting*, Czech existential novelist Milan Kundera (1999) suggests that the act of forgetting is a preview of death:

> This is the great private problem of man: death as the loss of the self. But what is this self? It is the sum of everything we remember. Thus what terrifies us most about death is not the loss of the future but the loss of the past. In fact, forgetting is a form of death always present within life.

Illness, too, offers a nodding acquaintanceship with our mortality. Have you ever been so sick that you thought you were dying—or wished you were? Illness serves to remind us that our bodies aren't invincible. Especially if we're quite ill—with a bad case of the flu or COVID-19, for example—we're forced to confront the fragility of life and our vulnerability to illness and death. If we're sick enough to be rendered bedridden, we have the opportunity to practice death-bed skills, such as asking for help, letting go of productivity ("being vs. doing"), and turning inward. Though unpleasant and unwelcome, being "flat out" with temporary illness is preparation for one day being "laid to rest."

As discussed in Chapter 12, humans have experimented with mind-altering substances since the beginning of time. From using those occurring in nature to those produced in a laboratory, human beings are inclined to explore the bounds of consciousness, expand the mind, and peer beyond the material world. Though motivations range from escapism (from a painful or mundane existence) to spiritual enlightenment, inducing an altered state of consciousness is arguably another preview of death—the ultimate alteration of consciousness.

La petite mort (the little death) is a French expression that means "the brief loss or weakening of consciousness; a state or event resembling or prefiguring death." The first attested use of the expression in English was in the late 1500s, meaning "fainting fit" and, later, "nervous spasm" (Oxford University Press, 2023). In Elizabethan England, Shakespeare and others used "die" as a euphemism for orgasm. In modern usage, the term describes the post-orgasmic state of momentary unconsciousness, likened to death. Indeed, both orgasm and death are a climactic conclusion—one to sex and the other to life. The act of sneezing has likewise been referred to as la petite mort, likely due to its involuntary and convulsive nature. As with orgasm, one loses agency over their body for a few brief seconds during a sneeze. Similar also in affording release, a sneeze is, essentially, a nasal orgasm. Both are common mini-previews of death.

Losses are also living deaths. Consider the many losses you've experienced over your lifetime. Some losses are tangible, such as the death of a loved one, a breakup, or a professional failure. Others are more abstract, such as the losses associated with aging, parenting, or significant life transitions. There are also so-called ambiguous losses such as infertility, chronic illness, or estrangement. Some of us, under particular circumstances, may have even experienced a loss of self. Life is full of losses. Large or small, actual or symbolic, these are the deaths of everyday life. In this way, we die many times over before the final curtain.

Through considering all of these common examples of dress rehearsals—mini-deaths or pre-deaths—you can see that you're actually more familiar with the experience of dying than you might have thought. You've had plenty of practice. There's great comfort in knowing that many aspects of your lived experience have prepared you for death—that when you die, it won't be completely foreign to you.

Nature's Way

> In the cycle of Nature, there is no such thing as victory or defeat; there is only movement.—Paulo Coelho

The natural world has much to teach us about death, and how to temper our dreadful perceptions of it. The cycle of life, as observed in plants, animals, and humans, provides us with a master class in impermanence. The last time you walked through the woods—recently, I hope—you undoubtedly saw signs of new life, growth, and decay. If you had the patience, you could observe a single leaf progress from a bud, to a green leaf, to a brown leaf, no longer able to hang on. You'd then watch that fallen leaf decompose on the forest floor, providing nourishment for future vegetation. Death and decay are intrinsic to the natural world—daily, seasonally, annually, and generationally. Whether through age, disease, or predation, everything that lives eventually dies. And everything that dies provides new life for something else. Indeed, the lives of many living things depend on the deaths of others. This recycling process is part of the natural balancing of any ecosystem, as is the food chain, wherein food energy is transferred from one animal or plant to another.

Though it may be unpleasant to think about, humans are as much part of this recycling process as any other element of nature.

Our bodies will eventually decay and provide a food source for billions of microorganisms that nourish the soil that nourishes the plants that nourish the animals, thereby perpetuating the cycle of life. When we unnaturally preserve ourselves, as in modern burial practices of embalming and vaulting, we simply delay this natural, but inevitable, process. The Earth is finite—in space and resources. So die we must, to make room for the next generation of humans. "A hundred years from now? All new people," quips Anne Lamott.

Eva Saulitis, naturalist and marine biologist, recently died of metastatic breast cancer at age 52. During her cancer journey, she spent much of her time immersed in nature, allowing it to companion and comfort her on her short path from vibrancy to end of life. She wrote prolifically, right up until the end, sharing nature-inspired pearls of wisdom about facing mortality:

> The salmon dying in their stream tell me I am not alone. The evidence is everywhere: in the skull of an immature eagle I found in the woods; in the bones of a moose in the gully below my house; in the corpse of a wasp on the windowsill; in the fall of a birch leaf from its branch. These things all tell me death is true, right, graceful; not tragic, not failure, not defeat [Saulitis, 2014].

Saulitis believed that, just like the salmon, she would know how to die. She understood that death is nature and took comfort in the fact that nature endures, despite her own death.

When we think of our death as a return to nature, the end of our life is not the end. This fact is quite independent of what we believe about the afterlife or immortality of the soul. In the natural world, death always gives way to new life. Nature doesn't know extinction, only rebirth and regrowth. According to the first law of thermodynamics, energy cannot be created or destroyed, only changed. Nothing disappears without a trace. Viewed through a naturalist lens, ideas of "self" and the finality of death are illusions. Our bodies live on in nature's great cycle, affirming our deep connection to the world around us. Understanding that we're one small piece of the much larger and enduring, even infinite, web of life can be a great comfort to those who fear death—even those who don't believe that consciousness transcends the physical body. We remember that we exist perpetually—in the dust, the wind, and the rain. Poet John Roedel (2022) captures the essence of impermanence and transformation in this endless circle of life and death:

> "This isn't how I planned for my life to look like," I whispered under my breath as I walked to my car.
> "Tell me about it," an eavesdropping cloud replied to me from above.
> I looked up and watched the cloud billow between looking like a dove and an open hand.
> The cloud continued:
> "I used to be a snowfield in Montana.
> I used to be a dewdrop kiss on a lily.
> I used to be a puddle in a parking lot.
> I used to be a river in Mexico.
> I used to be a glacier.
> I used to be a waterfall mist in a jungle.
> I used to be so many things."
> "Doesn't that make you sad?" I asked the cloud.
> "It used to—but not anymore," the cloud replied while wrapping herself around me like a scarf.
> "I don't think either of us was created to stay the same form our entire life."

At a cellular and molecular level, we're continually dying and being reborn, trillions of times in one "lifetime." Whether it's shedding skin or growing new hairs, the human body is in constant flux. Of the nearly 30 trillion cells we have in our bodies, most are being replaced on a regular, sometimes daily, basis. Astoundingly, the *average* age of all cells in the human body is seven to ten years (Opfer & Throutner, 2022). That's a lot of turnover. This means you're not the same person you were last year, or even last week. The death of the body is just another transformation—*trans* being the Latin prefix meaning "across," "beyond," or "through." Hence, according to Marcus Aurelius (ca. 161–180/2003), representing the characteristic Stoic attunement with nature, we needn't fear death:

> Accept death in a cheerful spirit, as nothing but the dissolution of the elements from which each living thing is composed. If it doesn't hurt the individual elements to change continually into one another, why are people afraid of all of them changing and separating? It's a natural thing. And nothing natural is evil.

Creature Features

> It's so good to get up in the morning and see a donkey—they're just unbelievably beautiful and funny. My donkey Hector laughs when I walk towards him; he knows mortality when he sees it.—John Nettles, British actor

Animals, a beloved part of nature, have much to teach us about death, behaviorally and attitudinally. Consider the cat, for example. Cats know how to fall. When a cat falls out of a tree, it lets go of itself; it relaxes and lands softly. If it were to become tense and rigid, to resist, a fall would break its bones. As Alan Watts (2000), British-American philosopher, points out:

> We are all falling off a tree, at every moment of our lives. As a matter of fact, the moment we were born, we were kicked off a precipice, and we are falling, and there is nothing that can stop it. So instead of living in a state of chronic tension, and clinging to all sorts of things that are actually falling with us because the whole world is impermanent, be like a cat. Don't resist it.

Consider, also, the buffalo. Buffalo know how to weather a storm. When a storm approaches, they run directly into it rather than try to outrun it or seek shelter. Though counterintuitive, this strategy enables them to minimize their exposure to the storm's most dangerous parts and to get through it more quickly. Consider, finally, the mayfly. Mayflies are aquatic insects with the shortest lifespan of any creature in the animal kingdom—typically just one day. To ensure the survival of their species, these highly ephemeral critters can lay as many as 10,000 eggs before they die. They've no time to waste.

Clinging, running away, and taking life for granted are our natural, instinctive human responses to mortality, are they not? What if, instead of bracing against our inevitable fall, we relaxed into it? What if, instead of retreating from the menacing storm, we faced it head-on? What if, instead of frittering time away as if unlimited, we made the most of it?

But our relationship with mortality contains more than fear, doesn't it? Indeed, fear of death is invariably accompanied by sadness and despair at the prospect of loss. Animals have no such angst or self-pity about their impermanence, nor concerns about an afterlife. Living fully in the present moment, they accept death much more graciously than we humans. When indulging in a pity party about the limits and vicissitudes of my earthly existence, I often take a note from critters, as poignantly and pithily expressed by D.H. Lawrence (1929) in his poem "Self-pity":

> I never saw a wild thing
> sorry for itself.
> A small bird will drop frozen dead from a bough
> without ever having felt sorry for itself.

Throughout this book, we've explored the fear-busting potential of changing our relationship with death. Animals afford us a model, at least metaphorically. In facing mortality, perhaps it would serve us to be more like a cat, or a buffalo, or a bird. And, when life seems too short, to remember the mayfly.

Zooming Out

> You're a ghost driving a meat-coated skeleton made from stardust; what do you have to be scared of?—Anonymous

Considering our mortality "in the grand scheme" is another powerful way to reframe our relationship with death. When we zoom out and adopt a big-picture perspective of our place in the universe, the infinitesimal speck that is us, fear is often replaced with humility and gratitude. And, perhaps, a bit of awe.

In the opening of his book *Unweaving the Rainbow*, British evolutionary biologist Richard Dawkins (2000) offers us such a perspective on mortality:

> We are going to die, and that makes us the lucky ones. Most people are never going to die because they are never going to be born. The potential people who could have been here in my place but who will in fact never see the light of day outnumber the sand grains of Arabia. Certainly those unborn ghosts include greater poets than Keats, scientists greater than Newton. We know this because the set of possible people allowed by our DNA so massively exceeds the set of actual people. In

the teeth of these stupefying odds it is you and I, in our ordinariness, that are here. We privileged few, who won the lottery of birth against all odds, how dare we whine at our inevitable return to that prior state from which the vast majority have never stirred?

What a compelling, quantifiable way to articulate the preciousness of our being. If you're mathematically inclined and wish to internalize the lottery win of your existence, I invite you to contemplate, if not calculate, the odds of you being alive. Think of the chances of your parents meeting and procreating, followed by your grandparents, and each previous generation in your ancestral line. For you to exist, your ancestors for thousands of years had to survive a multitude of threats (e.g., predation, starvation, illness, wars) to remain alive long enough to reproduce. And they had to be in the mood. The variables of time, place, choice, and chance that influence the calculation are seemingly infinite, the cumulative effect of which makes the probability of you being born minuscule, calculated by some scientists to be one in 400 trillion.

Our existence is unfathomable, really. And yet, we take it for granted and bemoan its limit. Death is seen as unfair or tragic, depriving us of something we believe we're guaranteed. But what if, instead, we were to focus on the astronomical unlikelihood of our unique DNA sequence even existing? What if we shifted our perspective to one of gratitude that we're alive at all—that we're among the lucky, unlikely few who have the privilege of dying?

Not only is your existence statistically *miraculous* (i.e., so unlikely as to be almost impossible), but from a cosmic perspective, you're ageless and timeless. Atomically speaking, your body is billions of years old. The hydrogen in your body was produced in the big bang 13.7 billion years ago, and heavier atoms such as carbon and nitrogen were created from "star stuff" over 4.5 billion years ago. Nearly all elements in the human body were forged from stars in the cosmos, and many have come into existence through supernovas (Sexton, 2022).

Now that I've suggested that you're lucky by merely existing, and special because you're made from stardust, I'm about to inform you that you're insignificant. Wait, what? Am I not the center of the universe? Does my life not matter in the grand scheme? Read on for the plot twist.

Dawkins (2017) offers us another bit of perspective in his imaginative exercise illustrating the timeline of life on Earth:

> Spread your arms wide. The tip of your left hand marks the beginning of evolution and the tip of your right hand marks today. The span from the tip of your left hand all the way to your right shoulder brings forth nothing more than bacteria. The first invertebrates make their entrance near your right elbow. The dinosaurs appear in the middle of your right palm, and die out near your outermost finger joint. Homo erectus and homo sapiens appear at the white part of your fingernails. And all of recorded human history—the Cro Magnon caves of Europe, the neolithic Fertile Crescent, the god-kings of Assyria and Mesoamerica, all the spreading trade routes and codified laws and languages of the world, the rise of nation-states and the fall of the Roman empire, right up to the Rolling Stones and reality TV—all of it would be erased by the single stroke of a nail file.

In his book *Ultimate Questions*, British philosopher Bryan Magee (2016) invites us to ponder our existence by zooming out in yet another way. If we divide the six-thousand-year history of human civilization into 100-year portions, each representing one centenarian's lifespan, a mere 20 lifetimes take us back to Jesus, 10 lifetimes take us back before the Norman Conquest, and the Renaissance is only a half dozen people away. Human history, seemingly unfathomably long based on our limited experience of time, isn't long at all.

High school chemistry teacher Keith Karraker has imagined planet Earth having the lifespan of a typical human (Kottke, 2017). By this comparison, Earth is middle-aged, about 40, or halfway through its lifespan. Humans on 40-year-old Earth have been using tools for about a week and a half, and developed spines just over four years ago. All of human history occurred in the last half hour. Scaling out your frame of reference, your personal existence is just a blink of an eye, cosmically inconsequential and irrelevant. The cosmos rambled on long before you and will do so long after.

When life and death are considered in the context of deep time, you realize that you're just one in a long line of billions to briefly exist in the history of the universe. You're "a tiny pinprick of consciousness on a modestly sized planet, hurtling through infinite eons across infinite space," as vividly expressed by Oliver

Burkeman (2021), British author and journalist. In his brilliant book *Four Thousand Weeks: Time Management for Mortals*, he offers a perspective-shifting take on our radically finite lives: the concept of *cosmic insignificance therapy*. Here's where the plot twists. On the face of it, our insignificance seems like a bad thing. But only because we typically think of it in terms of our status relative to others. In contrast, Burkeman sees our *cosmic* insignificance as a liberating construct.

Our cultural programming—reinforced by social media—suggests that a meaningful life involves accomplishing something extraordinary, fulfilling our obligations, and "realizing our potential." According to Burkeman, when we believe that what we do or fail to do is exceedingly consequential, the stakes are too high to enjoy life. Overvaluing the significance of our existence, succumbing to the pressure of fulfilling some cosmically significant life purpose, gives rise to a paralyzing grandiosity. But if our vantage point is high and wide enough, that thing we're fretting about isn't such a big deal, that big life decision we're agonizing over doesn't really matter in the grandest of schemes. The universe doesn't give a damn about how we're using our finite time. Rather than devolving into a nihilistic perspective, this realization allows us to breathe a sigh of relief, recalibrate the yardstick with which we measure what's really important, and focus on what we care about most deeply. Says Burkeman (2021),

> To be reminded of your cosmic insignificance therefore isn't just relaxing, but actively empowering. Because once you remember the stakes aren't anywhere near that high, you're free to take meaningful risks, to let unimportant things slide, and to let other people deal with how they might feel about your failing to live up to their expectations.

Embracing your cosmic insignificance can be like putting down a heavy burden you didn't even realize you were carrying. For Burkeman, the key to living a fulfilling and meaningful life isn't meeting the impossible standard of "remarkableness," but rather resolving to live a "modestly meaningful life."

For those whose fear of death centers around the shortness of life—inadequate time to have all the experiences, finish all the projects, hit all the milestones—Burkeman offers a refreshing perspective on time. His book's title—*Four Thousand Weeks*—confronts the reader with the sobering reality of the number of weeks in an 80-year lifespan. He explores the mismatch between being a finite human and existing in a world of infinite possibilities. We have an adversarial relationship with time, do we not? Propelled by an optimization mindset, we worship efficiency and base our worth on how much we accomplish. Hence, we're perpetually stressed over how to best spend our limited time. Through "time management"—the ostensible theme of Burkeman's book—we attempt to control and master time (and, therefore, the future). Do you recognize the Stoic illusion of control in this pursuit? In some sense, time management is yet another way of running from death and chasing the future, both of which remove us from the present moment. Rather than responding to our finitude with frenetic busyness and productivity, Burkeman suggests embracing our temporal limits as the key to a more fulfilling life. We confront our fear of death with a reframe: "I *only* have four thousand weeks" becomes "I *get to* have four thousand weeks." What are the chances?!

Laughter, the Best Medicine

> Laughter allows us to get past the fear of death.—Deepak Chopra

You've undoubtedly heard the expression "funny as a heart attack." As in, not funny. We think of death as a grim, serious subject—but it doesn't have to be. Research suggests that humor naturally and effectively down-regulates stressful or traumatic experiences and that contemplating death can even make us funnier and more creative. When participants were subliminally primed to think about either death or pain and then asked to caption cartoons, outside raters found the death-primed participants' captions to be significantly funnier (Long & Greenwood, 2013).

What makes something funny is not so much its subject matter, but its relatability. And what could be more relatable, universally so, than death? So let's top off this compendium of approaches to death anxiety by highlighting the lighter side of death. Laughter works a bit like gratitude, as being incompatible with fear. As Stephen Colbert, comedian extraordinaire, wisely observes, "You can't laugh and be afraid at the same time—of anything. If you're laughing, I defy you to be afraid." Among alternative perspectives on mortality, comedy is an unexpectedly powerful one. Humor diffuses fear by exaggerating our anxieties, enabling us to laugh at our human condition and get some distance from the absurdities of life and death.

I've compiled some of my favorite quips and quotes about death for your amusement—and perspective.

- I am not afraid of death, I just don't want to be there when it happens. (Woody Allen)
- There is no such thing as inner peace. There is only nervousness or death. (Fran Lebowitz)
- Life is hard. Then you die. Then they throw dirt in your face. Then the worms eat you. Be grateful it happens in that order. (David Gerrold)
- If my doctor told me I had only six minutes to live, I wouldn't brood, I'd type a little faster. (Isaac Asimov)
- I do not want to attain immortality by my works. I want to achieve it by not dying. (Woody Allen)
- Remember, when you are dead, you do not know you are dead. It is only painful for others. The same applies when you are stupid. (Ricky Gervais)
- What happens after you die? Lots of things happen after you die—they just don't involve you. (Louis C.K.)
- He died a modern death, in hospital, after medical science had prolonged his life to a point where the terms on which it was being offered were unimpressive. (Julian Barnes)
- I'm a Frisbeetarian. We believe that when you die, your soul goes up on the roof and you can't get it down. (Steve Martin)
- Inscription on a tombstone: I TOLD YOU I WAS SICK!
- I intend to live forever or die trying. (Groucho Marx)
- I'm always relieved when someone is delivering a eulogy and I realize that I'm listening to it. (George Carlin)

- For three days after death, hair and fingernails continue to grow but phone calls taper off. (Johnny Carson)
- I don't want to live on in the hearts of my countrymen. I want to live on in my apartment. (Woody Allen)
- I am prepared to meet my maker. Whether my maker is prepared for the great ordeal of meeting me is another matter. (Winston Churchill)
- He is one of those people who would be enormously improved by death. (H.H. Munro)
- When I die, I'm leaving my body to science fiction. (Steven Wright)
- What I look forward to is continued immaturity followed by death. (Dave Barry)
- Death is caused by swallowing small amounts of saliva over a long period of time. (George Carlin)
- I want to die peacefully in my sleep, like my grandfather. Not screaming and yelling like the passengers in his car. (Bob Monkhouse)
- The trouble with quotes about death is that 99.9% of them are made by people who are still alive. (Joshua Burns)

Some of the funniest words ever uttered are final ones. People on their deathbeds say the damnedest things and tend not to mince words. If those people happen to be famous cultural or historical figures, their parting thoughts are invariably noted and recorded. Sometimes they're wise, poignant, or profound. But often they're witty, clever, or ironic. We tend to be fascinated by the things people say as they take their exits, perhaps because they give us a window into that mysterious liminal space between life and death. Perhaps they give us hope about facing death with dignity, even humor. Here are a few of my favorite "famous last words":

- Die, my dear? Why that's the last thing I'll do. (Groucho Marx, American humorist, before dying of pneumonia)
- Jakie, is it my birthday, or am I dying? (Viscountess Nancy Astor, upon waking and seeing her family around her bedside)

Chapter 15. More(tality)

- Monsieur, I beg your pardon. I did not do it on purpose. (Marie Antoinette, after stepping on her executioner's foot on the way to the guillotine to be beheaded)
- Here I am, dying of a hundred good symptoms. (Alexander Pope, to the doctor who said that he was doing better)
- Is it the Fourth? (Thomas Jefferson, from his deathbed on the evening of July 3, 1826)
- I'm so bored with it all. (Winston Churchill, to his son-in-law who had offered him some champagne, before suffering a fatal stroke)
- I'm ashamed of you, dodging that way. They couldn't hit an elephant at this dist—(Major General John Sedgwick of the Union Army, before being shot under the eye by a Confederate sniper and killed instantly)
- Ow, fuck! (Roald Dahl, British children's author, after his nurse injected him with morphine to ease his passing)
- I want nothing but death. (Jane Austen, when asked by her sister if she wanted anything)
- You see, this is how you die. (Coco Chanel, to her maid, as she died in her bed at the Hotel Ritz)
- I hope the exit is joyful and hope to never return. (Frida Kahlo, iconic Mexican artist, recorded in her diary a few days before her death)
- Go on, get out! Last words are for fools who haven't said enough. (Karl Marx, shouted to his housekeeper who asked if he had anything he wanted to say)
- What the devil do you mean to sing to me, priest? You are out of tune. (French composer Jean-Philippe Rameau, objecting to a song sung at his bedside by a tone-deaf priest)
- One last drink, please. (Jack Daniel, whiskey distiller, before dying of blood poisoning from an infected toe)
- I'm a fucking doctor. (R.D. Laing, to people shouting "Get a doctor!" when he suffered a fatal heart attack in public)
- Dammit, don't you dare ask God to help me! (Joan Crawford, to her housekeeper who had begun praying aloud at the actor's bedside)

- My wallpaper and I are fighting a duel to the death. One or the other of us has to go. (Oscar Wilde, Irish playwright, to friends in the weeks leading up to his death)
- Stopped. (Surgeon Joseph Henry Green, checking his own pulse as he lay dying)
- This is no time to be making new enemies. (Voltaire, French Enlightenment philosopher, after a priest asked him if he wanted to renounce Satan)
- I have offended God and mankind because my work did not reach the quality it should have. (Leonardo da Vinci, Renaissance painter and polymath, on his deathbed)
- I'm going to the bathroom to read. (Elvis Presley, to his fiancé Ginger Alden, before suffering a fatal heart attack on the toilet)
- Hey fellas! How's this for a headline for tomorrow's paper? "French Fries!" (James French, convicted murderer, to a reporter moments before his execution by electric chair)
- Good. A woman who can fart is not dead. (Princess Marie Thérèse Louise de Savoie-Carignan, who let one rip as she was dying)
- On that subject I am coy. (Aaron Burr, an atheist, in response to the efforts of his friend, the Rev. Van Pelt, to get him to state that there was a God)
- Turn me over—I'm done on this side. (Saint Lawrence of Rome, while being burned alive as a martyr of Christian persecution)
- A dying man can do nothing easily. (Benjamin Franklin, to his daughter's suggestion that he change position on his deathbed to breathe more easily)
- On the contrary. (Henrik Ibsen, Norwegian playwright, to his wife's remark that his condition was looking improved, just before he died)
- I did not get my Spaghetti-O's; I got spaghetti. I want the press to know this. (Convicted murderer Thomas J. Grasso, complaining about his last meal before execution)
- I knew it! I knew it! Born in a hotel room and, goddamn

it, dying in a hotel room. (Pulitzer Prize-winning playwright Eugene O'Neill, born in a room at the Broadway Hotel and died in a Boston hotel)
- I'm looking for loopholes. (W.C. Fields, comedian, when asked why he was reading the Bible on his deathbed)

Though all of these famous exit lines are memorable for various reasons, I've saved the best last words for last. Not "best" as in funniest; rather, supremely comforting and inspiring for those who fear death. Steve Jobs (2005), inventor and co-founder of Apple, memorably described death as "very likely the single best invention of life" and "life's change agent." He had been diagnosed with pancreatic cancer at the time, conferring ultimate credibility to opine on mortality and the preciousness of time. When Jobs died in 2011 at age 56, his sister spoke of his final moments as part of her eulogy. She lauded his enormous capacity for awe and wonderment that lived alongside his legendary technical acumen and work ethic. Notably, his last words were monosyllables, repeated three times. Though we'll never know what he was experiencing, with a lingering look at his family, he uttered, simply, "Oh wow. Oh wow. Oh wow."

Epilogue: The Last Bite

As you've made your way through this buffet of offerings, I hope you've come away with food for thought and fuel for action, as well as appetite for further exploration. Ideally, your fear of death has been tempered, and mindfulness of mortality has sparked your resolve to make the most of whatever time you have in this life. Making peace with your mortality is a lifelong process, and I'm honored to accompany you on this leg of your journey. I may be a few steps ahead of you on the path, but we're traveling together.

Other fellow travelers, knocking on death's door, have served as models of the inextricable interdependence of life and death, illuminating the way for those of us still circling the neighborhood. Memorable among them is Warren Zevon, the American rock musician who died of lung cancer at age 56. In his final appearance on David Letterman's late-night television show less than a year before his death, he was asked what he had learned about life since his terminal diagnosis. Zevon looked directly into the camera and said, "You put more value in every minute. You're reminded to enjoy every sandwich." *Enjoy every sandwich.*

But first, dessert. Because life is uncertain. If you're anything like me, you'll agree that one of life's greatest pleasures is savoring the very last bite of a soft-serve ice cream cone. You know, the one where the last bit of ice cream has melted into the bottom of the softened cone, yielding the perfect ratio of cream to cone. We relish that last bite because we're aware that the pleasure of it is singular and fleeting. Life can be like that if we remain mindful of its limit. And only the prospect of death can make it so.

Memento Mori.
~~~
Memento Vivre.

When death finds you, may it find you alive.
—African Proverb

Appendix: The Revised Collett-Lester Scale

How disturbed or made anxious are you by the following aspects of death and dying? Read each item and answer it quickly. Don't spend too much time thinking about your response. We want your first impression of how you think right now. Circle the number that best represents your feeling.

	Very	Somewhat			Not
Your Own Death					
1. the total isolation of death	5	4	3	2	1
2. the shortness of life	5	4	3	2	1
3. missing out on so much after you die	5	4	3	2	1
4. dying young	5	4	3	2	1
5. how it will feel to be dead	5	4	3	2	1
6. never thinking or experiencing anything again	5	4	3	2	1
7. the possibility of pain and punishment during life-after-death	5	4	3	2	1
8. the disintegration of your body after you die	5	4	3	2	1
Your Own Dying					
1. the physical degeneration involved in a slow death	5	4	3	2	1
2. the pain involved in dying	5	4	3	2	1
3. the intellectual degeneration of old age	5	4	3	2	1
4. that your abilities will be limited as you lay dying	5	4	3	2	1
5. the uncertainty as to how bravely you will face the process of dying	5	4	3	2	1

	Very	Somewhat			Not
6. your lack of control over the process of dying	5	4	3	2	1
7. the possibility of dying in a hospital away from friends and family	5	4	3	2	1
8. the grief of others as you lay dying	5	4	3	2	1
The Death of Others					
1. the loss of someone close to you	5	4	3	2	1
2. having to see their dead body	5	4	3	2	1
3. never being able to communicate with them again	5	4	3	2	1
4. regret over not being nicer to them when they were alive	5	4	3	2	1
5. growing old alone without them	5	4	3	2	1
6. feeling guilty that you are relieved that they are dead	5	4	3	2	1
7. feeling lonely without them	5	4	3	2	1
8. envious that they are dead	5	4	3	2	1
The Dying of Others					
1. having to be with someone who is dying	5	4	3	2	1
2. having them want to talk about death with you	5	4	3	2	1
3. watching them suffer from pain	5	4	3	2	1
4. having to be the one to tell them that they are dying	5	4	3	2	1
5. seeing the physical degeneration of their body	5	4	3	2	1
6. not knowing what to do about your grief at losing them when you are with them	5	4	3	2	1
7. watching the deterioration of their mental abilities	5	4	3	2	1
8. being reminded that you are going to go through the experience also one day	5	4	3	2	1

Calculate your score by adding up all of the numbers you circled.

References

Agin-Liebes, G.I., Malone, T., Yalch, M.M., Mennenga, S.E., Ponté, K.L., Guss, J., Bossis, A.P., Grigsby, J., Fischer, S., & Ross, S. (2020). Long-term follow-up of psilocybin-assisted psychotherapy for psychiatric and existential distress in patients with life-threatening cancer. *Journal of Psychopharmacology, 34*(2), 155–166.

Al Boukhary, R., Hallit, R., Postigo, A., & Malaeb, D. (2024). The effect of gratitude on death anxiety is fully mediated by optimism in Lebanese adults following the 2023 earthquake. *BMC Psychology, 12*(2).

American Psychiatric Association. (2013). *Diagnostic and statistical manual of mental disorders* (5th ed.).

American Psychological Association. (2015). *APA dictionary of psychology* (2nd ed.).

Association for Contextual Behavioral Science (n.d.). *Cognitive defusion (deliteralization)*. https://contextualscience.org/cognitive_defusion_deliteralization

Aurelius, M. (2003). *Meditations*. (G. Hayes, Trans.) Modern Library. (Original work published ca. 161–180 CE.)

Baldoni, J. (Director). (2016). *My last days*. [Film]. Wayfarer Entertainment in association with SoulPancake.

Baruchello, G. (2002). Montaigne and Nietzsche: Ancient and future wisdom. University of Alberta. *Symposium, 6*, 79–91. http://www.artsrn.ualberta.ca/symposium/files/original/d9a662efdd6d70cd6e2c46ec335eb83d.PDF

Becker, E. (1973). *The denial of death*. The Free Press.

Benson, H. (2000). *The relaxation response*. William Morrow.

Bering, J. (2002). Intuitive conceptions of dead agents' minds: The natural foundations of afterlife beliefs as phenomenological boundary. *Journal of Cognition and Culture, 2*(4), 263–308.

Bering, J. (2008). The end? *Scientific American Mind, 19*(5), 34–41.

Bering, J. (2011). *The belief instinct: The psychology of souls, destiny, and the meaning of life*. W.W. Norton.

Bouchrika, I. (2024, February 8). *35 Scientific benefits of gratitude: Mental health research findings in 2024*. Research.com https://research.com/education/scientific-benefits-of-gratitude

Brewer, J.A., Worhunsky, P.D., Gray, J.R., Tang, Y.Y., Weber, J., & Kober, H. (2011). Meditation experience is associated with differences in default mode network activity and connectivity. *PNAS, 108*(50), 20254–20259.

Brooks, A.C. (2023, May 25). Think about your death and live better. *The Atlantic*. https://www.theatlantic.com/ideas/archive/2023/05/death-memento-mori-happiness/674158/

Burke, B.L., Martens, A., & Faucher, E.H. (2010). Two decades of terror management theory: A meta-analysis of mortality salience research. *Personality and Social Psychology Review, 14*(2), 155–195.

Burkeman, O. (2012). *The antidote: Happiness for people who can't stand positive thinking*. Farrar, Straus and Giroux.

Burkeman, O. (2021). *Four thousand weeks: Time management for mortals*. Farrar, Straus and Giroux.

Carhart-Harris, R.L., & Friston, K.J. (2019). REBUS and the anarchic brain: Toward a unified model of the brain action of psychedelics. *Pharmacological Reviews, 71*(3), 316–344.

Carlson, L.E. (2012). Mindfulness-based interventions for physical conditions: A narrative review evaluating levels of evidence. *ISRN Psychiatry*, 651583.

Carlson, L.E., & Garland, S.N. (2005). Impact of mindfulness-based stress reduction (MBSR) on sleep, mood, stress and fatigue symptoms in cancer outpatients. *International Journal of Behavioral Medicine, 12*(4), 278–285.

Cave, S. (2012). *Immortality: The quest to live forever and how it drives civilization*. Crown.

Chapman University. (2023). *The Chapman University Survey of American Fears, Wave 9*. Orange, CA: Earl Babbie Research Center.

Ciarrochi, J., Hayes, L., Quinlen, G., Sahdra, B., Ferrari, M., & Yap, K. (2022). Letting go, creating meaning: The role of Acceptance and Commitment Therapy in helping people confront existential concerns and lead a vital life. In R.G. Menzies, R.E. Menzies, & G. Dingle (Eds.), *Existential concerns and cognitive-behavioral procedures. An integrative approach to mental health* (pp. 283–302). Springer.

Collins, J. (2001). *Good to great*. Harper Business.

Conversation Project National Survey. (2018). *The conversation project*. Institute for Healthcare Improvement. https://theconversationproject.org/wp-content/uploads/2018/06/TCP_OnePager.pdf

Critchley, S. (2008). *The book of dead philosophers*. Granta.

Danaher, J. (2013, January 24). *The Lucretian symmetry argument (Part One)*. Philosophical Disquisitions. https://philosophicaldisquisitions.blogspot.com/2013/01/the-lucretian-symmetry-argument-part-one.html

Davazdahemami, M.H., Bayrami, A., Petersen, J.M., Twohig, M.P., Bakhtiyari, M., Noori, M., & Kheradmand, A. (2020). Preliminary evidence of the effectiveness of Acceptance and Commitment Therapy for death anxiety in Iranian clients diagnosed with obsessive-compulsive disorder. *Bulletin of the Menninger Clinic, 84*(Supplement A), 1–11.

Dawkins, R. (2000). *Unweaving the rainbow: Science, delusion, and the appetite for wonder*. Mariner.

Dawkins, R. (2017). *Science in the soul: Selected writings of a passionate rationalist*. Random House.

Demjén, Z., Semino, E., & Koller, V. (2016). Metaphors for "good" and "bad" deaths: A health professional view. *Metaphor and the Social World, 6*(1), 1–19.

DeWall, C.N., & Baumeister, R.F. (2007). From terror to joy: Automatic tuning to positive affective information following mortality salience. *Psychological Science, 18*(11), 984–990.

Diamond, S.A. (2016, May 11). *Got death anxiety? Psychology Today*. https://www.psychologytoday.com/au/blog/evil-deeds/201605/got-death-anxiety

Ding, F., Tian, X., Chen, L., & Wang, X. (2020). The relationship between physical health and fear of death in rural residents: The mediation effect of meaning in life and mental health. *Death Studies, 46*, 1–9.

Dresser, S. (2020, August 19). *How to not fear your death*. Psyche. https://psyche.co/guides/how-to-use-philosophy-to-overcome-the-fear-of-your-own-death

Emmons, R.A. (2010, November 16). Why gratitude is good. *Greater Good Magazine*. https://greatergood.berkeley.edu/article/item/why_gratitude_is_good

Emmons, R.A., & McCullough, M.E. (2003). Counting blessings versus burdens: An experimental investigation of gratitude and subjective well-being in daily life. *Journal of Personality and Social Psychology, 84*(2), 377–389.

Emmons, R.A., & McCullough, M.E. (2004). *The psychology of gratitude*. Oxford University Press.
The epic of Gilgamesh (M.G. Kovaks, Trans.). (1998). Academy of Ancient Texts. (Original work published ca. 2750–2500 BCE)
Epictetus. (2004). *Enchiridion*. (G. Long, Trans.) Dover Publications. (Original work published ca. 125 CE)
Epictetus. (2008). *Discourses and selected writings*. (R. Dobbin, Trans.) Penguin Classics. (Original work published ca. 108 CE)
Epicurus. (2019). *Principal doctrines and the letter to Menoeceus*. (Yonge, C.D., & Hicks, R.D., Trans.) Adansonia Publishing.
Fenwick, P. (2017). *Perceptions of beyond the near death experience and at the end of life*. Royal College of Psychiatrists. https://www.rcpsych.ac.uk/docs/default-source/members/sigs/spirituality-spsig/spsig-archive-fenwick-perceptions-of-beyond-in-the-near-death-experience-and-at-the-end-of-life.pdf?sfvrsn=7b6e14f3_2
Ferrigio, D. (Host). (2023, April 21). Life, death, and 911 (No. 102) [Audio podcast episode]. In *Dead Talks Podcast*.
Firestone, R., & Catlett, J. (2009). *Beyond death anxiety: Achieving life-affirming death awareness*. Springer.
Fowler, J.H., & Christakis, N.A. (2008). Dynamic spread of happiness in a large social network: Longitudinal analysis over 20 years in the Framingham Heart Study. *British Medical Journal, 337*, a2338, 1–9.
Frankl, V.E. (2006). *Man's search for meaning*. Beacon.
Friend, C. (2017, March 27). Silicon valley's quest to live forever. *The New Yorker*. https://www.newyorker.com/magazine/2017/04/03/silicon-valleys-quest-to-live-forever
Goranson, A., Ritter, R.S., Waytz, A., Norton, M.I., & Gray, K. (2017). Dying is unexpectedly positive. *Psychological Science, 28*(7), 988–999.
Greenberg, J., Vail, K., & Pyszczynski, T. (2014). Terror management theory and research: How the desire for death transcendence drives our strivings for meaning and significance. *Advances in Motivation Science, 1*, 85–134.
Griffith, J.D., Gassem, M., Hart, C.L., Adams, L.T., & Sargent, R. (2018). A cross-sectional view of fear of death and dying among skydivers. *OMEGA—Journal of Death and Dying, 77*(2), 173–187.
Griffiths, R.R., Johnson, M.W., Carducci, M.A., Umbricht, A., Richards, W.A., Richards, B.D., Cosimano, M.P., & Klinedinst, M.A. (2016). Psilocybin produces substantial and sustained decreases in depression and anxiety in patients with life-threatening cancer: A randomized double-blind trial. *Journal of Psychopharmacology, 30*(12), 1181–1197.
Griffiths, R.R., Richards, W.A., McCann, U., & Jesse, R. (2006). Psilocybin can occasion mystical-type experiences having substantial and sustained personal meaning and spiritual significance. *Journal of Psychopharmacology, 187*(3), 268–283.
Harris, R. (2022). *The happiness trap: How to stop struggling and start living*. Shambhala.
Hayes, S.C. (2009, January 1). *Human life is not a problem to be solved. Psychology Today*. https://www.psychologytoday.com/us/blog/get-out-your-mind/200901/human-life-is-not-problem-be-solved
Herzog, E. (2001). *Psyche and death: Death-demons in folklore, myths, and modern dreams*. Spring Publications.
Holiday, R. (n.d.). *How to not fear death*. Daily Stoic. https://dailystoic.com/how-to-not-fear-death/
Irvine, W.B. (2008). *A guide to the good life: The ancient art of Stoic joy*. Oxford University Press.
Isaacson, B. (2015, March 5). Silicon Valley is trying to make humans immortal—and finding some success. *Newsweek*. https://www.newsweek.com/2015/03/13/silicon-valley-trying-make-humans-immortal-and-finding-some-success-311402.html
Iverach, L., Menzies, R.G., & Menzies, R.E. (2014). Death anxiety and its role in

psychopathology: Reviewing the status of a transdiagnostic construct. *Clinical Psychology Review, 34*, 580–593.

Jobs, S. (2005, June 12). "You've got to find what you love," Jobs says. *Stanford News*. https://news.stanford.edu/2005/06/12/youve-got-find-love-jobs-says/

Jonas, E., Schimel, J., Greenberg, J., & Pyszczynski, T. (2002). The Scrooge effect: Evidence that mortality salience increases prosocial attitudes and behavior. *Personality and Social Psychology Bulletin, 28*(10), 1342–1353.

Jones, J.M. (2023, September 22). In U.S., 47% identify as religious, 33% as spiritual. *Gallup News*. https://news.gallup.com/poll/511133/identify-religious-spiritual.aspx

Jong, J. (2021). Death anxiety and religion. *Current Opinion in Psychology, 40*, 40–44.

Jong, J., Ross, R., Philip, T., Si-Hua Chang, S-H., Simons, N., & Halberstadt, J. (2018). The religious correlates of death anxiety: A systematic review and meta-analysis. *Religion, Brain & Behavior, 8*(1), 4–20.

Joshu, E. (2023, August 13). *Want to feel thrilled to be alive? Try death meditation: It involves wrapping yourself in sheets like a "mummy" and imagining looking at your dead body*. Daily Mail. https://www.dailymail.co.uk/health/article-12394153/Want-feel-thrilled-alive-Try-death-meditation-involves-wrapping-sheets-like-mummy-imagining-looking-dead-body.html

Kabat-Zinn, J. (2013). *Full catastrophe living: Using the wisdom of your body and mind to face stress, pain, and illness*. Bantam.

Kabat-Zinn, J. (2017, January 11). *Jon Kabat-Zinn: Defining mindfulness*. Mindful. https://www.mindful.org/jon-kabat-zinn-defining-mindfulness/

Kahneman, D. (2011). *Thinking, fast and slow*. Farrar, Straus and Giroux.

Karnes, B. (2014, February 18). *Labor of the dying*. bkbooks.com https://bkbooks.com/blogs/something-to-think-about/labor-of-the-dying

Kastenbaum, R. (2000). *The psychology of death* (3rd ed.). New York: Springer Publishing.

Kerr, S. [@sacreddeathcare]. (2023, July 16). *What does dying feel like?* [Post]. The Centre for Sacred Deathcare. Instagram.

Korb, A. (2012, November 20). *The grateful brain: The neuroscience of giving thanks*. Psychology Today. https://www.psychologytoday.com/us/blog/prefrontal-nudity/201211/the-grateful-brain

Korb, A. (2015) *The upward spiral: Using neuroscience to reverse the course of depression*. New Harbinger.

Kottke, J. (2017, February 28). *What if the Earth were a middle-aged adult and other comparisons*. Kottke.org. https://kottke.org/17/02/what-if-the-earth-were-a-middle-aged-adult-and-other-comparisons#

Kübler-Ross, E. (2014). *On death and dying: What the dying have to teach doctors, nurses, clergy and their own families*. Scribner.

Kundera, M. (1999). *Book of laughter and forgetting*. Harper Perennial Modern Classics.

Kurzweil, R. (2005). *The singularity is near: When humans transcend biology*. Viking.

Lau, R.W.L., & Cheng, S.T. (2011). Gratitude lessens death anxiety. *European Journal of Ageing, 8*(3), 169–175.

Lawrence, D.H. (1929). *Pansies: Poems*. Knopf.

Lawton, G. (2019, November 20). Why almost everyone believes in an afterlife—even atheists. *New Scientist*. https://www.newscientist.com/article/mg24432570-500-why-almost-everyone-believes-in-an-afterlife-even-atheists/

League of the Lexicon (2022). Two Brothers Games, Ltd (UK).

LeBon, T. (2022, February 11). *Report on Stoic Week 2022*. Modern Stoicism. https://modernstoicism.com/report-on-stoic-week-2022-by-tim-lebon/

LeBon, T. (2023, April 23). The Stoic dichotomy of control in practice. *Psychology Today*. https://www.psychologytoday.com/intl/blog/365-ways-to-be-more-stoic/202304/the-stoic-dichotomy-of-control-in-practice

Lepinskie, B. (2022, February 28). Endocannibalism: The mortuary ritual of consuming the dead. *Talk Death*. https://talkdeath.com/endocannibalism-mortuary-ritual-consuming-dead/

Lester, D. (1990). The Collett-Lester fear of death scale: The original version and a revision. *Death Studies, 14*(5), 451–468.

Long, C., & Greenwood, D. (2013). Joking in the face of death: A terror management approach to humor production. *Humor, 26*(4), 493–509.

Lucas, S. (2023, October 7). *Death meditation can reduce anxiety and improve your life*. Healthnews. https://healthnews.com/family-health/end-of-life-care/death-meditation-can-reduce-anxiety-and-improve-your-life/

Lucretius. (2007). *On the nature of things* (A.E. Stallings, Trans.) Penguin Classics. (Original work published ca. 60–55 BCE)

Maden, J. (2020, June). *Why death is nothing to fear: Lucretius and Epicureanism*. Philosophy Break. https://philosophybreak.com/articles/why-death-is-nothing-to-fear-lucretius-epicureanism/

Magee, B. (2016). *Ultimate questions*. Princeton University Press.

Magnusson, M. (2020). *The gentle art of Swedish death cleaning*. Canongate Books.

Malinowski, B. (1948). *Magic, science and religion and other essays*. Beacon.

McCraty, R., & Childre, D. (2004). The grateful heart: The psychophysiology of appreciation. In R.A. Emmons, & M.E. McCullough (Eds.), *Series in affective science. The psychology of gratitude* (pp. 230–255). Oxford University Press.

McGregor, H.A., Lieberman, J.D., Greenberg, J., Solomon, S., Arndt, J., Simon, L., & Pyszczynski, T. (1998). Terror management and aggression: Evidence that mortality salience motivates aggression against worldview-threatening others. *Journal of Personality and Social Psychology, 74*(3), 590–605.

Menzies, R.E., & Menzies, R.G. (2020). Death anxiety in the time of COVID-19: Theoretical explanations and clinical implications. *The Cognitive Behaviour Therapist, 13*, e19.

Menzies, R.E., & Veale, D. (2022). *Free yourself from death anxiety: A CBT self-help guide for a fear of death and dying*. Jessica Kingsley.

Menzies, R.E., & Whittle, L.F. (2022). Stoicism and death acceptance: Integrating Stoic philosophy in cognitive behaviour therapy for death anxiety. *Discover Psychology, 2*(11).

Menzies, R.E., Sharpe, L., & Dar-Nimrod, I. (2019). The relationship between death anxiety and severity of mental illnesses. *British Journal of Clinical Psychology, 58*, 452–467.

Menzies, R.E., Zuccala, M., Sharpe, L., & Dar-Nimrod, I. (2018). The effects of psychosocial interventions on death anxiety: A meta-analysis and systematic review of randomised controlled trials. *Journal of Anxiety Disorders, 59*, 64–73.

Metcalf, P. (1987). Wine of the corpse: Endocannibalism and the great feast of the dead in Borneo. *Representations, 17*, 96–109.

Mikulincer, M., Florian, V., & Tolmacz, R. (1990). Attachment styles and fear of personal death: A case study of affect regulation. *Journal of Personality and Social Psychology, 58*(2), 273–280.

Montaigne, M. (1993). *The complete essays of Michel de Montaigne*. (M.A. Screech, Trans.) Penguin Classics. (Original work published ca. 1580)

Moore, C.C., & Williamson, J.B. (2003). The universal fear of death and the cultural response. In C.D. Bryant (Ed.), *Handbook of death and dying*, Volume I, Chapter 1. Sage Publications.

Moser, J.S., Hartwig, R., Moran, T.P., Jendrusina, A.A., & Kross, E. (2014). Neural markers of positive reappraisal and their associations with trait reappraisal and worry. *Journal of Abnormal Psychology, 123*(1), 91.

Nabokov, V. (1989). *Speak, memory: An autobiography revisited*. Vintage.

National Institute of Mental Health. (n.d.). *Specific phobia*. U.S. Department of Health and Human Services. https://www.nimh.nih.gov/health/statistics/specific-phobia

Newberg, A.B., & Iversen, J. (2003). The neural basis of the complex mental task of meditation: Neurotransmitter and neurochemical considerations. *Meditation Hypotheses, 61*(2), 282–291.

Nhat Hanh, T. (2002). *No death, no fear: Comforting wisdom for life.* Riverhead Books.

Nietzsche, F. (2001). *The gay science.* (J. Nauckhoff, Trans.) Cambridge University Press. (Original work published 1882)

Nietzsche, F. (2005). *Thus spoke Zarathustra.* (G. Parkes, Trans.) Oxford University Press. (Original work published 1885)

Nili, U., Goldberg, H., Weizman, A., & Dudai, Y. (2010). Fear thou not: Activity of frontal and temporal circuits in moments of real-life courage. *Neuron, 66*(6), 949–62.

Norem, J.K., & Cantor, N. (1986). Defensive pessimism: Harnessing anxiety as motivation. *Journal of Personality and Social Psychology, 51*(6), 1208–1217.

O'Leary, S. (2023, December 13). *This Dutch university dug a grave for its students (and they love it).* Dutch Review. https://dutchreview.com/culture/radboud-university-grave-for-students/

Opfer, C., & Throutner, A. (2022, September 22). *Does your body really replace itself every seven years?* How Stuff Works. https://science.howstuffworks.com/life/cellular-microscopic/does-body-really-replace-seven-years.htm

Otto, A.K., Szczesny, E.C., Soriano, E.C., Laurenceau, J.P., & Siegel, S.D. (2016). Effects of a randomized gratitude intervention on death-related fear of recurrence in breast cancer survivors. *Health Psychology, 35*(12), 1320–1328.

Oxford University Press. (2023). Petite mort. In *Oxford English Dictionary.*

Oxford University Press. (2024). Ritual. In *Oxford English Dictionary.*

Pannu, J., & Swett, J. (2023, May 28). What if there was never a pandemic again? *New York Times.* https://www.nytimes.com/2023/05/28/opinion/lastpandemic.html

Petruzzi, D. (2023, September 11). *Revenue of the cosmetic and beauty industry in the U.S. 2002–2022.* Statista. https://www.statista.com/statistics/243742/revenue-of-the-cosmetic-industry-in-the-us/

Pew Research Center. (2021, November 23). *Views on the afterlife.* https:/www.pewresearch.org/religion/2021/11/23/views-on-the-afterlife/

Plato. (1977). *Plato's Phaedo* (G.M.A. Grube, Trans.; Second edition). Hackett. (Original work published ca. 360 BCE)

Pollan, M. (2015, February 2). The trip treatment. *The New Yorker.* https://www.newyorker.com/magazine/2015/02/09/trip-treatment

Ralls, E. (2023, May 2). *Millions of near-death experiences validated by new study.* Earth. https://www.earth.com/news/millions-of-near-death-experiences-validated-by-new-study/

Reed, B. (2008, June 10). Simon Critchley's top 10 philosophers' deaths. *The Guardian.* https://www.theguardian.com/books/2008/jun/11/top10s.philosophers.deaths

Rickles, D. (2022). *Life is short: An appropriately brief guide to making it more meaningful.* Princeton University Press.

Roach, M. (2006). *Spook: Science tackles the afterlife.* W.W. Norton.

Robertson, D.J. (2019). *How to think like a Roman emperor.* St. Martin's Press.

Roedel, J. (2022, January 7). *This isn't how I planned for my life to look like.* [Post]. John Roedel—A Short Writer. Facebook.

Rosenberg, L. (1994, Spring). Shining the light of death on life: Maranasati meditation (Part I). *Insight Journal.* Barre Center for Buddhist Studies.

Rosenblatt, A., Greenberg, J., Solomon, S., Pyszczynski, T., & Lyon, D. (1989). Evidence for terror management theory: I. The effects of mortality salience on reactions to those who violate or uphold cultural values. *Journal of Personality and Social Psychology, 57*(4), 681–690.

Ross, S., Bossis, A., Guss, J., Agin-Liebes, G., Malone, T., Cohen, B., Mennenga, S.E., Belser, A., Kalliontzi, K., Babb, J., Su, Z., Corby, P., & Schmidt, B.L. (2016). Rapid and sustained symptom reduction following psilocybin treatment for anxiety and depression in patients with life-threatening cancer: A randomized controlled trial. *Journal of Psychopharmacology, 30*(12), 1165–1180.

Roth, B. (2007, November 12). *Family dharma: The elephant's footprint.* Tricycle. https://tricycle.org/article/family-dharma-the-elephants-footprint/

Rowe, A. (2023, March 21). *Study reveals average person has 100 passwords.* Tech.co. https://tech.co/password-managers/how-many-passwords-average-person

Russac, R.J., Gatliff, C., Reece, M., & Spottswood, D. (2007). Death anxiety across the adult years: An examination of age and gender effects. *Death Studies, 31*(6), 549–561.

Russell, B. (2015). *The conquest of happiness.* Routledge.

Safran, J.D., & Segal, Z.V. (1990). *Interpersonal process in cognitive therapy.* Basic Books.

Sang-Hun, C. (2016, October 26). South Koreans, seeking new zest for life, experience their own funerals. *The New York Times.* https://www.nytimes.com/2016/10/27/world/what-in-the-world/korea-mock-funeral-coffin.html?smid=nytcore-ios

Sarazin, S. (2023, October 27). The reality of mortality: Why we aren't talking about death. *Psychology Today.* https://www.psychologytoday.com/us/blog/soulbroken/202310/the-reality-of-mortality-why-we-arent-talking-about-death

Saulitis, E. (2014, March 5). *Wild darkness.* Orion Magazine. https://www.orionmagazine.org/article/wild-darkness/

Scott, C. (2021, August 1). *The philosophy of death: Is it rational to fear death?* The Collector. https://www.thecollector.com/philosophy-of-death/

Seneca. (1969). *Letters from a Stoic* (R. Campbell, Trans.) Penguin Classics. (Original work published ca. 65 CE)

Seneca. (2005). *On the shortness of life* (C.D.N. Costa, Trans.) Penguin. (Original work published ca. 49 CE)

Seneca. (2017). *On consolation to Helvia, Marcia, and Polybius: Seneca's complete consolations.* (F. Miller, Trans.) Independently published. (Original work published ca. 40–45 CE)

Sexton, C. (2022, December 3). *Earth, humans, and all living creatures are made from stars.* Earth. https://www.earth.com/video/earth-humans-and-all-living-creatures-are-made-from-stars/

Sexton, C. (2023, July 29). *Fountain of youth pill created by Harvard scientists reverses aging.* Earth. https://www.earth.com/news/harvard-scientists-fountain-of-youth-pill-sparks-controversy/

Slater, L. (2012, April 20). How psychedelic drugs can help patients face death. *The New York Times Magazine.* https://www.nytimes.com/2012/04/22/magazine/how-psychedelic-drugs-can-help-patients-face-death.html

Smith, A. (1863). *Dreamthorp: A book of essays written in the country.* Quotidiana. http://essays.quotidiana.org/smith_a/death_and_the_fear_of_dying/

Solomon, S., Greenberg, J., & Pyszczynski, T.A. (2015). *The worm at the core: On the role of death in life.* Random House.

Stoddard, J.A., & Afari, N. (2014). *The big book of ACT metaphors: A practitioner's guide to experiential exercises and metaphors in Acceptance and Commitment Therapy.* New Harbinger.

Sweeney, M.M., Nayak, S., Hurwitz, E.S., Mitchell, L.N., Swift, T.C., & Griffiths, R.R. (2022). Comparison of psychedelic and near-death or other non-ordinary experiences in changing attitudes about death and dying. *PLOS ONE, 17*(8), e0271926.

Tarrant, J. (2022, May 20). *The therapeutic potential of altered states of consciousness.* Psychology Today. https://www.psychologytoday.com/us/blog/choosing-your-meditation-style/202205/the-therapeutic-potential-altered-states-consciousness

Taylor, S. (2021). *Extraordinary awakenings.* New World Library.

Tigunait, P.R. (n.d.) *Dissolving our fear of death through meditation.* Yoga International. https://yogainternational.com/article/view/dissolving-our-fear-of-death-through-meditation/

Tolstoy, L. (2008) *The death of Ivan Ilyich and other stories.* (A. Briggs, D. McDuff, & R. Wilks, Trans.) Penguin Classics. (Original work published 1886)

Tung, L. (2019, November 21). *Your brain on gratitude: How a neuroscientist used his research to heal from grief.* The Pulse. https://whyy.org/segments/your-brain-on-gratitude-how-a-neuroscientist-used-his-research-to-heal-from-grief/

2045 Initiative. (n.d.). *About us.* https://www.2045.com/about

UMNCSH (Producer). (2015, December 8). *Mindfulness as a love affair with life: An interview with Jon Kabat-Zinn* [Video]. YouTube. https://www.youtube.com/watch?v=F2LebuLJmmA

Updike, J. (1989). *Self-consciousness.* Knopf.

Varanasi, L. (2023, December 7). Tech billionaires trying to hack longevity, live forever. *Business Insider.* https://www.businessinsider.com/richest-wealthiest-entrepreneurs-ceo-billionaires-tech-searching-hacking-longevity

Walter, T. (2019). The pervasive dead. *Mortality, 24*(4), 389–404.

Ware, B. (2019). *Top five regrets of the dying: A life transformed by the dearly departing.* Hay House.

Watts, A. (2000). *What is Tao?* New World Library.

Weiner, E. (2022, February 24). *Bhutan's dark secret to happiness.* BBC. https://www.bbc.com/travel/article/20150408-bhutans-dark-secret-to-happiness

Weingarten, E. (2011, June 2). *A short history of skulls as decor.* Slate. https://slate.com/culture/2011/06/a-short-history-of-skulls-as-decor.html

Wilson, R. (2023). *Soul boom: Why we need a spiritual revolution.* Hachette Go.

Wolfe, S.E., & Tubi, A. (2019). Terror management theory and mortality awareness: A missing link in climate response studies. *WIREs Climate Change, 10,* 566.

Wong, P.T. (2016, December 23). *From death anxiety to death acceptance.* International Network on Personal Meaning. https://www.meaning.ca/article/from-death-anxiety-to-death-acceptance/

Wong, P.T., Reker, G.T., & Gesser, G. (1993). Death attitude profile-revised: A multidimensional measure of attitudes toward death. In R.A. Neimeyer (Ed.), *Death anxiety handbook: Research, instrumentation and application* (pp. 121–148). Taylor & Francis.

Wong P.T. (2007). Meaning management theory and death acceptance. In A. Tomer, G.T. Eliason, & T.P. Wong (Eds.), *Existential and spiritual issues in death attitudes* (pp. 91–114). Psychology Press.

Wood, A.M., Froh, J.J., & Geraghty, A.W. (2010). Gratitude and well-being: A review and theoretical integration. *Clinical Psychology Review, 30*(7), 890–905.

World Health Organization. (2019). *International statistical classification of diseases and related health problems* (11th ed.).

World Population Review. (2024). *Deaths-per-day.* https://worldpopulationreview.com/countries

Wu, J. (2020, September 2). *Why we fear death and how to overcome it. Psychology Today.* https://www.psychologytoday.com/us/blog/the-savvy-psychologist/202009/why-we-fear-death-and-how-overcome-it

Wutzler, A., Mavrogiorgou, P., Winter, C., & Juckel, G. (2011). Elevation of brain serotonin during dying. *Neuroscience Letters, 498*(1), 20–21.

Yalom, I.D. (2008). *Staring at the sun: Overcoming the terror of death.* Jossey-Bass.

Yang, J. (2024, May 22). *Revenue of cosmetic procedures in the U.S. by type 2022.* Statista. https://www.statista.com/statistics/281346/total-revenue-on-cosmetic-procedures-in-the-united-states-by-type/

Zahn, R., Garrido, G., Moll, J., & Grafman, J. (2014). Individual differences in posterior cortical volume correlate with proneness to pride and gratitude. *Social Cognitive and Affective Neuroscience, 9*(11), 1676–1683.

Zahn, R., Moll, J., Krueger, F., Huey, E.D., Garrido, G., & Grafman, J. (2007). Social concepts are represented in the superior anterior temporal cortex. *Proceedings of the National Academy of Sciences, 104*(15), 6430–6435.

Index

Acceptance and Commitment Therapy (ACT) 45, 137, 155–164, 189, 194; relation to Cognitive Behavioral Therapy (CBT) 157–158, 161, 164, 189; *see also* cognitive defusion; cognitive fusion; mindfulness
advance care planning 218–222; Advance Directive 218–220; DNR 220; Healthcare Power of Attorney 219, 222, 223; HIPAA Release 221; Living Will 219–220, 222, 223; organ/tissue donation 221; POLST/MOLST 221; *see also* preparation, death
after-death (final arrangements) 229–230; *see also* burial; cremation; embalming; eulogy; funerals; human composting; obituary; preparation, death; rituals, death
afterlife 16, 24, 32, 35, 46, 50, 53–54, 56, 63, 107–116, 121–122, 124, 125, 235, 238; bio-social-evolutionary theory of 114–115; fear of punishment in 32, 46, 53, 54, 110–111; non-religious beliefs about 113–115; *see also* reincarnation; religion; resurrection
aging 21–23, 35, 37, 204, 218, 233; *see also* anti-aging
Agnosticism 111, 115; *see also* religion
Allende, Isabel 199
amor fati 102, 195; *see also* Nietzsche, Friedrich
Angelou, Maya 66, 88, 182–183
anti-aging 21–23; ageism 22; fear of getting old (FOGO) 21; *see also* defiance, death; life extension movement
anxiety 2–3, 30, 32, 64, 65, 70, 82, 88, 91, 93, 94, 139, 141, 146, 149–150, 157, 176, 186, 187, 191, 193, 198, 217; *see also* avoidance; mental illness; panic; phobias
Arendt, Hannah 204

artificial intelligence (AI) 23
Atheism 35, 111, 115; *see also* religion
attachment 70–74, 89–90, 129, 133, 135, 181, 192; detachment 65, 130, 132, 133, 161–162, 188–189, 192, 193–194; *see also* Buddhism; Epictetus; impermanence; Stoic philosophy
attachment styles (relational) 35–36, 41, 44
attentional bias *see* cognitive biases
Aurelius, Marcus 61, 63, 83, 84–86, 89, 236; *see also Meditations*; Stoic philosophy; time, relationship with
automatic thoughts *see* cognitive biases
avoidance: consequences of 43–44, 74, 146–149, 216; in maintenance of death anxiety 146–149; as part of anxiety 14, 21, 27, 30, 31, 117–118, 146–148; *see also* anxiety; denial, death; maintenance of death anxiety
awakening experiences 98, 188, 206–207; *see also* mortality awareness; mortality triggers; near-death experiences (NDE)

Becker, Ernest 40, 113; *see also The Denial of Death*; Terror Management Theory (TMT)
Bhutan 14, 167, 169
De Brevitate Vitae (On the Shortness of Life) 80, 83; *see also* Seneca; time, relationship with
Bromberg, Peter 208
Buddhism 71, 108, 120, 121, 125, 130–135, 167, 183, 192, 204, 231; relation to Stoic philosophy 71, 99, 130, 134, 135, 167, 231; *see also* attachment; impermanence; meditation; religion; rituals, death
Buffet, Jimmy 19
burial 5, 13, 14, 117, 120–122, 123, 132,

261

229–230, 235; green burial 211, 229–230; *see also* after-death; preparation, death
Burkeman, Oliver 93, 240–242; *see also* cosmic insignificance therapy; time, relationship with
Byron, George Gordon (Lord) 232

Camus, Albert 70
cancer 18, 19, 20, 25–26, 87, 142, 160, 177, 178, 186–187, 203, 216, 235, 247, 248; *see also* disease; illness; National Cancer Act
Canus, Julius 50; *see also* Stoic philosophy
celebrities, death of 25–26, 211; *see also* curiosity, death
The Chapman University Survey of American Fears (CSAF) 28–29
Chopra, Deepak 242
Christianity 53, 108–109, 204; Protestant Reformation 109; *see also* afterlife; religion
A Christmas Carol 96, 98; *see also* awakening experiences; Dickens, Charles
Chrysippus 50, 91; *see also* Stoic philosophy
Cicero, Marcus Tullius 50, 176; *see also* Stoic philosophy
Coelho, Paulo 79, 234
Cognitive Behavioral Therapy (CBT) 138–154; Rational-Emotive Behavior Therapy 88–89; relation to Acceptance and Commitment Therapy (ACT) 157–158, 161, 189; relation to Stoic philosophy 62, 66, 88, 93–94, 139, 154, 231; *see also* cognitive biases; cognitive distortions; cognitive restructuring; exposure and response prevention (ERP); self-talk
cognitive biases 140–141; attentional bias 141, 177; confirmation bias 140; *see also* Cognitive Behavioral Therapy (CBT); cognitive distortions
cognitive defusion 158–164, 189–190, 193–194; application to death anxiety 159–164; *see also* Acceptance and Commitment Therapy (ACT); mindfulness
cognitive distortions 140, 141–143, 147; related to death anxiety 142–143; *see also* Cognitive Behavioral Therapy (CBT); cognitive biases
cognitive fusion 158–159; *see also* Acceptance and Commitment Therapy (ACT); cognitive defusion

cognitive restructuring 139–145, 153–154, 189–190; application to death anxiety 142–145; challenge questions 141, 144; *see also* Cognitive Behavioral Therapy (CBT)
Colbert, Stephen 243; *see also* humor
Collett-Lester Fear of Death Scale 47, 251–252
comedy *see* humor
compulsions 2, 32, 64, 147–148, 150, 153, 217; *see also* maintenance of death anxiety; obsessive-compulsive disorder (OCD)
confirmation bias *see* cognitive biases
consciousness 54–56, 97, 98, 109, 111, 114–116, 130, 135, 157, 167, 188–189, 201, 207, 232, 233, 236, 240; covert 207; *see also* consciousness, altered states; unconscious state
consciousness, altered states 185–195, 206, 233; *see also* meditation; psychedelics
control, dichotomy of 64–70; application to death anxiety 69–70; definition 64–65; errors of classification 65–66; in the face of tragedy 68; opportunity cost 66; relation to Cognitive Behavioral Therapy (CBT) 139; relation to hope 93; relation to mental health 68–69, 70; thought experiment 67–68; *see also* control, illusion of; Epictetus; Stoic philosophy
control, illusion of 63–64, 65, 73–74, 82, 93, 95, 102, 142–143, 217, 242; relation to mental illness 65; *see also* control, dichotomy of
Controlled Substances Act 186, 190; *see also* psychedelics; Right-To-Try laws
The Conversation Project 209; *see also* conversations, death
conversations, death 20, 31, 151, 208–212, 228, 230; guidelines 210–212; resources 208–210; *see also* Death Cafe
cosmic insignificance therapy 241; *see also* Burkeman, Oliver
cosmology 59, 161–162, 197, 238–242; *see also* cosmic insignificance therapy; overview effect
cosmos *see* cosmology
Cotard's syndrome 43; *see also* mental illness
COVID-19 *see* pandemic
cremation 120–122, 123, 134, 229–230; water cremation (alkaline hydrolysis) 229; *see also* after-death; preparation, death

curiosity, death 3, 7, 25–26, 162, 212; *see also* celebrities, death of; illiteracy, death

Dalai Lama 180, 200
Darwin, Charles 81
Dawkins, Richard 238–240; *see also* cosmology
death anxiety *see* thanatophobia
Death Cafe 4, 5, 208–209; *see also* conversations, death
The Death Deck 210; *see also* conversations, death
The Death of Ivan Ilych 98–99; *see also* dying, experience of; Tolstoy, Leo
Death Over Dinner 209; *see also* conversations, death
death positive movement 5, 208, 210
deathbed visioning 205–206; *see also* dying, phenomena
de Botton, Alain 86, 204
decentering 193; *see also* cognitive defusion
de Champaigne, Philippe 172
default-mode network (DMN) 189, 193; *see also* consciousness, altered states; meditation; neuroscience; psychedelics
defensive pessimism 94; *see also* premeditatio malorum
defiance, death 1, 14, 21–24, 27; *see also* anti-aging; life extension movement
deliteralization *see* cognitive defusion
denial, death 1, 3, 5, 14, 17, 20, 21, 24–27, 40–42, 43–45, 112, 118, 216; *see also* avoidance; Terror Management Theory (TMT)
The Denial of Death 40; *see also* Becker, Ernest; Terror Management Theory (TMT)
depression 2, 32, 65, 87, 136, 138–139, 176, 180, 186–187, 191; *see also* mental illness
developmental theory 38–39; *see also* Erikson, Erik
Diagnostic and Statistical Manual of Mental Disorders (DSM-V) 29–31
Dickens, Charles 96, 98; *see also* *A Christmas Carol*
Dillard, Annie 81
Discourses 73, 85, 93; *see also* Epictetus
disease 18–20, 25–26, 31, 46, 170, 199, 201, 202, 204, 218, 234; *see also* cancer; illness
Doughty, Caitlin *see* death positive movement; The Order of the Good Death

doula, death 3, 5, 6, 229; *see also* death positive movement
Dyer, Wayne 66
dying, experience of 199–205; active dying 202; agonal (Cheyne–Stokes) breathing 202; death rattle 201–202; Ilych, Ivan 98–99; metaphors for 200–201; Montaigne, Michel de 97–98; pain 200, 202, 204; research 203; terminal secretions 201; *see also* hospice; Karnes, Barbara
dying, phenomena 205–208; *see also* deathbed visioning; near-death experiences (NDE); out-of-body experiences; terminal lucidity (the rally)

education, death 4, 25, 198–208; resources 212–214; *see also* conversations, death; illiteracy, death; myths, death
Eliot, T.S. 202
Elliot, Jim 216
Ellis, Albert *see* Rational-Emotive Behavior Therapy
embalming 13, 230, 235; *see also* after-death; preparation, death
Emerson, Ralph Waldo 78, 198
emotional contagion *see* rippling
Enchiridion (Handbook) 64, 69, 72; *see also* Epictetus
endocannibalism 120–121; *see also* rituals, death
The Epic of Gilgamesh 9, 21
Epictetus 61, 63, 64–65, 66, 69, 71–74, 85, 89, 93; *see also* control, dichotomy of; Stoic philosophy
Epicurean philosophy 52–60, 61, 63, 109; *see also* Epicurus; experiential blank argument; Lucretius; symmetry argument
Epicurus 52, 53–56, 59; *see also* Epicurean philosophy; experiential blank argument
Era, Dasho Karma 14; *see also* Bhutan
Erikson, Erik 38; *see also* developmental theory
Ertz, Susan 79
Essais 97–98; *see also* Montaigne, Michel de
estate planning 31, 37, 222–225; Durable/Financial Power of Attorney 223; Last Will and Testament 219, 222–224; Living Trust 223–224; Pet Trust 224; transfer-on-death (TOD) 224–225; *see also* preparation, death
eternal recurrence *see* eternal return

eternal return 100–103, 176; *see also* Nietzsche, Friedrich
eudaemonia 54, 61; *see also* Stoic philosophy
eulogy 18, 29, 151, 229, 230, 247; *see also* after-death; preparation, death
euphemisms, death 15–17, 21, 208, 211; *see also* language, death; metaphors, death
existential philosophy 96, 100, 165; *see also* Montaigne, Michel de; Nietzsche, Friedrich
existential psychology 10, 39, 68, 98, 107, 165, 168, 179, 180; *see also* freedom; gratitude; meaning; *memento mori*; rippling
experiential blank argument 52, 53–56; *see also* Epicurean philosophy; Epicurus
exposure and response prevention (ERP) 145–154; application to death anxiety 150–154; behavioral experiment 149, 153; exposure tasks 149, 150–153, 212; fear hierarchy 149, 150; imaginal exposure 88, 149, 151; *in vivo* exposure 149, 151; response prevention 150; *see also* Cognitive Behavioral Therapy (CBT)

fear of death *see* thanatophobia
Ferriss, Tim 81
fight or flight 117; *see also* avoidance; denial, death
File of Life 218; *see also* preparation, death
Five Wishes 221–222; *see also* advance care planning; preparation, death
Forster, E.M. 174
Fox, Glenn 178; *see also* gratitude
Frankl, Viktor 39, 68, 165; *see also* existential psychology
freedom 21, 49, 66, 70, 90, 100, 156, 158, 241; from anxiety 8, 54, 84, 93, 130, 200; existential 39, 68, 96, 165; free will 39, 53–54, 62, 102; relation to control 66; *see also* existential psychology
Freud, Sigmund 38, 113; *see also* psychoanalytic theory
Frost, Robert 145
Fulghum, Robert 138
funerals 5, 13–14, 47, 114, 118, 145, 151, 229, 230; cross-cultural funerary rituals 120–124, 126; home funerals 230; living funerals 5, 229; *see also* after-death; preparation, death

Gale, Zona 134
generativity *see* rippling
Glorious, Princely H. 16; *see also* language, death
good death 21, 49–50, 56, 91, 97, 98–99, 130, 199–203, 228–229, 247
gratitude 73, 165, 167, 174–179, 188, 228, 238, 239, 243; neuroscience of 177, 178; practices 178–179; *see also* existential psychology
Greece, ancient 21, 29, 49–50, 52, 53, 61, 171, 232; *see also* Stoic philosophy
Greenberg, Jeff 40; *see also* Terror Management Theory (TMT)
grief 16, 46, 55, 71, 72, 73, 113, 119, 123, 178; *see also* loss
Groundhog Day 100; *see also* eternal return; Nietzsche, Friedrich

habit reversal training 177; *see also* gratitude
habit stacking 172–173; *see also* *memento mori*; mortality awareness
Halifax, Roshi Joan 134; *see also* Buddhism
Harris, Dan 195; *see also* meditation
Hawkins, A.J. 133
Hayes, Steven C. 155, 157; *see also* Acceptance and Commitment Therapy (ACT)
health anxiety 2, 32, 44, 148, 160
healthspan 170; *see also* lifespan
Hemingway, Ernest 200; *see also* dying, experience of
heuristics *see* cognitive biases
Hinduism 108, 121, 122, 124; *see also* religion
Holocaust 68, 92
Homer 232; *see also* Hypnos; Thanatos
hope 92–93; *see also* optimism paradox; *premeditatio malorum*
Horace 52; *see also* Epicurean philosophy
hospice 20, 21, 26, 99, 105, 145, 151, 199–200, 202, 205, 227; *see also* dying, experience of; Karnes, Barbara; palliative care
human composting (natural organic reduction) 229; *see also* after-death; preparation, death
humor 50–51, 242–247; famous last words 244–247
Huxley, Aldous 205
hypervigilance 44, 141, 189; *see also* anxiety
Hypnos 232; *see also* Thanatos
hypochondriasis *see* health anxiety

Iliad see Homer
illiteracy, death 14, 24–27; *see also* curiosity, death; myths, death
illness 18–20, 28–29, 32, 34, 44, 148, 160, 201, 232–233, 234; terminal 18, 20, 32, 34, 36, 84, 151, 190, 203, 219, 221; *see also* disease
illness anxiety disorder *see* health anxiety
Ilych, Ivan *see The Death of Ivan Ilych*
immortality 13, 14, 21–24, 37, 41–42, 56, 79, 112–113, 184; *see also* soul, immortality of the; symbolic immortality
impermanence 17, 71–74, 79, 129–131, 133–135, 136, 161, 172, 173–174, 184, 234, 236, 238; *see also* attachment; Buddhism; Epictetus; Stoic philosophy
International Classification of Diseases (ICD) 12
intrusive thoughts 31, 135, 159–160; *see also* obsessive-compulsive disorder (OCD); obsessive rumination
Isherwood, Christopher 70
Islam 108–109, 167; *see also* religion
Itskov, Dmitri 23; *see also* 2045 Initiative

James, William 10, 184
Jobs, Steve 84, 247
Judaism 108–109; *see also* religion

Kabat-Zinn, Jon 157, 192, 195; *see also* meditation; mindfulness; Mindfulness-Based Stress Reduction
Karnes, Barbara 199–200, 203; *see also* dying, experience of; hospice
Kübler-Ross, Elizabeth 200; *see also* dying, experience of
Kurzweil, Ray 23; *see also* artificial intelligence (AI); defiance, death; life extension movement

Lamott, Anne 127, 235
language, death 15–21, 25, 203, 206; *see also* euphemisms, death; metaphors, death
Leary, Timothy 186; *see also* psychedelics
legacy projects 229; *see also* preparation, death
Lennon, John 200; *see also* dying, experience of
Letters from a Stoic 76, 90; *see also* Seneca
life after death *see* afterlife

life calendars 169–170; *see also memento mori*; mortality awareness
life expectancy *see* lifespan
life extension movement 22–23; superagers 22; *see also* anti-aging; defiance, death
Life Support 210; *see also* conversations, death; education, death
lifespan 12, 13, 75, 77–78, 80, 169–170, 237, 240, 242; *see also* longevity
Lincoln, Abraham 203
literacy, death *see* education, death
Logos 61–62, 72, 77; *see also* Stoic philosophy
London, Jack 53
longevity 21–22, 79, 83–84; *see also* life extension movement; lifespan
Lorca, Federico Garcia 231
loss 35, 37, 44, 46, 53, 64, 68, 71–74, 76, 84, 86, 89–92, 98, 151, 160, 204, 211–212, 232–233, 237; *see also* attachment; grief
Lovecraft, H.P. 24
LSD *see* psychedelics
Lucretius (Titus Lucretius Carus) 52, 57–60, 84; *see also* Epicurean philosophy; symmetry argument
Luther, Martin 109; *see also* Christianity

magic mushrooms *see* psychedelics
magical thinking 3, 16, 44, 142–143, 147; *see also* cognitive distortions
maintenance of death anxiety 146–149, 153–154; compulsions 147–148, 150, 153; reassurance-seeking 32, 148, 150; safety-seeking (superstitious) behaviors 32, 147–148, 150, 153; thought suppression 148, 160; *see also* avoidance
Marley, Bob 100
Marx, Karl 52, 106
Mary, Queen of Scots 171–172; *see also memento mori*
May, Rollo 39, 165; *see also* existential psychology
meaning 2, 7, 35, 37, 38–39, 43–44, 79, 83, 111–113, 119, 120, 127, 128, 139, 165, 168, 170, 176–177, 179, 183–184, 187–188, 190, 203, 241–242; *see also* existential psychology
Meaning Management Theory (MMT) 39, 63, 177; *see also* meaning; Wong, Paul T.P
meditation: benefits of 191, 193–194; corpse 132–133; death 129–136, 152, 167; gratitude 179; *Maranasati*

130–132, 134, 167; mindfulness 191–195; neuroscience of 192–193; relation to psychedelics 192–194; *see also* Buddhism; consciousness, altered states; mindfulness; Mindfulness-Based Stress Reduction
Meditations 85–86; *see also* Aurelius, Marcus
memento mori 130, 165–174, 248; habit formation 172–173; life calendars 169–170; mindfulness 173–174; visual cues 170–172; WeCroak app 168–169; *see also* existential psychology; mortality awareness; Stoic philosophy
Menoeceus 55; *see also* Epicurus
mental health 35, 61, 62, 68–69, 191; *see also* resilience, psychological
mental illness 2–3, 7, 32–33, 34, 62, 65, 138–140, 186, 193; *see also* anxiety; depression; phobias; obsessive-compulsive disorder (OCD); post-traumatic stress disorder (PTSD)
metaphors, death 200–201; Acceptance and Commitment Therapy (ACT) 45, 155–156, 160; battle 18–21; end-of-life care 21; impermanence 74; *see also* language, death; euphemisms, death
mindfulness: in Acceptance and Commitment Therapy (ACT) 157–159, 162–163, 193–194; meditation 158–159, 185, 191–195; of mortality 76, 78, 103, 129, 135, 168, 173–174, 248; *see also* meditation; *memento mori*; Mindfulness-Based Stress Reduction; mortality awareness
Mindfulness-Based Stress Reduction 192; *see also* Kabat–Zinn, Jon; meditation; mindfulness
Mitchell, Joni 37
Montaigne, Michel de 52, 58, 83, 96–100, 171, 188; *see also* dying, experience of; *Essais*; existential philosophy
Monty Python and the Holy Grail 117; *see also* denial, death; avoidance
Moody, Raymond A., Jr. 207; *see also* near-death experiences (NDE)
Moral Letters to Lucilius 77; *see also* Seneca
mortality, acceptance of 20–21, 24, 35, 45, 63, 86, 98, 102, 136, 177, 187, 188, 189–190, 193, 195, 299; neutral orientation (Meaning Management Theory) 39, 63
mortality awareness 9–10, 36–37, 39, 40–42, 43–44, 83, 85, 99–100, 110, 129–130, 134–135, 165–168, 173–174, 208, 248; benefits of 130, 135, 165–168, 174; paradox 10; *see also* awakening experiences; *memento mori*; mindfulness, of mortality; mortality salience; mortality triggers
mortality salience 36–37, 41, 113, 167; *see also* mortality awareness; mortality triggers; Terror Management Theory (TMT)
mortality triggers 26, 32, 36–37, 44, 146, 149, 152; *see also* awakening experiences; mortality awareness; mortality salience
mythology 16, 21, 53, 111, 232; *see also* Hypnos; Thanatos
myths, death 15, 25–27, 202–204; *see also* illiteracy, death

National Cancer Act 18; *see also* cancer
Native Americans 125, 167; *see also* rituals, death
nature 24, 37, 58, 61, 63, 98, 136, 176, 197, 201, 205, 207, 234–236; animals 235, 237–238; cycle of life 63, 120, 133, 134, 234–236; *see also* Stoic philosophy
near-death experiences (NDE) 97–99, 187, 190, 194, 205, 206–208; *see also* dying, phenomena; Moody, Raymond A., Jr.; out-of-body experiences; psychedelics
negative thinking *see premeditatio malorum*
negative visualization *see premeditatio malorum*
Nettles, John 237
neuroplasticity 150, 189; *see also* neuroscience
neuroscience 94, 114–115, 149–150, 173, 175, 177–178, 188–190, 192–193, 195, 202, 207–208; *see also* neuroplasticity; neurotransmitters
neurotransmitters 178, 188, 192, 202; cortisol 178, 192; dopamine 178, 192; GABA 192; neurohormones 192; serotonin 178, 188, 192, 202; *see also* meditation; neuroscience; psychedelics
Nhat Hanh, Thich 134; *see also* Buddhism
Nichols, David E. 185
Niebuhr, Reinhold *see The Serenity Prayer*
Nietzsche, Friedrich 96, 100–103, 176, 195; *see also amor fati*; eternal return; existential philosophy

Index

Nixon, President 18, 186; *see also* Controlled Substances Act; National Cancer Act

obituary 18, 25, 151, 228; *see also* after-death; preparation, death
obsessive-compulsive disorder (OCD) 2, 32, 160; *see also* compulsions; intrusive thoughts; mental illness; obsessive rumination
obsessive rumination 7, 31, 44, 64, 65, 91, 138, 158, 160, 193, 217; *see also* intrusive thoughts; obsessive-compulsive disorder (OCD); self-talk; worry
Of Consolation to Helvia 90–91; *see also* Seneca
On Consolation to Marcia 77, 90–91; *see also* Seneca
optimism paradox 91–93; *see also* hope; positive thinking; *premeditatio malorum*
The Order of the Good Death 5; *see also* death positive movement
organ donation 182, 221, 229; *see also* preparation, death
Osmond, Humphry 185; *see also* psychedelics
out-of-body experiences 152, 187, 190, 194, 206; *see also* dying, phenomena; near-death experiences (NDE); psychedelics
overview effect 194; *see also* consciousness, altered states; cosmology; meditation; psychedelics

palliative care 20, 199, 202, 210; *see also* hospice
pandemic 12, 37, 64, 70, 171; COVID–19 6, 13, 18, 37, 41, 182, 210, 233
panic 2, 31; *see also* anxiety; phobias
Peale, Norman Vincent 86; *see also* positive thinking
la petite mort 233; *see also* rehearsal, death
phobias 2, 30–31, 34, 133, 149; athazagoraphobia 31; necrophobia 31; specific 30–31, 33; symptoms 31; taphephobia 31; xenophobia 41; *see also* anxiety; thanatophobia
plague *see* pandemic
planning, death *see* preparation, death
Plato 49, 53; *see also* soul, immortality of the
positive psychology 39, 176
positive thinking 86–87, 91–92, 93–94,

145, 157, 177; *see also* hope; optimism paradox; *premeditatio malorum*
post-traumatic stress disorder (PTSD) 2, 32, 191; *see also* mental illness
Potts, Malcolm 107
premeditatio malorum (premeditation of evils) 87–94; application to mortality 89–91, 99–100; contemporary thinkers/research 93–94; distinct from anticipatory anxiety 91; negative visualization 91; optimism paradox 92–93; practice of 88–89; relation to Cognitive Behavioral Therapy (CBT) 88, 94, 139, 154; *see also* Stoic philosophy
preparation, death 152, 197, 216–230; after-death 229–230; legacy projects 229; legal/financial 222–225; material 225–226; medical 218–222; practical 226–228; relational 228–229; *see also* advance care planning; after-death; estate planning; Swedish death cleaning
psychedelics 185–190, 192, 193, 194, 195, 206; LSD 186, 187, 191; psilocybin 186–190; psilocybin-assisted psychotherapy 187–188, 190; relation to ACT and CBT 189–190; *see also* consciousness, altered states; Controlled Substances Act; default-mode network (DMN); neuroscience; neurotransmitters; Right-To-Try laws
psychoanalytic theory 38; *see also* Freud, Sigmund
Pyszczynski, Tom 40; *see also* Terror Management Theory (TMT)

Quarles, Francis 215

Ram Dass 21
Rank, Otto 39, 165; *see also* existential psychology
Rational-Emotive Behavior Therapy 88–89
regret 7, 38, 45, 46, 55, 85, 86, 102, 155, 174–179, 184, 228; *see also* Ware, Bronnie
rehearsal, death 89–91, 99–100, 130, 136, 167, 188, 231–233; *see also* Buddhism; Cognitive Behavioral Therapy (CBT); Stoic philosophy
reincarnation 108, 114, 115; *see also* afterlife; religion
relaxation response 192; *see also* meditation
religion 53, 96, 100, 102, 105–106, 107; cognitive science of 114–115;

non-believers 111–112; relation to death anxiety 34, 35, 110–111; and Terror Management Theory (TMT) 42, 112–113; world/organized religions 105–106, 107–110, 118–119; *see also* afterlife; soul, immortality of the; rituals, death

Renault, Mary 87; *see also premeditatio malorum*

De Rerun Natura (On the Nature of Things) 52, 57; *see also* Lucretius

resilience, psychological 61, 70, 94, 168, 176, 191, 194, 195; *see also* mental health

resurrection 108, 109; *see also* afterlife; religion

Right-To-Try laws 190; *see also* psychedelics

rippling 180–184; *see also* existential psychology; Yalom, Irvin

rituals, death 13, 14, 113, 114, 117–119, 126–128; ancestral veneration 124–126; cross-cultural funerary rituals 120–124; *Dia de los Muertos* (Day of the Dead) 124–125, 170–171; *see also* after-death; religion

Rogers, (Mister) Fred 27

Roman Empire 58, 61, 80, 84, 166, 171, 240; *see also* Stoic philosophy

samurai 167; *see also memento mori*

Scrooge, Ebenezer *see* awakening experiences; *A Christmas Carol*

Secular Humanism 111–112; *see also* religion

self-esteem 34, 37, 40; *see also* mental health

self-talk 138, 141, 143; *see also* Cognitive Behavioral Therapy (CBT)

Seneca the Younger 51, 58, 61, 63, 76–78, 80–84, 85, 88, 89, 90–91, 92–93; *see also premeditatio malorum*; Stoic philosophy; time, relationship with

The Serenity Prayer 65; *see also* control, dichotomy of

Shakespeare, William 139, 166, 204, 232, 233

Sikhism 108; *see also* religion

Silicon Valley 21, 23; *see also* anti-aging; defiance, death; life extension movement

Sinclair, David 22; *see also* anti-aging; defiance, death; life extension movement

the singularity *see* artificial intelligence (AI)

Sisyphus 21

Skepticism 97; *see also* Montaigne, Michel de

skull iconography 125, 170–172; *see also memento mori*

Smith, Dominic 185

Socrates 49–50, 53–54, 56, 69; *see also* soul, immortality of the

Solomon, Sheldon 40; *see also* Terror Management Theory (TMT)

soul, immortality of the 49, 53–54, 56, 108–109, 116, 235; *see also* afterlife; Plato; religion; Socrates

soul, mortality of the 53–56, 63, 111, 116; materialism 54, 109, 111, 207; *see also* Epicurean philosophy; Epicurus; experiential blank argument; Lucretius; Stoic philosophy; symmetry argument

specific phobias *see* phobias; thanatophobia

Stanford Letter Project 228; *see also* preparation, death

stigma, death *see* taboo, death

Stockdale paradox *see* optimism paradox

Stoic philosophy 50–51, 52, 58, 61–63, 64–65, 68–69, 71–74, 77, 80–81, 85–93, 94–95, 99, 109, 130, 134, 135, 166, 171, 188, 231, 236, 242; relation to Buddhism 71, 99, 130, 134, 135, 167, 231; relation to psychology 62–63, 65, 68–69, 81, 88, 91, 94, 139, 154, 157, 231; *see also* Aurelius, Marcus; control, dichotomy of; Epictetus; *memento mori*; *premeditatio malorum*; Seneca; soul, mortality of the; time, relationship with

suicide 2, 50, 69, 91, 180, 199

superstitious thinking *see* magical thinking

suppression 62, 70, 148, 157, 159–160, 162–164, 192, 194; *see also* Acceptance and Commitment Therapy (ACT); avoidance

Swedish death cleaning 5, 226; *see also* preparation, death

symbolic immortality 24, 40, 112; *see also* Terror Management Theory (TMT)

symmetry argument 52, 56–60; *see also* Epicurean philosophy; Lucretius

taboo, death 4, 5, 14, 15, 17, 21, 27, 36, 172, 208, 212

terminal lucidity (the rally) 205, 207; *see also* dying, phenomena

Terror Management Theory (TMT) 40–42, 112, 177; *see also* Becker, Ernest; denial, death; mortality salience
thanatology 3
thanatophobia: assessment of 45–47, 251–252; components/bases of 32, 39, 45–47; consequences of 42–45; defense mechanisms against 31–32, 33, 40–42, 43–45, 112–113, 146–149; definition of 29–31; development of 33–34; and other mental health conditions 2–3, 31, 32–33; risk factors 34–36; symptoms of 30–32; theories of 38–42; triggers 36–37; *see also* anxiety; avoidance; maintenance of death anxiety; mortality triggers; phobias
Thanatos 29, 232; *see also* Hypnos
Thomas, Dylan 18
time, relationship with 59, 65, 75–78, 79–84, 85–86, 240–242; presence in the moment 76, 82, 86, 93, 157, 174, 176, 177, 178, 188, 191–193, 195, 238, 242; scarcity principle 83; time management 76–77, 242; urgency 6, 77, 85, 134, 217; *see also* Aurelius, Marcus; *De Brevitate Vitae* (On the Shortness of Life); Burkeman, Oliver; Seneca; Stoic philosophy
Tolle, Eckhart 66, 191
Tolstoy, Leo 99, 165–166, 200; *see also The Death of Ivan Ilych*; dying, experience of
Tutu, Desmond 218
Twain, Mark 56, 88
2045 Initiative 23; *see also* anti-aging; defiance, death; Itskov, Dmitri; life extension movement
Tyson, Neil deGrasse 59; *see also* Epicurean philosophy; symmetry argument
unconscious (subconscious) mind 3, 16, 33, 37, 38, 41, 43, 56, 127, 168, 188, 192
unconscious state 97, 201–202, 219, 232, 233

Vanitas 172; *see also memento mori*
Voltaire 15
Voskamp, Ann 174

Ware, Bronnie 102, 175; *see also* hospice; regret
Washington, Booker T. 80
Waterhouse, John William 232; *see also* Hypnos; Thanatos
Webster, John 12
WeCroak app 168–169; *see also memento mori*; mortality awareness
Western culture 4, 5, 13–14, 17, 21, 24, 27, 118, 119, 120, 123, 127, 135, 172, 208, 220, 230
Williams, Patricia J. 117
wind phone 127; *see also* rituals, death
Wong, Paul T.P. 39; *see also* Meaning Management Theory (MMT)
worm at the core 10, 11, 40
worry 31–32, 59, 62, 65, 66, 84, 88, 91, 135, 138, 141, 154, 159–160, 162, 193, 217; *see also* anxiety, intrusive thoughts; obsessive rumination

Yalom, Irvin 10, 56, 98, 107, 165, 180–181, 184; *see also* existential psychology; rippling

Zeno of Citium 61; *see also* Stoic philosophy
Zevon, Warren 248

www.ingramcontent.com/pod-product-compliance
Ingram Content Group UK Ltd.
Pitfield, Milton Keynes, MK11 3LW, UK
UKHW041931140426
5217IPUK00014B/418